Collins

AQA GCSE 9-1 Combined Science Trilogy Higher

Ian Honeysett, Sam Holyman and Ed Walsh

Exam Skills and Practice

How to use this book

This Exam Skills and Practice book puts the spotlight on the different types of command word – the instructional word or phrase in a question – you can expect to find in your GCSE papers. Each section has worked examples and lots of timed practice to help build your exam technique.

Top Tips offer nuggets of information to keep in mind when answering each type of question.

Scan the **QR code** to test your understanding of the command word and see a worked solution to the example question on that page.

Each question shows the paper P1 P2, the part of the specification and grade range you are working at. Look out for maths skills and practical skills being tested.

Complete the example to take the next step in your practice. Parts of the workings and/or answers are given for you to finish. Helpful hints also steer you in the right direction.

Each **command word** is defined in easy-to-understand language.

Example questions show the command words in context. Use the QR code to access worked video solutions and commentary for them.

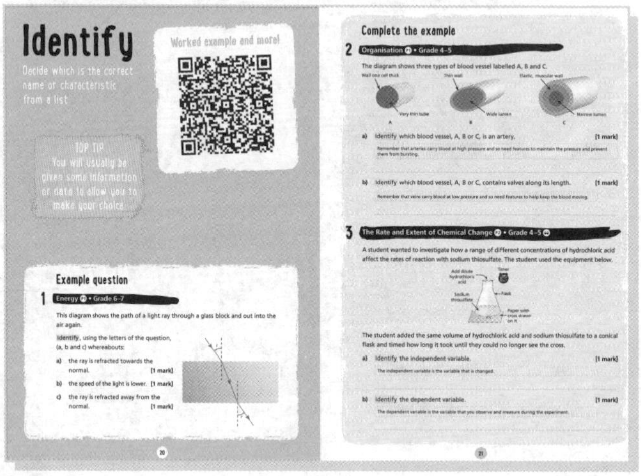

Exam practice questions enable you to delve deeper into each command word across a range of topics and grade levels. There is a target time for doing these at exam speed.

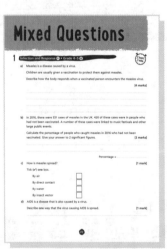

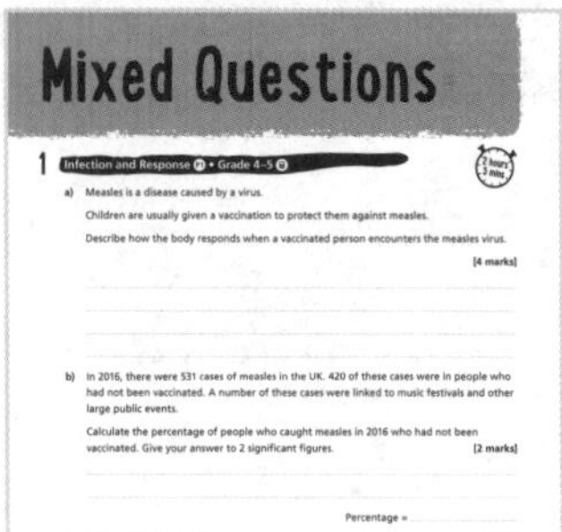

Mixed questions help to refine your exam skills with practice that recaps a variety of the command words.

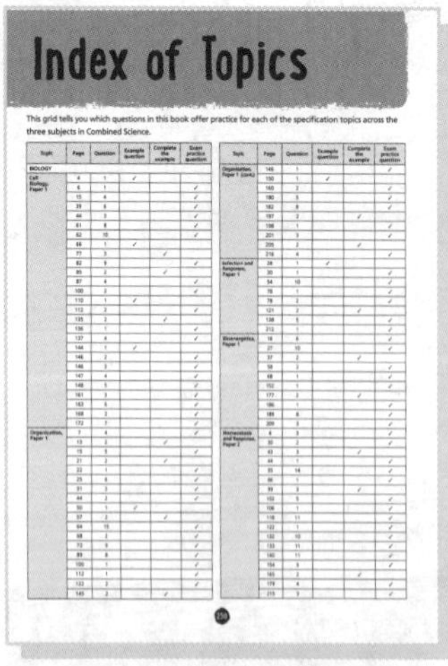

An **index of topics** enables you to quickly find questions within the book from particular parts of the AQA GCSE specification.

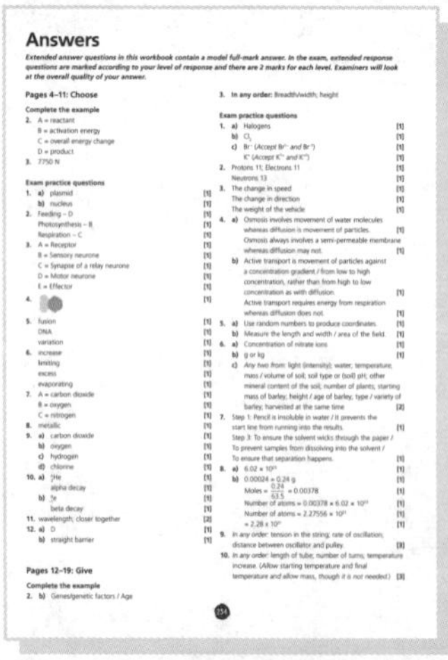

Answers are given at the back of the book so that you can check and mark your own work.

Contents

Revise by command word!

Choose

Select your answer from a list of alternatives. These questions are usually targeted at lower grades as they give you a choice of answers.

Worked example and more!

TOP TIP
Use the options given, not your own words.

Example question

1 **Cell Biology P1 • Grade 4–5**

Water can enter or leave a cell through the cell membrane.

Choose words from the list to complete the sentences about movement of water. **[3 marks]**

active transport	concentrated	diffusion	dilute
impermeable	osmosis	partially permeable	respiration

Water can enter a cell by the process of ....

This happens when the cytoplasm of the cell is more .... than the solution outside the cell.

The water enters through the cell membrane, which is ....

Complete the example

2 Energy Changes P1 • Grade 4–5

Charcoal is a fuel that can be combusted. This is an exothermic reaction.

The figure shows the reaction profile for the combustion of charcoal.

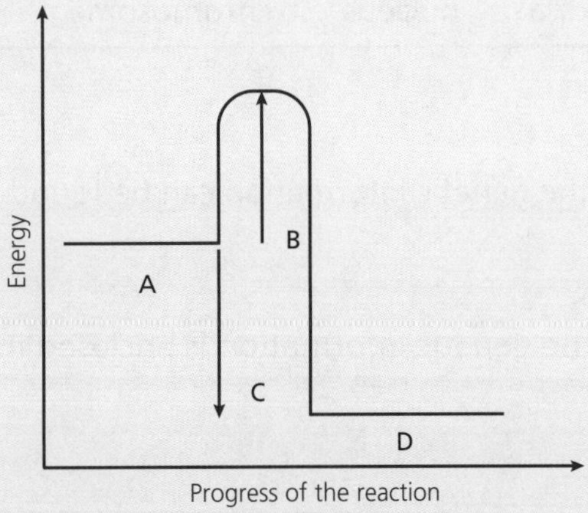

What do the labels A, B, C and D represent?

Choose answers from the box. **[4 marks]**

reactant	product	activation energy	overall energy change
time	energy	catalyst	

A = ...

B = ...

C = ...

D = ...

3 Forces P2 • Grade 4–5

This question is about motion.

Complete the sentence.

Choose the answer from the box. **[1 mark]**

7750 N	8500 N	10 000 N	12 250 N

An engine is applying 10 000 N to a train in a forwards direction. The motion is being opposed by friction of 750 N and air resistance of 1500 N.

The resultant force acting on the train is

....

Exam practice questions

34

1 **Cell Biology P1 • Grade 4–5**

Cells are the basic unit of all forms of life.

Choose words from the box to complete the sentences about cell structure.

mitochondria	nucleus	chromosome	plasmid	ribosome

[2 marks]

a) In prokaryotic cells the genetic information can be found in a subcellular structure known as a

....

b) In eukaryotic cells the genetic information is enclosed in a subcellular structure known as a

....

2 **Ecology P2 • Grade 4–5**

The diagram shows some parts of the carbon cycle.

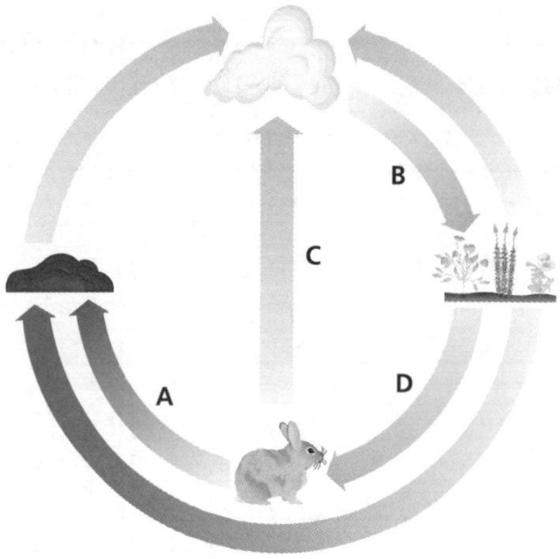

Choose the letter from the diagram that corresponds with each process. **[3 marks]**

Feeding ....

Photosynthesis ....

Respiration ....

3 **Homeostasis and Response P1 • Grade 4–5**

The diagram shows the human reflex arc.

Choose words from the box to label the main structures in the reflex arc. **[5 marks]**

Receptor	Effector	Effect	Stimulus	Motor neurone
Synapse of a relay neurone		Sensory neurone	Impulse	Brain

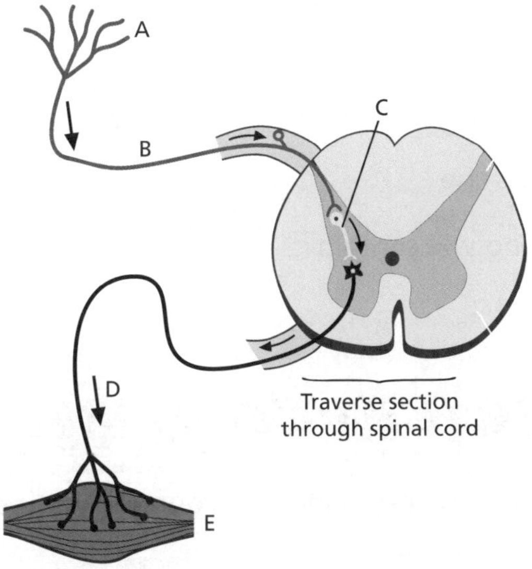

A = ...

B = ...

C = ...

D = ...

E = ...

4 Organisation P1 • Grade 4–5

Enzymes are biological catalysts that are used in the digestive system to break down large, insoluble molecules into small, soluble molecules.

Look at the diagram of an enzyme.

Choose which substrate would bind to the active site of the enzyme shown.

Tick (✔) one box. **[1 mark]**

 ☐

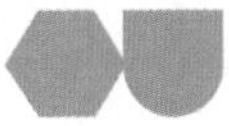 ☐

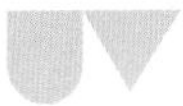 ☐

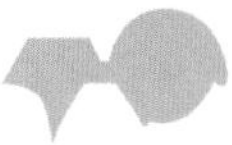 ☐

 ☐

5 Inheritance, Variation and Evolution P1 • Grade 4–5

Choose the correct words from the box to complete each sentence. **[3 marks]**

DNA	enzymes	variation	fertilisation	division
separation	fusion	cells	differentiation	

Sexual reproduction is the .... of the male and female gametes.

The resulting offspring will contain .... from both parents.

This gives rise to ....

6 Chemical Changes P1 • Grade 4–5

A student can make a pure, dry sample of copper(II) sulfate by reacting copper(II) oxide.

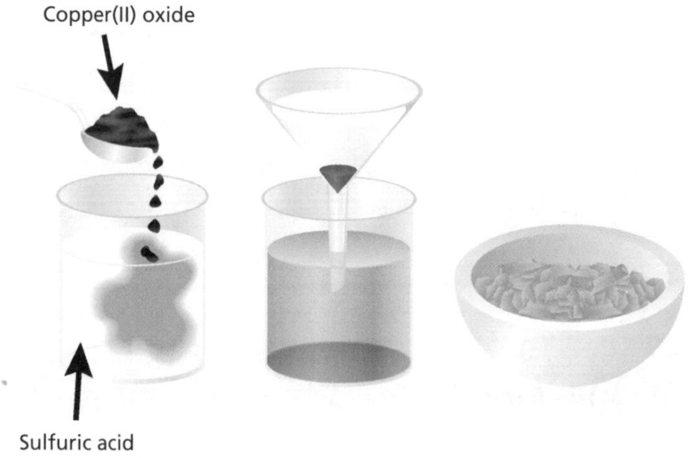

Complete the sentences to explain the steps in the practical.

Choose the answers from the box. **[4 marks]**

boiling	condensing	decrease	evaporating	excess
increase	filtrate	limiting	residue	

Sulfuric acid is heated up to .... the rate of reaction.

As the sulfuric acid is the .... reagent, the reaction mixture is filtered to remove the .... copper(II) oxide.

The copper(II) sulfate crystals are obtained from the filtrate by .... the water.

7 Chemistry of the Atmosphere P2 • Grade 4–5

For 200 million years, the proportions of different gases in the atmosphere have been much the same as they are today.

The figure below is a pie chart which shows the composition of dry air.

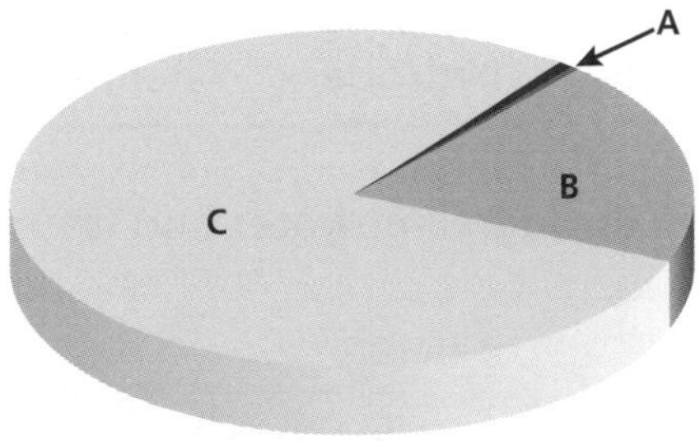

What do labels A, B and C represent?

Choose answers from the box. **[3 marks]**

hydrogen	nitrogen	oxygen	water
carbon dioxide	oxygen	chlorine	

A = ...

B = ...

C = ...

8 Atomic Structure and the Periodic Table P1 • Grade 4–5

This question is about the alkali metals and their compounds.

The table shows the melting points of some alkali metals.

Element	Melting point in °C
Lithium	181
Sodium	98
Potassium	63
Rubidium	39

Why does rubidium have a lower melting point than potassium?

Choose a word from the box to complete the sentence below. **[1 mark]**

ionic	covalent	metallic	intermolecular

Rubidium has weaker .... bonds than potassium.

9 Chemical Analysis P2 • Grade 4–5

Qualitative tests can be used to identify gases that are made in a chemical reaction.

Choose words from the box to complete the sentences about the identification of common gases. **[4 marks]**

oxygen	methane	hydrogen	helium	carbon dioxide	chlorine

a) When the gas is blown through limewater and it turns cloudy, the gas is

....

b) When the gas causes a glowing splint to relight, the gas is

....

c) When a burning splint causes the gas to burn rapidly with a pop sound, the gas is

....

d) When the gas causes damp litmus paper to bleach, the gas is

....

10 Atomic Structure P1 • Grade 6–7

Complete the equations and sentences.

Choose the answers from the box. **[4 marks]**

$^{4}_{2}He$	$^{2}_{4}He$	$^{0}_{1}e$	$^{0}_{-1}e$
alpha decay	beta decay	gamma decay	biological decay

a) Uranium 238 decays to Thorium 234.

The equation for this is: $^{238}_{92}U \rightarrow ^{234}_{90}Th +$ ....

Uranium 238 decaying to Thorium 234 is an example of ....

b) Thorium 234 decays to Protactinium 234.

The equation for this is: $^{234}_{90}Th \rightarrow ^{234}_{91}Pa +$ ....

Thorium 234 decaying to Protactinium 234 is an example of ....

11 Waves P2 • Grade 6–7

This question is about light.

Complete the sentence.

Choose the answers from the box. **[2 marks]**

wavelength	amplitude	direction	further apart
	reversed	closer together	

Light is refracted when it enters a denser medium. This causes the .... to be reduced and the wave fronts to be ....

12 Waves P2 • Grade 8–9

Some students are using a ripple tank to explore the reflection of straight waves from a barrier.

They are trying to find out if the relationship between the incident and reflected waves in the water is the same as the relationship for light rays being reflected by a plane mirror.

They need to produce a steady sequence of straight waves and must choose the best method to do this.

a) Complete the sentence.

Choose the answer from the box. **[1 mark]**

Method A:	**Method B:**	**Method C:**	**Method D:**
Have a single dipper* from the beam making contact with the water.	Have a pair of dippers* from the beam making contact with the water.	Have a row of dippers* from the beam making contact with the water.	Have the beam making contact with the water.

*Dippers are attached to the motorised beam on a ripple tank

The students need to produce a steady sequence of straight waves. The ripple tank has a motor on a beam to produce oscillations.

To get this to make straight waves they need to choose **method** ....

b) The students need to place something in the water in the way of the waves. This will represent the plane mirror.

Complete the sentence.

Choose the answer from the box. **[1 mark]**

curved barrier	straight barrier	piece of plastic mesh
	piece of metal gauze	

The most suitable object to represent the plane mirror is a .... placed in the water.

Total score: .... / 34

Give

Only a short answer is required, not an explanation or a description.

Worked example and more!

TOP TIP
Read the question carefully.

Example question

1 **Bonding, Structure, and the Properties of Matter P1 • Grade 4–5**

Fullerenes are molecules of carbon atoms with hollow shapes.

a) Give the name of the first fullerene that was discovered. **[1 mark]**

b) Give **one** use of this fullerene. **[1 mark]**

Complete the example

2 Organisation P1 • Grade 4–5

Read the passage about different types of cancer.

> Cancer can cause tumours to form in the body.
>
> There are two types of tumours caused by cancer. Benign tumours are contained in one area but another type of tumour can spread.
>
> Various lifestyle factors, such as sunbathing, can act as risk factors for cancer.

Answer these questions about the passage.

a) Give the name of the type of tumour that can spread. **[1 mark]**

Malignant

b) Give a risk factor for cancer that is **not** a lifestyle factor. **[1 mark]**

....

3 Particle Model of Matter P1 • Grade 4–5

A student is determining the density of the rectangular solid block shown. They have been provided with the block, a ruler and a weighing balance.

Give **four** measurements they will need to take to enable them to calculate the density. **[4 marks]**

1 *Length*

2 *Mass*

3 ....

4 ....

Exam practice questions

33

1 Atomic Structure and the Periodic Table P1 • Grade 4–5

The elements in Group 7 and Group 1 can react together to make ionic compounds.

Group 1 elements are all examples of alkali metals.

a) Give the name used to describe all elements in Group 7. **[1 mark]**

....

b) Group 7 elements make molecules consisting of two atoms.

Give the formula of a molecule of chlorine. **[1 mark]**

....

c) Give the formula of the ions formed when potassium and bromine react to form an ionic compound. **[2 marks]**

....

2 Atomic Structure and the Periodic Table P1 • Grade 4–5

An isotope of sodium can be represented by the symbol $^{24}_{11}Na$.

Give the number of each subatomic particle in this atom of sodium. **[2 marks]**

Protons: ....

Neutrons: ....

Electrons: ....

3 Forces P2 • Grade 4–5

The diagram shows a set of apparatus that is set up to investigate the acceleration of a vehicle along a horizontal air track.

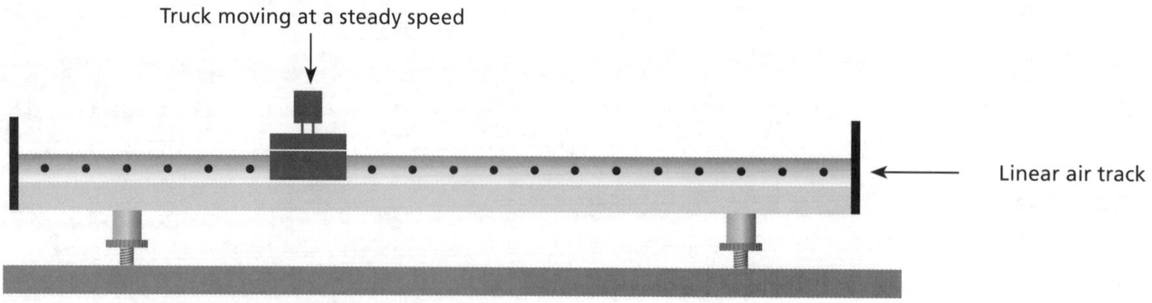

Air is being blown up through the track to support the vehicle.

Give **three** factors that will affect the acceleration of the vehicle. **[3 marks]**

1 ....

2 ....

3 ....

4 Cell Biology P1 • Grade 6–7

a) Give **two** differences between osmosis and diffusion. **[2 marks]**

1 ....

....

....

2 ....

....

....

b) Give **two** differences between diffusion and active transport. **[2 marks]**

1 ....

....

....

2 ....

....

....

5 Organisation P1 • Grade 6–7

A student is investigating the population size of dandelion plants on a football field.

This is their method:

1. Place a $0.25\ m^2$ quadrat at random on the field.
2. Count the number of dandelion plants in the quadrat.
3. Repeat this process ten times.
4. Calculate a mean for the number of dandelion plants in each quadrat.

a) Give a method for placing the quadrat at random on the field. **[1 mark]**

....

b) Give a further measurement that the student needs to make before they can estimate the population size of dandelion plants on the football field. **[1 mark]**

....

6 Bioenergetics P1 • Grade 6–7

Barley plants use nitrate ions that are absorbed from the soil to make protein.

Scientists investigated the yield of barley in different soils.

This is the method used:

1. A large box of soil was used to grow the barley plants.
2. No nitrate ions were put in the box.
3. All the barley from each plant in the box was removed and weighed.
4. The mean mass of barley per plant was calculated.
5. Steps 1 to 4 were repeated for boxes containing soil with different concentrations of nitrate ions.

a) Give the independent variable for this investigation. **[1 mark]**

....

b) Give a suitable unit for the dependent variable in this investigation. **[1 mark]**

....

c) Give **two** variables that scientists should have controlled in this investigation. **[2 marks]**

1 ....

2 ....

Chemical Analysis P2 • Grade 6–7

A student investigated the colours of some food colourings.

The diagram shows the equipment used.

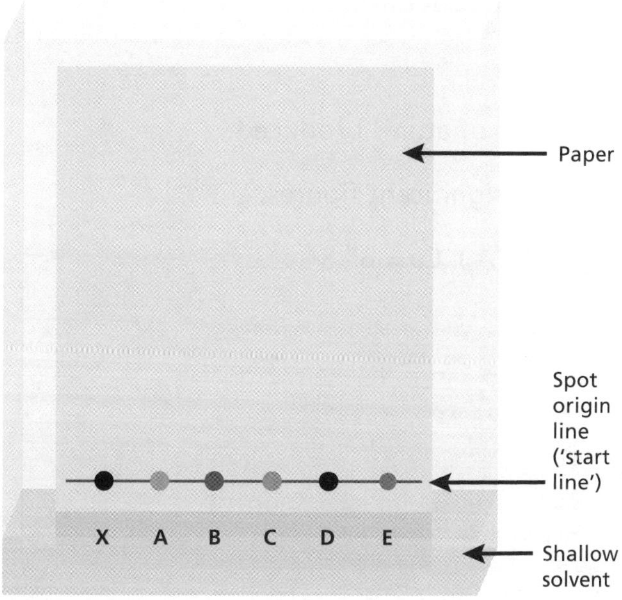

This is the method used:

1. Draw a 'start line', in pencil, on a piece of absorbent paper.
2. Put samples of five known food colourings (A, B, C, D and E) and the unknown substance (X) on the 'start line'.
3. Dip the edge of the paper into the water, ensuring the water level is below the start line.
4. Wait for the solvent to travel to the top of the paper.
5. Identify substance X by comparing the horizontal spots with the results of A, B, C, D and E.

Give **one** reason for:

- Step 1
- Step 3 **[2 marks]**

Step 1 ....

....

Step 3 ....

....

8 Quantitative Chemistry P1 • Grade 8–9

Copper(II) nitrate solution was electrolysed for 20 minutes with a current of 0.6 A.

0.00024 kg of copper was collected at the cathode.

a) Give the value of the Avogadro constant. **[1 mark]**

....

b) Determine the number of atoms produced. **[5 marks]**

Give your answer to 3 significant figures.

Relative atomic mass (A_r): Cu = 63.5

....

....

....

....

....

9 Waves P2 • Grade 6–7

The diagram shows a set of apparatus used to study waves on a stretched string.

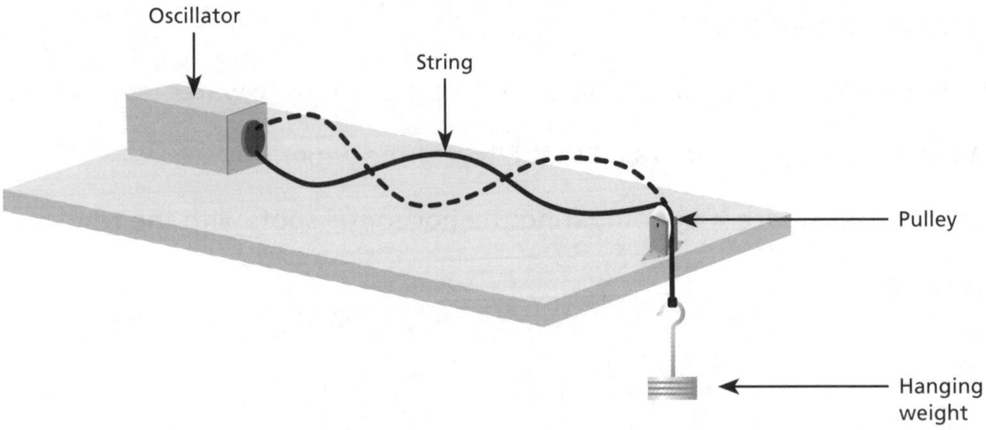

When the equipment is set up correctly and the oscillator is turned on, standing waves can be seen on the string.

Give **three** variables that need to be adjusted correctly to get standing waves to appear when the oscillator is turned on. **[3 marks]**

1 ....

2 ....

3 ....

10 Energy P1 • Grade 8–9

A student is investigating the specific heat capacity of lead.

The student puts small pieces of lead in a cardboard tube that is closed at both ends. The student repeatedly turns the tube upside down and notices that the tube gets hotter.

Give **three** things they should measure that will be useful in determining the specific heat capacity of lead. **[3 marks]**

1 ....

2 ....

3 ....

Total score: .... / 33

Identify

Decide which is the correct name or characteristic from a list.

Worked example and more!

TOP TIP
You will usually be given some information or data to allow you to make your choice.

Example question

1 **Energy P1 • Grade 6–7**

This diagram shows the path of a light ray through a glass block and out into the air again.

Identify, using the letters of the question, (a, b and c) whereabouts:

a) the ray is refracted towards the normal. **[1 mark]**

b) the speed of the light is lower. **[1 mark]**

c) the ray is refracted away from the normal. **[1 mark]**

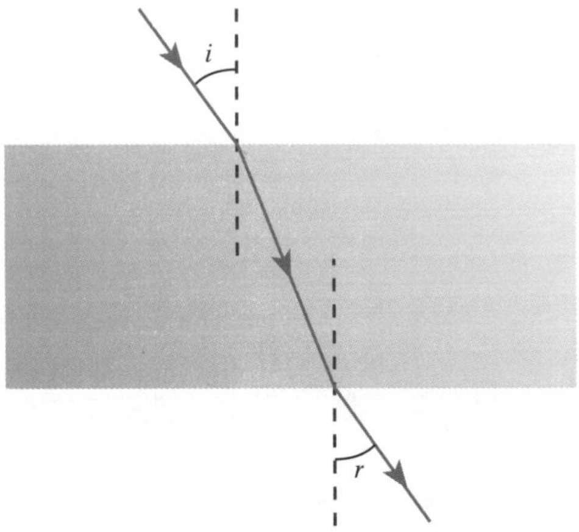

Complete the example

2 Organisation P1 • Grade 4–5

The diagram shows three types of blood vessel labelled A, B and C.

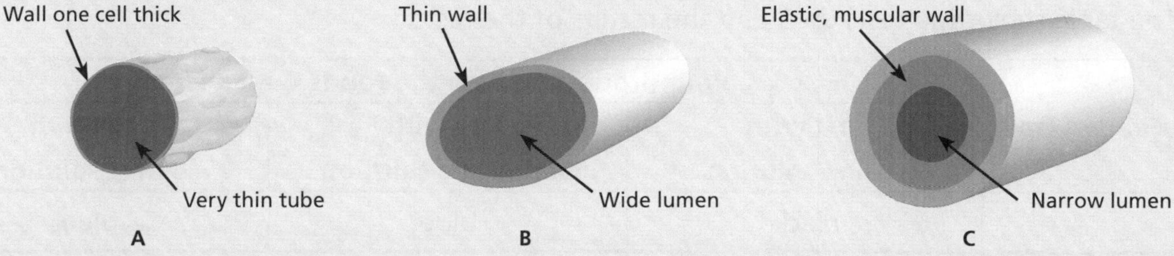

a) Identify which blood vessel, A, B or C, is an artery. **[1 mark]**

Remember that arteries carry blood at high pressure and so need features to maintain the pressure and prevent them from bursting.

....

b) Identify which blood vessel, A, B or C, contains valves along its length. **[1 mark]**

Remember that veins carry blood at low pressure and so need features to help keep the blood moving.

....

3 The Rate and Extent of Chemical Change P2 • Grade 4–5

A student wanted to investigate how a range of different concentrations of hydrochloric acid affect the rates of reaction with sodium thiosulfate. The student used the equipment below.

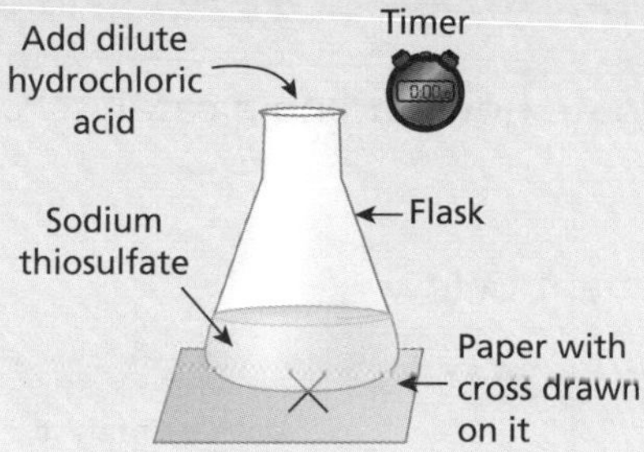

The student added the same volume of hydrochloric acid and sodium thiosulfate to a conical flask and timed how long it took until they could no longer see the cross.

a) Identify the independent variable. **[1 mark]**

The independent variable is the variable that is changed.

....

b) Identify the dependent variable. **[1 mark]**

The dependent variable is the variable that you observe and measure during the experiment.

....

Exam practice questions

27

1 Organisation P1 • Grade 4–5

A student tested four samples of food for different biological molecules.

The table shows the tests used and the results of the tests.

Food sample	Colour produced when the foods were tested		
	Test with iodine solution	Test with Benedict's solution	Test with Biuret solution
A	black	blue	blue
B	brown	blue	purple
C	brown	blue	blue
D	brown	orange	blue

a) Identify which food sample contains starch. **[1 mark]**

....

b) Identify which food samples contain carbohydrates. **[2 marks]**

....

c) Identify which food sample may contain an enzyme. **[1 mark]**

....

2 The Rate and Extent of Chemical Change P2 • Grade 4–5

A student wanted to investigate how adding a catalyst to hydrogen peroxide affected the rate of reaction.

The student used the equipment below.

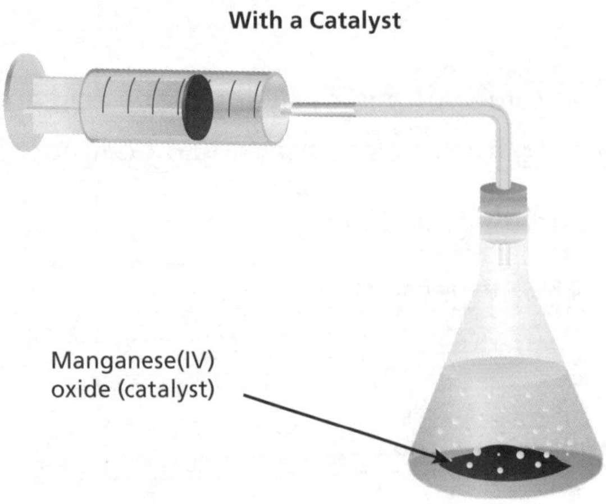

The student added hydrogen peroxide to a conical flask and recorded how much gas was collected every 10 seconds for two minutes.

The student did this experiment twice, once with a catalyst and once without.

a) Identify the dependent variable. **[1 mark]**

....

b) Identify a possible control variable. **[1 mark]**

....

....

3 Atomic Structure P1 • Grade 4–5

This diagram summarises information about different types of radioactive emissions and their ability to penetrate various materials.

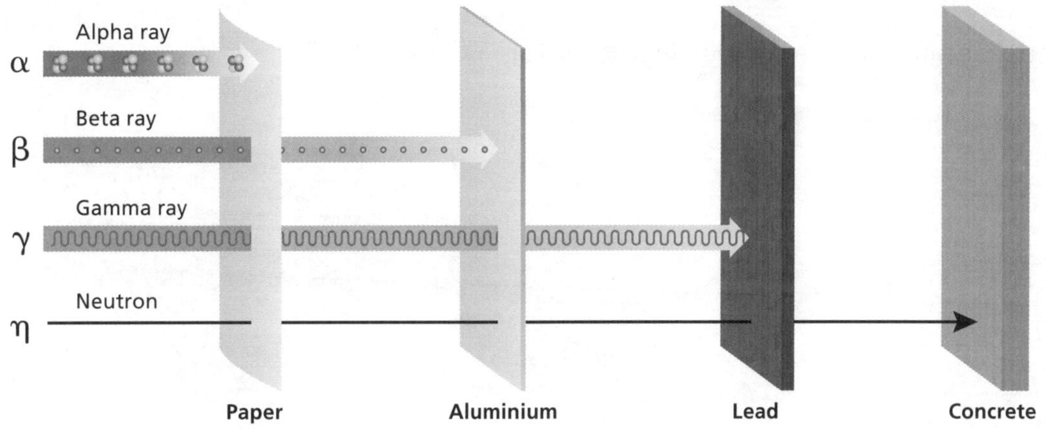

a) Identify which type of radiation cannot penetrate paper. **[1 mark]**

....

b) Identify which type of material can prevent both alpha and beta radiation but not gamma rays or neutrons. **[1 mark]**

....

c) Identify which type of radiation can penetrate aluminium but not lead. **[1 mark]**

....

d) Identify which material will prevent the passage of gamma rays but not neutrons. **[1 mark]**

....

4 Forces P2 • Grade 4–5

Identify which **two** of these factors will affect the amount of energy in the kinetic energy store of a moving object.

Tick (✔) **two** correct answers. **[2 marks]**

- Mass ☐
- Temperature ☐
- Height above ground ☐
- Velocity ☐
- Weight ☐
- Friction ☐

5 Magnetism and Electromagnetism P2 • Grade 6–7

The diagram shows a simple electric motor.

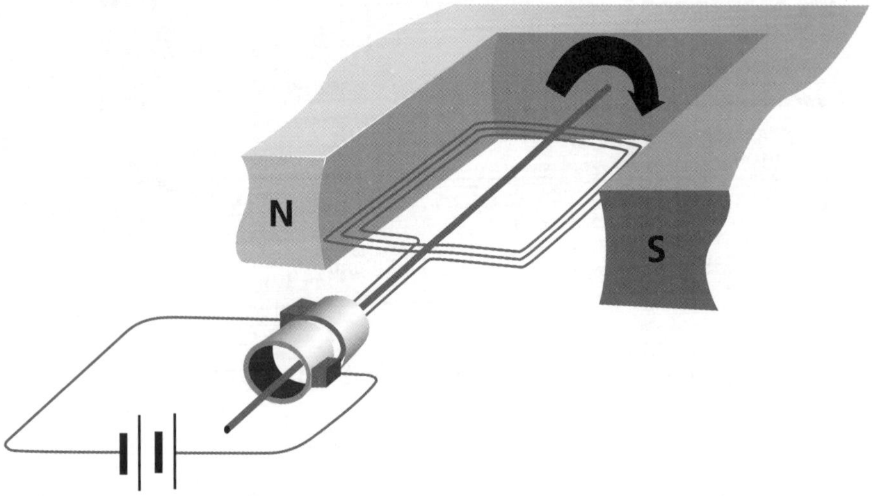

a) Identify the poles of the magnet, using the letter **A**. **[2 marks]**

b) Identify the coil of wire, using the letter **B**. **[1 mark]**

c) Identify the axis of rotation, using the letter **C**. **[1 mark]**

d) Identify the power supply, using the letter **D**. **[1 mark]**

6 Organisation P1 • Grade 6–7

A student used a potometer to measure water uptake by three shoots, P, Q and R. They took five measurements using each shoot.

The table shows their results.

	Volume of water taken up in mm^3				
Shoot	**1st result**	**2nd result**	**3rd result**	**4th result**	**5th result**
P	5	3	3	5	4
Q	9	9	7	6	9
R	9	7	7	10	7

Identify the shoot, P, Q or R, that gave results where the mean was the same as the median.

Show how you worked out your answer. **[2 marks]**

....

....

7 Chemical Changes P1 • Grade 6–7

This question is about the extraction of copper from its ore.

Malachite is a copper ore containing mainly copper(II) carbonate ($CuCO_3$).

The copper can be extracted in a two-stage process:

Stage 1: $CuCO_3 \rightarrow CuO + CO_2$

Stage 2: $2CuO + C \rightarrow 2Cu + CO_2$

a) Identify the type of chemical reaction in each stage of the copper extraction. **[2 marks]**

Stage 1: ....

Stage 2: ....

b) Identify the substance that is being oxidised in stage 2. **[1 mark]**

....

8 Chemical Changes P1 • Grade 6–7

Iron is extracted from iron ore in the blast furnace.

Coke is an impure form of carbon and reacts with the iron ore to make iron. The equation for this reaction is:

$2Fe_2O_3 + 3C \rightarrow 3CO_2 + 4Fe$

a) Identify the substance that is being reduced. **[1 mark]**

....

b) A neutralisation reaction is used to remove any acidic waste. Limestone is added to the blast furnace to neutralise acidic gases.

Identify the substance that will react with the limestone. **[1 mark]**

....

9 Chemical Changes P1 • Grade 6–7

A student carries out an experiment to find out what happens when an aqueous solution of sodium chloride is electrolysed.

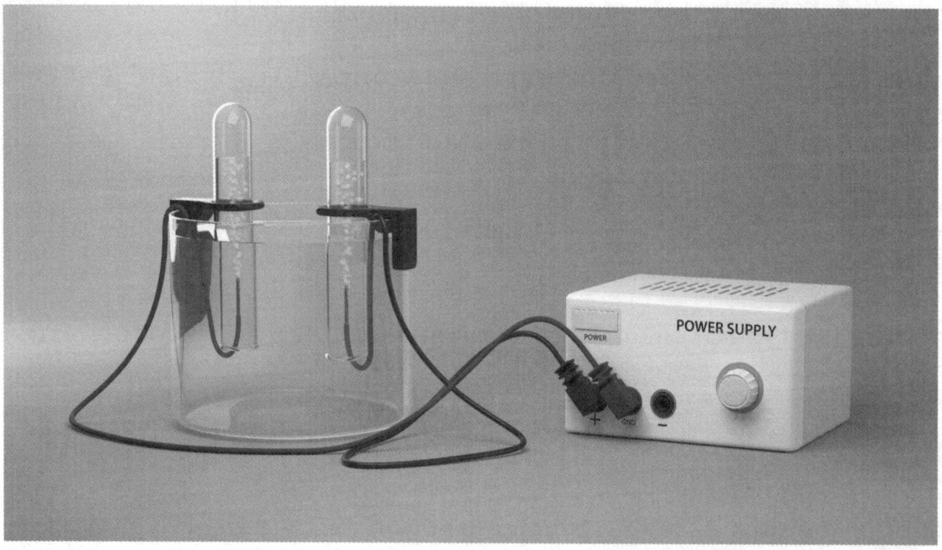

Identify the two positive ions present in an aqueous solution of sodium chloride. **[2 marks]**

....

....

The graph shows how light intensity affects the rate of photosynthesis in a plant.

The measurements were taken at three different carbon dioxide concentrations and different temperatures.

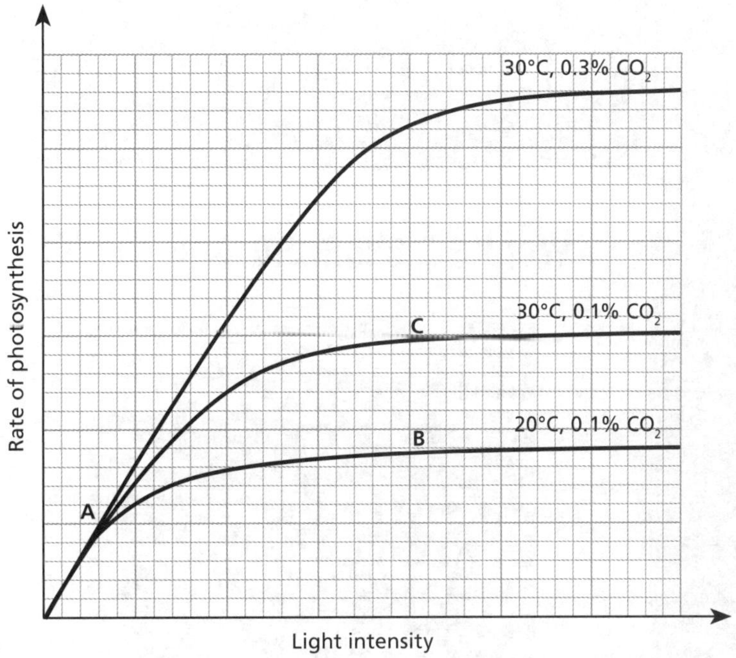

Identify the point, **A**, **B** or **C**, that shows where temperature is the limiting factor. **[1 mark]**

....

Total score: .... / 27

Name

Only a short answer is required, not an explanation or a description.

Worked example and more!

TOP TIP
A 'Name' question can often be answered with a single word, phrase or sentence.

Example question

1 **Infection and Response P1 • Grade 4–5**

Many drugs have been extracted from plants or microorganisms.

a) Name the drug that has been extracted from foxgloves. **[1 mark]**

b) Name the plant that is used to extract aspirin. **[1 mark]**

c) Name the scientist who discovered penicillin. **[1 mark]**

Example question

2 Chemical Changes P1 • Grade 4–5

A salt can be made by adding excess copper(II) oxide to sulfuric acid.

The salt solution must be separated from the unreacted copper(II) oxide using the equipment shown.

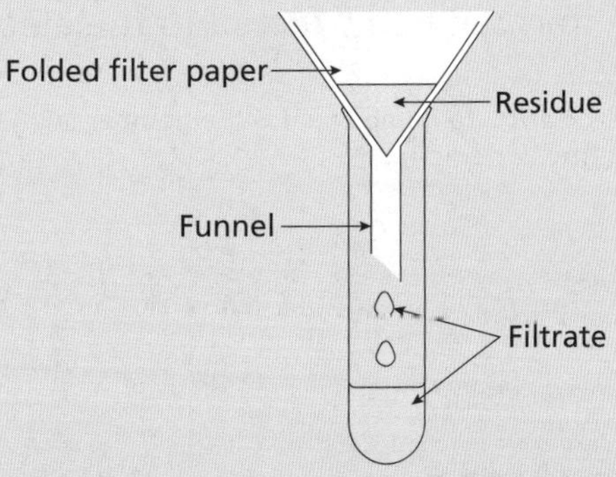

a) Name the separating technique shown in the diagram. **[1 mark]**

Filtering

b) Name the salt that is collected. **[1 mark]**

3 Magnetism and Electromagnetism P2 • Grade 4–5

The diagram shows an electromagnet attracting pieces of metal.

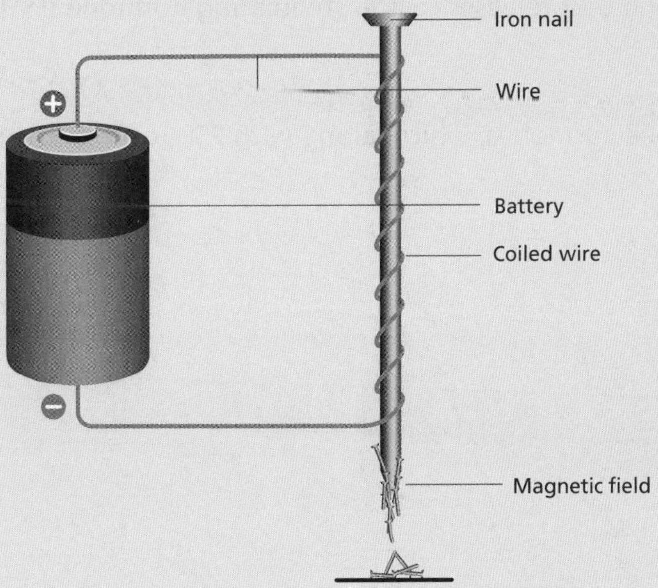

a) Name **two** metal elements that can be attracted to the electromagnet. **[2 marks]**

Look carefully at the question. You are being asked for the names of elements that are attracted to the magnet; these are substances listed on the Periodic Table. You could give their symbol, but you won't have a Periodic Table in your physics exam and if you incorrectly write the symbol you will get no marks. But if you spell the name of the metal element incorrectly you would still get the mark.

1 ....

2 ....

b) Name **one** metal alloy that can be attracted to the electromagnet. **[1 mark]**

This part of the question is asking you to name an alloy. Remember, alloys are mixtures of mainly metals and are not named on the Periodic Table.

....

Exam practice questions

30

1 Infection and Response P1 • Grade 4–5

Pathogens may be viruses, bacteria, protists or fungi.

Name the type of pathogen that causes each of these diseases. **[3 marks]**

Rose black spot ....

Malaria ....

Measles ....

2 Homeostasis and Response P2 • Grade 4–5

a) Name the gland that releases follicle stimulating hormone (FSH). **[1 mark]**

....

b) Name the **three** hormones, which, along with FSH, control the menstrual cycle. **[3 marks]**

1 ....

2 ....

3 ....

3 Organisation P1 • Grade 6–7

The diagram shows a model for enzyme action.

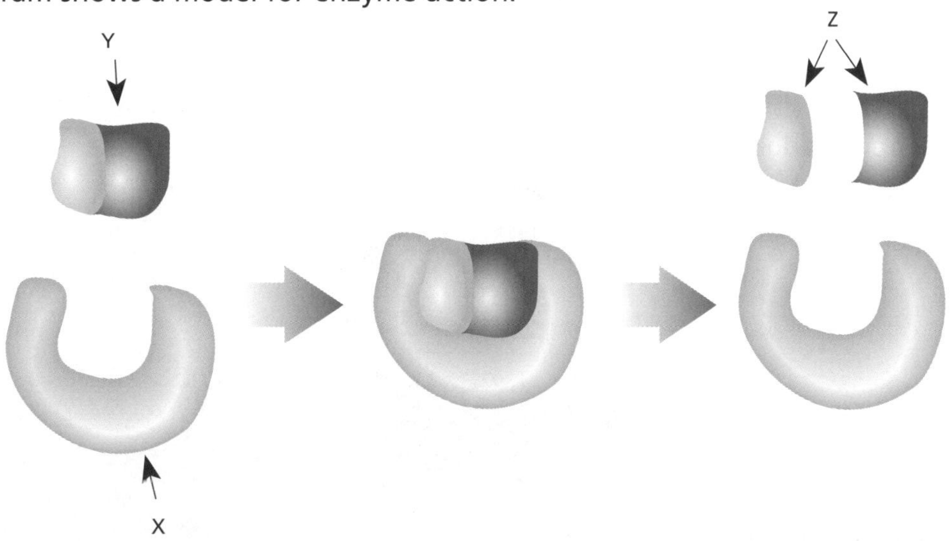

a) Name the type of molecule represented by X, Y and Z in the diagram. **[3 marks]**

X = ...

Y = ...

Z = ...

b) Name the theory that is represented by this model. **[1 mark]**

....

4 Organic Chemistry P2 / Chemistry of the Atmosphere P2 • Grade 4–5

Natural gas is a fossil fuel and is used in our homes for heating and cooking.

Natural gas is mainly made of an alkane with one carbon atom.

a) Name the main hydrocarbon found in natural gas. **[1 mark]**

....

b) Name the chemical reaction for when natural gas is used to cook your food. **[1 mark]**

....

c) Name the greenhouse gas that is made when natural gas is used. **[1 mark]**

....

5 Atomic Structure and the Periodic Table P1 • Grade 4–5

Early models of atoms showed them as tiny spheres that could not be divided into simpler substances.

In 1897, Thompson discovered that atoms contained small, negatively charged particles. He proposed a new model, shown below.

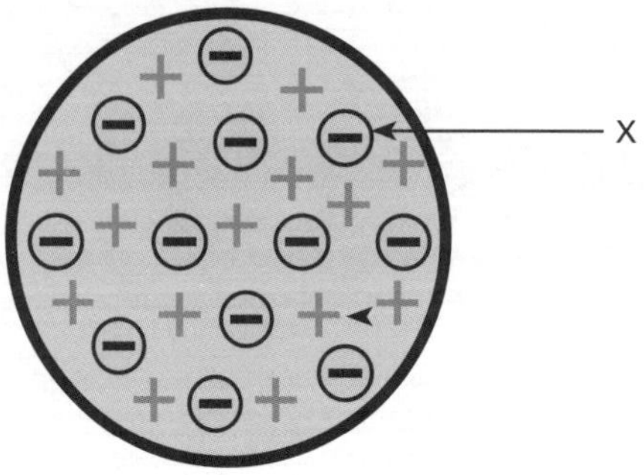

Name the particle labelled X. **[1 mark]**

....

6 Chemical Changes P1 • Grade 4–5

Lead bromide is an ionic compound. It can be separated by electrolysis, as shown in the diagram.

a) Name the element formed at the positive electrode during the electrolysis of molten lead bromide. **[1 mark]**

....

b) Name the element formed at the negative electrode during the electrolysis of molten lead bromide. **[1 mark]**

....

7 Electricity P1 • Grade 4–5

A student investigated the current through an ohmic conductor.

The student varied the potential difference across the resistor at constant temperature.

The diagram shows the circuit that the student used.

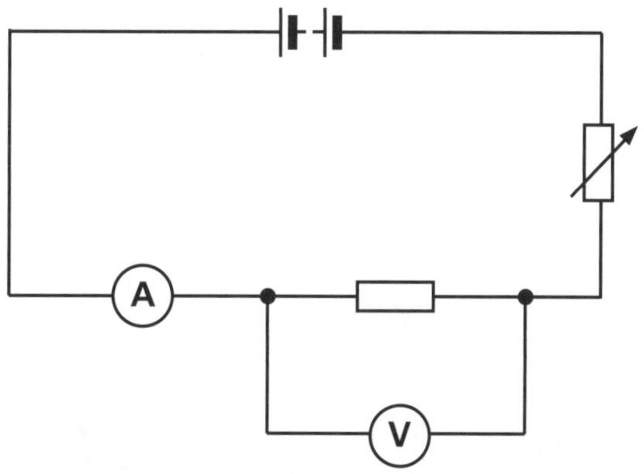

a) Name the component that can be used to change the potential difference in the circuit. **[1 mark]**

....

b) Name the type of relationship between potential difference and current for a resistor at constant temperature. **[1 mark]**

....

8 Bonding, Structure, and the Properties of Matter P1 • Grade 6–7

This question is about the metal sodium and its compounds.

a) Name the bonding in a sample of pure sodium. **[1 mark]**

....

b) Name the particle that carries electric charge in a sample of pure sodium. **[1 mark]**

....

c) Name the bonding in a pure sample of solid sodium chloride. **[1 mark]**

....

d) Name the particle that carries the electric charge during the electrolysis of sodium chloride solution. **[1 mark]**

....

9 Energy P1 / Particle Model of Matter P1 • Grade 6–7

Buildings can be fitted with an air source heat pump.

This increases the temperature of the air inside the building by transferring energy from the air outside a building.

The diagram shows an air source heat pump.

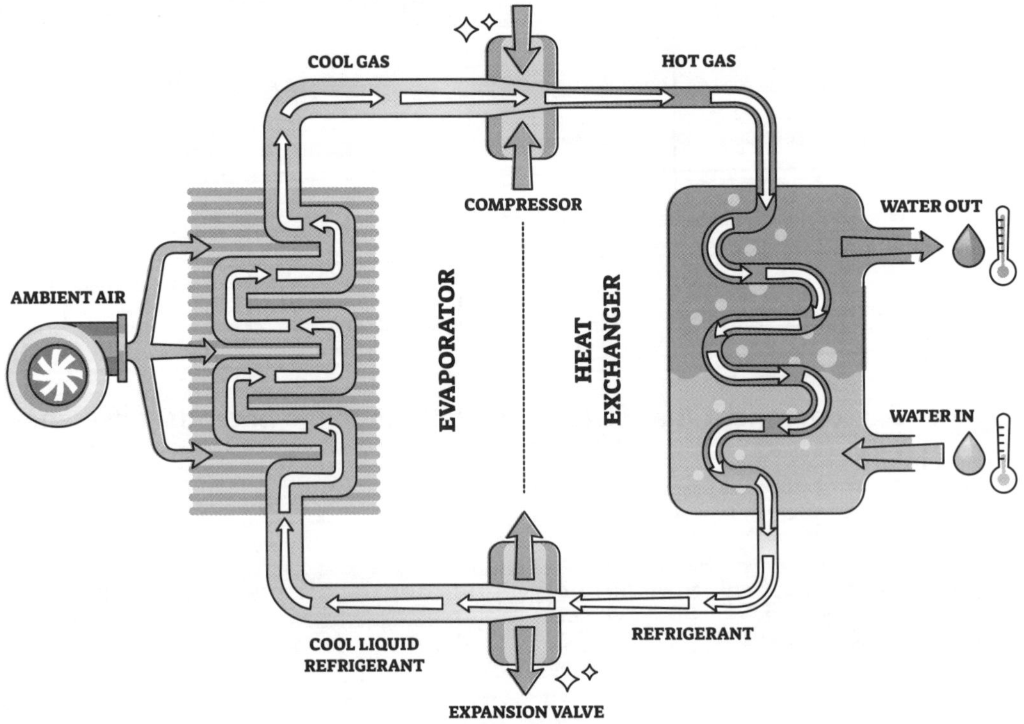

a) Name the physical change happening to the refrigerant in the heat exchanger. **[1 mark]**

....

b) Name the energy change accompanying the change of state of the refrigerant in the evaporator. **[1 mark]**

....

10 Energy P2 • Grade 6–7

The picture shows a narrow boat.

The narrow boat generates its own electricity to charge the battery on the boat.

Name **two** renewable sources of energy that could be used on the boat to generate electricity. **[2 marks]**

1 ....

2 ....

11 Organic Chemistry P2 • Grade 8–9

This question is about ethene.

a) Name the **two** processes used to make ethene from crude oil. **[1 mark]**

....

....

b) Name the **two** products when ethene undergoes complete combustion. **[1 mark]**

....

....

c) Name the product produced when ethene undergoes an addition reaction with steam. **[1 mark]**

....

Total score: .... / 30

Write

Recall a fact, definition or equation and write it down. Only a short answer is required, not an explanation or a description.

Worked example and more!

TOP TIP
The space provided will give an indication of the amount of detail required.

In Chemistry, 'write' is mostly used for chemical equations.

Example question

1 **Organic Chemistry P2 • Grade 4–5**

Methane is the main hydrocarbon found in natural gas. Natural gas is combusted in gas boilers in homes to provide heat.

Write a word equation for the complete combustion of methane. **[2 marks]**

Complete the example

2 Bioenergetics P1 • Grade 4–5

Anaerobic respiration in yeast cells is used to manufacture useful products.

a) Write the word equation for anaerobic respiration in yeast cells. **[1 mark]**

Glucose → .... + ...

b) Write **one** food and **one** drink that are produced using anaerobic respiration in yeast. **[1 mark]**

....

3 Magnetism and Electromagnetism P2 • Grade 6–7

The motor effect is caused when a current carrying wire interacts with another magnetic field.

Write down the equation that links magnetic flux density, current and length. **[1 mark]**

Remember that you have a formula sheet in the physics examination. This formula is for higher tier only and on the formula sheet.

....

....

Exam practice questions

33

1 Ecology P2 • Grade 4–5

Organisms in food webs can be named according to their trophic level.

a) Write the name given to herbivores that feeds on producers. **[1 mark]**

....

b) Write the name given to carnivores that do not have any predators. **[1 mark]**

....

c) Write the name given to carnivores that feed on herbivores. **[1 mark]**

....

2 Inheritance, Variation and Evolution P2 • Grade 4–5

Tom and Jake are identical twins. This means they have inherited the same genes from their parents.

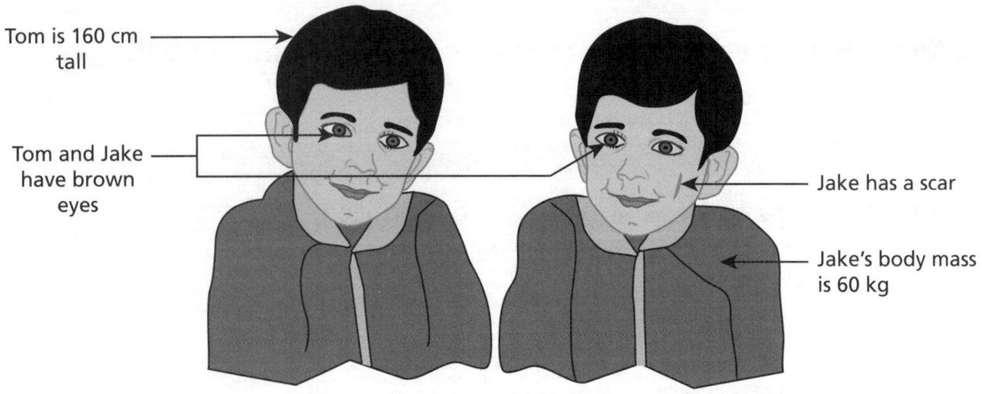
Tom is 160 cm tall
Tom and Jake have brown eyes
Jake has a scar
Jake's body mass is 60 kg

Write each of the characteristics from the image in the correct column of the table. **[4 marks]**

Controlled by their genes	Caused by the environment	Controlled by their genes and caused by the environment
....	....	....
....	....	....
....	....	....
....	....	....

3 Energy P1 • Grade 4–5

A solid material is at its melting point and is being melted.

Write down the **two** factors that will determine the amount of energy needed to melt it without raising its temperature. **[2 marks]**

1 ....

2 ....

4 Electricity P1 / Magnetism and Electromagnetism P2 • Grade 4–5

Write down the **three** factors which affect the strength of a solenoid. **[3 marks]**

1 ....

2 ....

3 ....

5 Inheritance, Variation and Evolution P2 • Grade 6–7

Organisms are classified into groups called:

- kingdom
- phylum
- class
- order
- family
- genus
- species.

a) Two of these groups form the biological name for each organism.

Write down these two groups. **[2 marks]**

....

b) Write down the name given to this system of naming organisms. **[1 mark]**

....

c) Carl Woese introduced a new level of classification above kingdom.

Write down the name of this level of classification. **[1 mark]**

....

6 Cell Biology P1 • Grade 6–7

Write down the name of the sub-cellular structure that fits each of these descriptions. **[3 marks]**

a) Small loops of DNA found in the cytoplasm ....

b) Structures where glucose is oxidised ....

c) Structures where a light endothermic reaction occurs ....

7 Atomic Structure and the Periodic Table P1 • Grade 6–7

Potassium is a Group 1 metal. When a small piece of potassium metal is put into water, it reacts to make potassium hydroxide and a gas.

The figure below shows the reaction.

Write a balanced symbol equation for the reaction between potassium metal and water.

You do **not** need to include state symbols. **[3 marks]**

....

8 Bonding, Structure, and the Properties of Matter P1 • Grade 6–7

Caesium atoms react with bromine atoms to produce caesium bromide (CsBr).

Describe what happens when a caesium atom reacts with a bromine atom.

Write about electron transfer in your answer. **[4 marks]**

....

....

....

....

9 **Forces P2 • Grade 6–7**

A truck is travelling along a road at a steady speed.

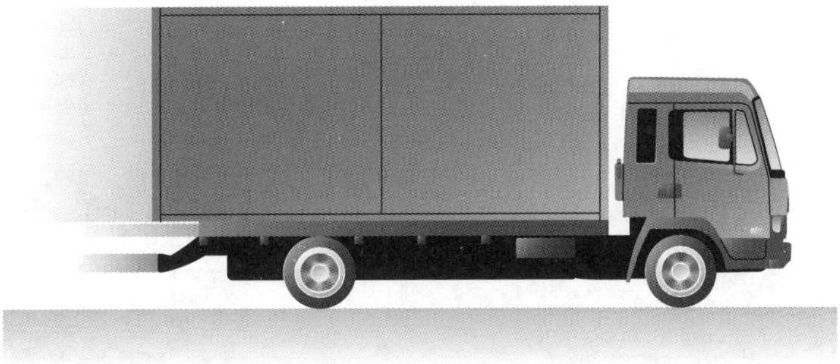

Write down the equation that can be used to calculate its momentum. **[1 mark]**

....

10 **Chemical Changes P1 • Grade 8–9**

A student electrolysed a solution of copper(II) chloride.

The figure below is a diagram of the equipment that they used.

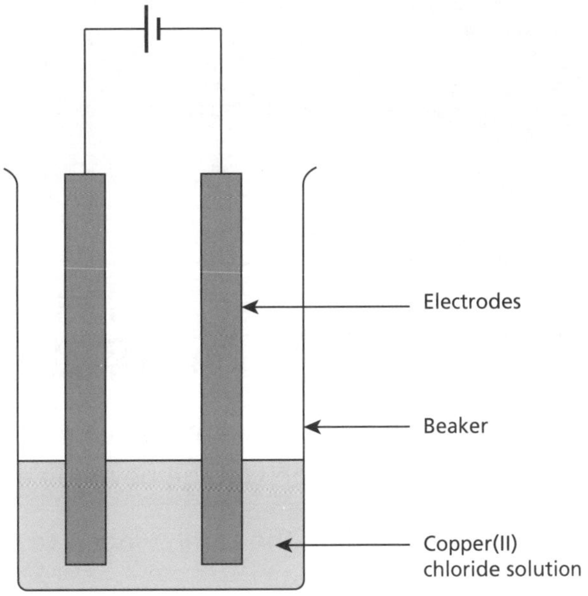

a) Write a half equation for the reaction at the anode. **[3 marks]**

....

b) Write a half equation for the reaction at the cathode. **[3 marks]**

....

Total score: .... **/ 33**

Complete

Write your answer in the space provided, for example on a diagram, in the gaps in a sentence or in a table.

Worked example and more!

TOP TIP
Fill in the gaps you know first. This can help narrow down the options for the remaining gaps.

Example question

1 **Electricity P1 • Grade 4–5**

This diagram shows how electricity generated in a power station can be distributed to consumers using high voltage power lines.

Complete the diagram by adding the correct labels to the boxes. **[4 marks]**

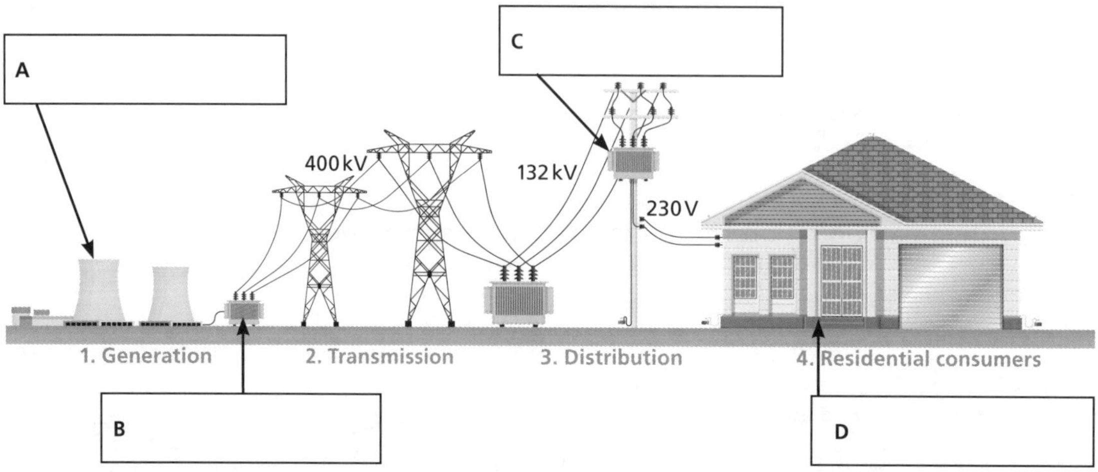

Complete the example

2 Organic Chemistry P2 • Grade 4–5

The figure below is a diagram of an organic molecule.

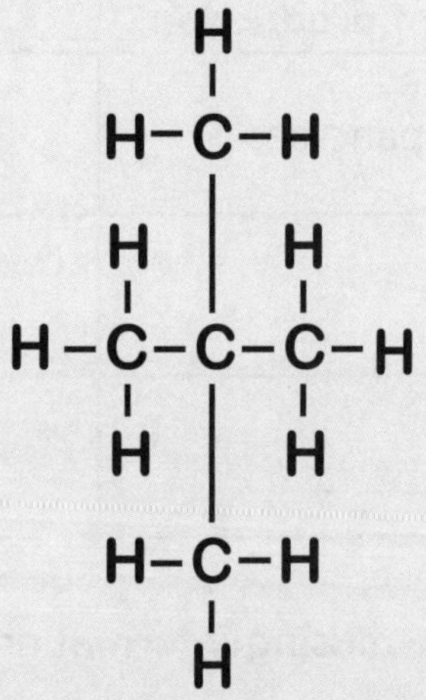

Complete the molecular formula for the molecule. **[1 mark]**

Molecular formula = C.................. H..................

3 Homeostasis and Response P2 • Grade 8–9

The diagram shows the levels of four hormones throughout the female menstrual cycle.

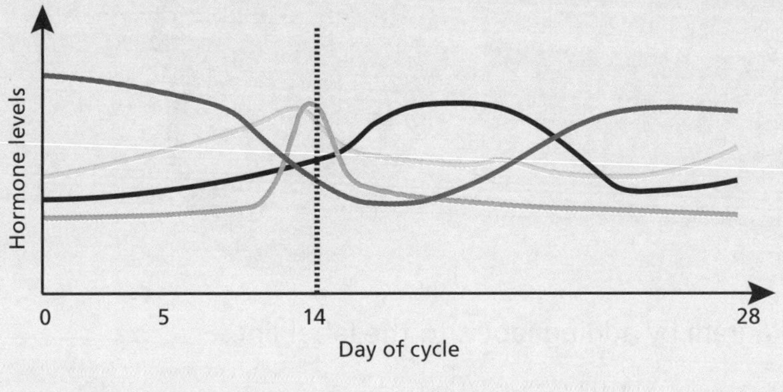

Key: — ....

— ....

— ....

— ....

Complete the diagram by writing in the names of the four hormones in the key. **[4 marks]**

Exam practice questions

52

1 Homeostasis and Response P2 • Grade 4–5

The table shows some details about different human hormones.

Hormone	Site of production	Function
insulin	pancreas	
testosterone		controls production of secondary sexual characteristics
thyroxine		

Complete the table by giving the missing information. **[4 marks]**

2 Organisation P1 • Grade 4–5

The diagram shows a section through the human heart.

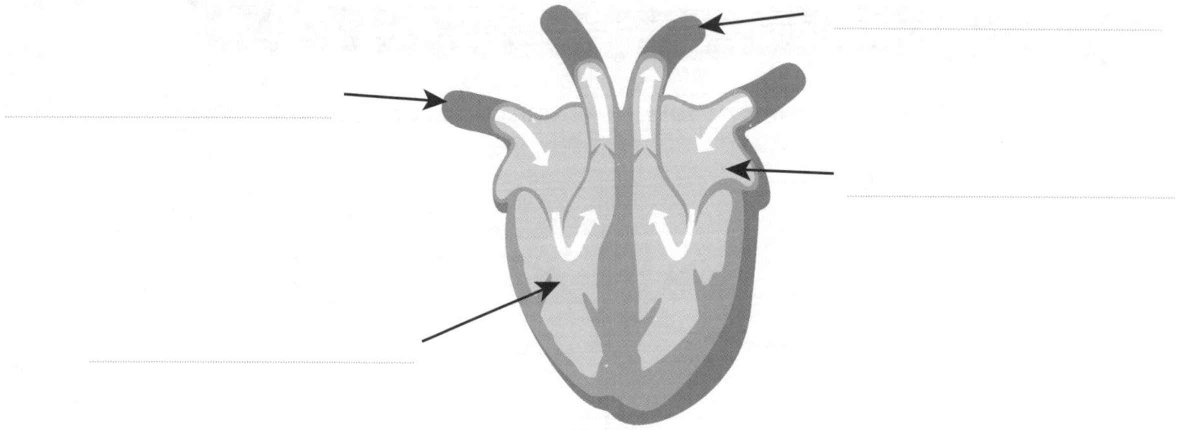

Complete the diagram by adding labels to the label lines. **[4 marks]**

3 Cell Biology P1 • Grade 4–5

In an osmosis experiment, potato cylinders are left in different concentrations of sugar solution.

The percentage change in mass of the cylinders is calculated.

The table shows the results of the experiment.

Concentration of sugar solution %	Percentage change in mass of cylinder
0	+10.1
0.2	+3.3
0.4	+1.2
0.6	–1.3
0.8	–4.5

Complete these sentences to explain the results of the experiment. **[4 marks]**

The cylinder in 0% sugar solution .... in mass.

This is because .... entered the cell through a .... permeable membrane.

The results show that the cytoplasm of the potato cells has a concentration approximately equivalent to a ....% sugar solution.

4 Energy Changes P1 • Grade 4–5

This question is about energy changes.

Complete the sentences. **[3 marks]**

An exothermic reaction is one that transfers energy to the ....

Endothermic reactions cause the temperature of the surroundings to ....

Hand warmers and self-heating cans are examples of everyday uses of ....

5 Bonding, Structure, and the Properties of Matter P1 • Grade 4–5

Magnesium is a metal and can form a compound with oxygen.

A magnesium atom contains two electrons in the outer shell.

An oxygen atom contains six electrons in the outer shell.

Complete the dot-and-cross diagram for the compound of magnesium oxide. Show the outer electrons only. **[4 marks]**

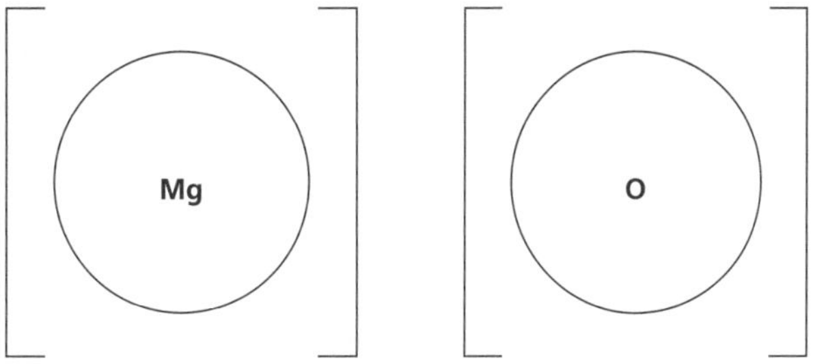

6 The Rate and Extent of Chemical Change P2 • Grade 4–5

A student wanted to investigate the reaction between magnesium and hydrochloric acid.

The student used the equipment shown in the figure below.

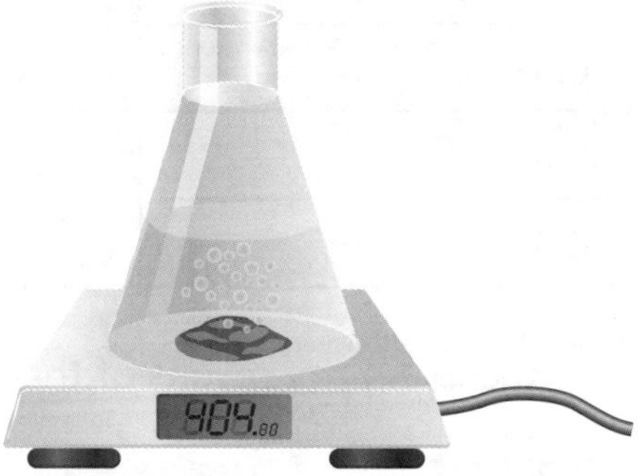

The student investigated different concentrations of hydrochloric acid and measured the mass change to determine the rate of reaction with magnesium metal.

a) Complete the word equation for this reaction. **[2 marks]**

magnesium + hydrochloric acid → .... + ...

b) Complete the sentences. **[2 marks]**

The independent variable is ....

The dependent variable is ....

7 Energy P1 • Grade 4–5

The table shows various situations in which energy is being transferred.

Complete the table by filling in the gaps. **[3 marks]**

Situation	An energy store that is being filled	An energy store that is being depleted
Weight being dropped from a height.	Kinetic	**a)** ....
Climber reaching the top of a hill.	**b)**	Chemical
Spring being stretched by weights being hung on it.	**c)**	Kinetic

8 Energy P1 • Grade 4–5

The melting point of wax is 80°C.

The graph shows how the temperature of a sample of wax changes as it cools down and freezes.

Complete the graph by labeling the different physical states of the wax. **[3 marks]**

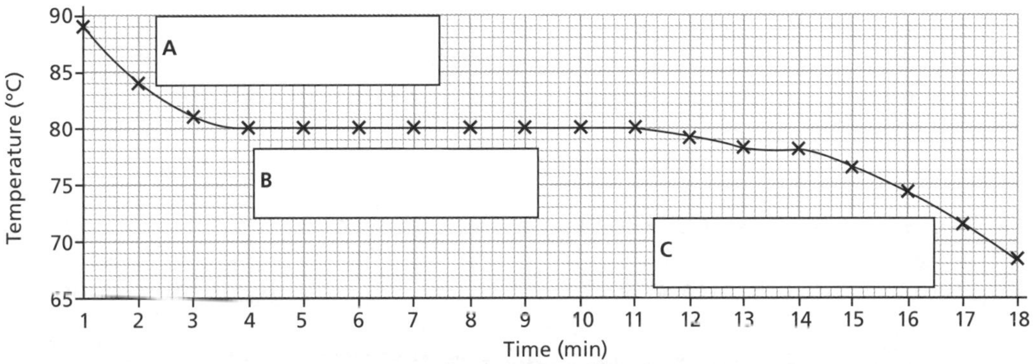

9 Energy P1 • Grade 4–5

This question is about energy stores.

Complete the sentence.

Choose the answer from the box. **[1 mark]**

gravitational potential	chemical	kinetic	strain potential

A toy car rolls down a ramp and off across the floor.

When it reaches the bottom of the ramp, its .... energy store is at its highest level for the whole journey.

10 Waves P2 • Grade 4–5

The diagram shows a ripple tank set up to demonstrate wave behaviour.

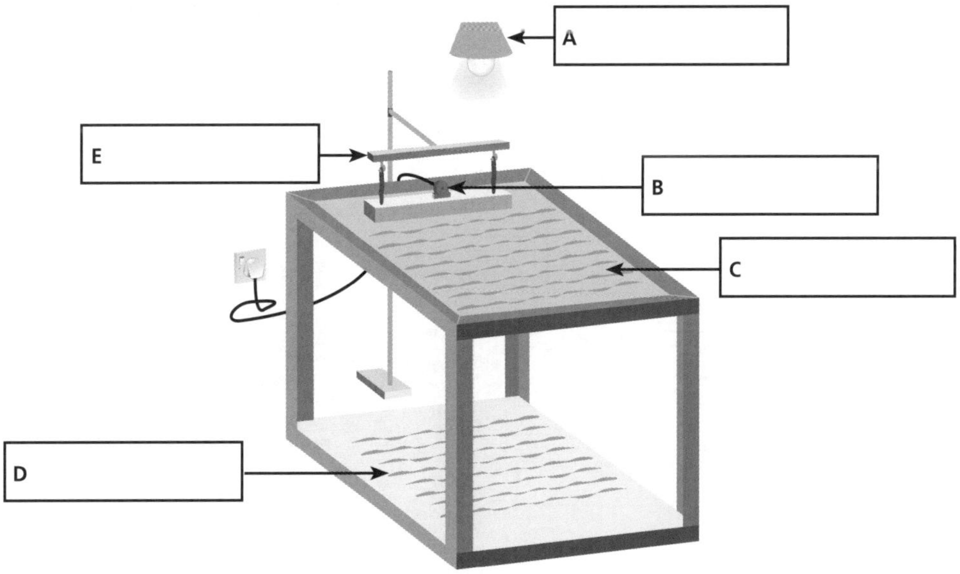

Complete the diagram by adding the correct labels. **[5 marks]**

11 Inheritance, Variation and Evolution P2 • Grade 6–7

Complete these sentences about gene expression in humans. **[6 marks]**

Some characteristics in humans are controlled by a single gene, such as ....

Each gene may have different forms called alleles.

The alleles present in a gene are called the ....

The characteristic that is expressed by the gene is called the ....

A .... allele is always expressed, even if only one copy is present.

If the two alleles for a gene are the same, the organism is .... for that trait.

Most characteristics are a result of .... genes interacting.

12 Quantitative Chemistry P1 • Grade 6–7

This question is about the amount of substance.

Complete the sentences. **[2 marks]**

a) Chemical amounts are measured in ....

b) The number of atoms, molecules or ions in a mole of a given substance is the

....

13 Atomic Structure and the Periodic Table P1 • Grade 6–7

This question is about halogen displacement reactions.

A student investigated the reactivity of the halogens.

The student mixed chlorine water with potassium bromide solution in a test tube.

a) Complete the sentence. **[1 mark]**

A more reactive halogen can displace a less reactive halogen from an aqueous solution of its ....

b) Complete the ionic equation for this reaction. **[2 marks]**

$2Br^{-}$ + ... → $2Cl^{-}$ + ...

14 Inheritance, Variation and Evolution P2 • Grade 8–9

The diagram shows stages in the production of genetically engineered bacteria to supply insulin.

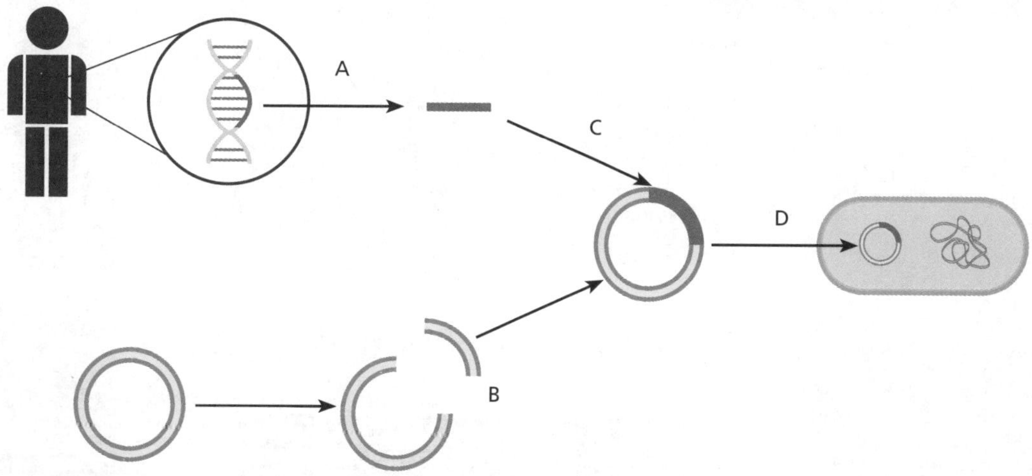

Complete this table to show the events occurring at each of the stages in the process. **[4 marks]**

Step	Events occurring
A	
B	
C	
D	

15 Bonding, Structure, and the Properties of Matter P1 / Organic Chemistry P2 • Grade 8–9

Acetylene is an unsaturated hydrocarbon that contains two carbon atoms and only two hydrogen atoms.

Complete the dot-and-cross diagram for a molecule of acetylene.

Show the outer electrons only. **[2 marks]**

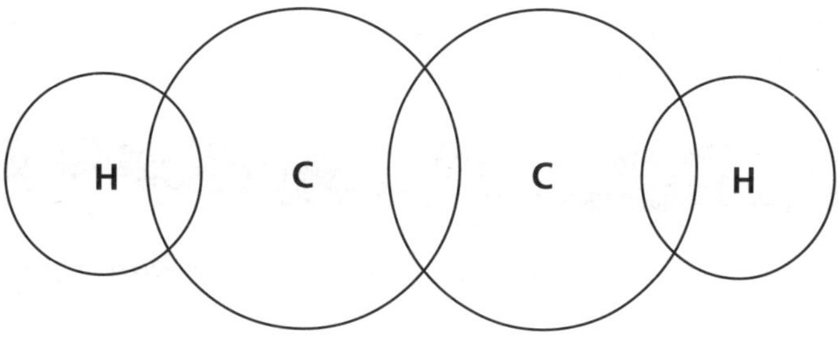

Total score: .... / 52

Define

Give the exact meaning of a term or idea.

Worked example and more!

TOP TIP
Defining something means being very clear about what that thing is.

Example question

1 **Organisation P1 • Grade 4–5**

Transport in plants involves the processes of transpiration and translocation.

a) Define **transpiration**. **[2 marks]**

b) Define **translocation**. **[2 marks]**

Complete the example

2 Forces P2 • Grade 4–5

Define the term acceleration. **[1 mark]**

The rate at which .... *changes.*

3 Chemical Changes P1 • Grade 6–7

The thermite reaction is used to weld railway tracks together.

Iron oxide is reduced by aluminium in a displacement reaction.

The balanced symbol equation for the reaction is:

$Fe_2O_3 + 2Al \rightarrow Al_2O_3 + 2Fe$

a) Define **oxidation.** **[2 marks]**

Gain of .... *and loss of* ....

b) Define **reduction.** **[2 marks]**

Loss of .... *and gain of* ....

Exam practice questions

22

1 Ecology P2 • Grade 4–5

In a pond ecosystem there is a varied community of organisms.

a) Define the term ecosystem. **[1 mark]**

....

....

b) Define the term community. **[1 mark]**

....

....

2 Organic Chemistry P2 • Grade 4–5

Methane is an example of a hydrocarbon and the first member of the alkane homologous series. The figure below is a diagram of a molecule of methane. Carbon is shown as black spheres and hydrogen is shown as white spheres.

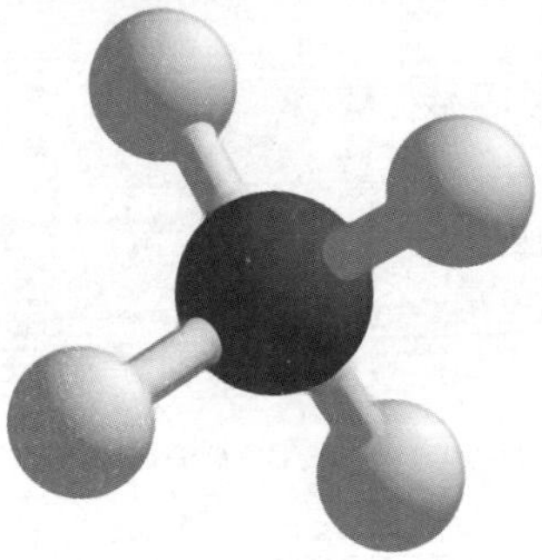

Define hydrocarbon. **[2 marks]**

....

....

3 Energy Changes P1 • Grade 4–5

Hydrocarbon fuels undergo combustion reactions when they are used.

Usually a spark or flame will provide the activation energy to start the combustion reaction.

a) Define exothermic. **[2 marks]**

....

....

b) Define activation energy. **[1 mark]**

....

....

4 Chemistry of the Atmosphere P2 • Grade 4–5

In the UK, potable water is produced from an unpolluted source of fresh water. Potable water contains low levels of dissolved substances.

Define potable water. **[1 mark]**

5 Waves P2 • Grade 4–5

Waves transfer energy between stores.

Motion of a wave can be described by frequency.

Define the term frequency. **[1 mark]**

6 Energy P1 • Grade 4–5

Energy is always conserved but can be transfered between energy stores.

Define the term kinetic energy store. **[1 mark]**

7 Energy P1 • Grade 4–5

Define the term specific heat capacity. **[1 mark]**

8 Atomic Structure P1 • Grade 4–5

Uranium 235 is a radioactive isotope.

$$^{235}_{92}\mathrm{U}$$

Define what is meant by the half life of a radioactive isotope. **[1 mark]**

9 Atomic Structure P1 • Grade 4–5

Foods are often irradiated to improve shelf life by reducing the number of microorganisms present.

Define the term irradiation. **[1 mark]**

....

....

10 Infection and Response P1 • Grade 6–7

Human health can be influenced by the environment. This may involve a disease which can be affected by various risk factors.

a) Define health. **[1 mark]**

....

....

b) Define risk factor. **[1 mark]**

....

....

11 Quantitative Chemistry P1 / Chemical Changes P1 • Grade 6–7

A student wanted to make a pure dry sample of copper(II) sulfate.

This is the method used:

1. React excess copper(II) oxide with sulfuric acid.
2. Filter off and crystallise the product from the filtrate.
3. Remove the crystals and dry with absorbent paper.

Sulfuric acid was the limiting reactant.

Define limiting reactant. **[1 mark]**

....

....

12 Forces P2 • Grade 6–7

Moving objects can be described in terms of momentum.

Define what is meant by momentum. **[1 mark]**

13 Electricity P1 • Grade 6–7

In a simple circuit, a voltmeter can be used to measure the potential difference of a component.

Define the term potential difference. **[1 mark]**

14 Homeostasis and Response P2 • Grade 8–9

Cells in the body can only survive within narrow physical and chemical limits.

The body constantly monitors and adjusts the composition of the blood and tissues.

a) Define homeostasis. **[2 marks]**

b) Define the term negative feedback. **[2 marks]**

Total score: / 22

Describe

You need to give the details of facts or processes in an organised way.

Worked example and more!

TOP TIP

In 'Describe' questions you are rewarded for giving a logical flow of information, so it can help to plan your answer as a bullet point list and think about the order you want to write the bullet points in.

Example question

1 **Atomic Structure and the Periodic Table P1 • Grade 4–5**

The model of the atom has changed over time as new scientific evidence has been collected. In 1897, J.J. Thomson discovered the electron.

Describe the atomic model of the atom that J.J. Thomson proposed. **[2 marks]**

Complete the example

2 Organisation P1 • Grade 4–5

Describe the functions of bile in digestion. **[3 marks]**

Bile is .... and so neutralises ....

released in the ....

Bile also ....

This means that bile .... the rate of ....

.. by lipase ....

3 Forces P2 • Grade 4–5

This graph shows the motion of an object.

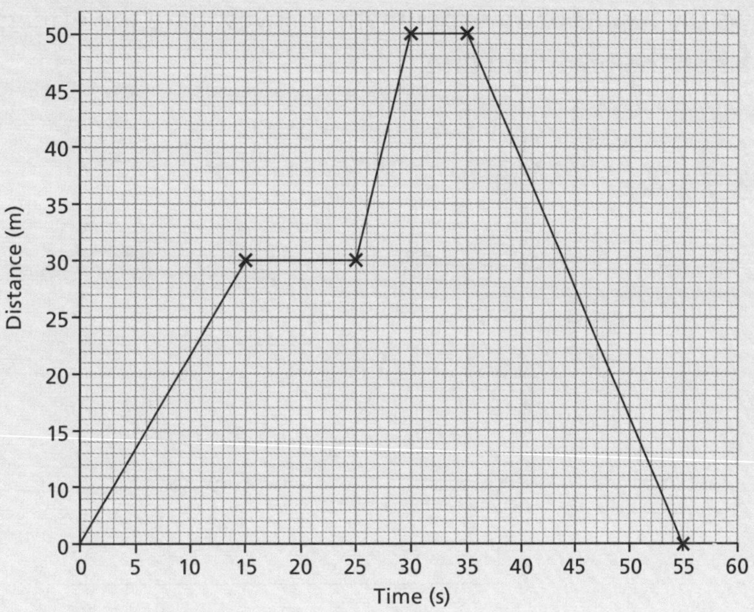

Describe the motion of the object. **[4 marks]**

The graph shows the relationship between distance and ....

On a graph like this if the line is horizontal it means that the object is

.. . If the line has a positive gradient it means that the

object is ....

In this graph the object starts off by travelling at a ....

and then .... It then moves at a greater .... ,

then .... and finally ....

Exam practice questions

67

1 Inheritance, Variation and Evolution P2 • Grade 4–5

Fossils are the remains of organisms from millions of years ago.

Describe how fossils can be formed. **[4 marks]**

2 Bioenergetics P1 • Grade 4–5

The graph shows the results of an experiment to investigate the effects of percentage of oxygen in the air on the breathing rate.

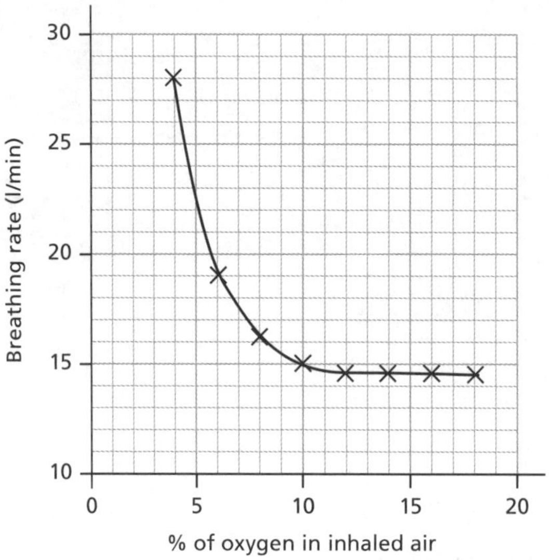

Describe the pattern of results shown by the graph.

Include data in your answer. **[3 marks]**

3 Atomic Structure and the Periodic Table (P1) • Grade 4–5

This question is about the Periodic Table.

a) Describe how elements were ordered before subatomic particles were discovered. **[1 mark]**

....

....

b) Describe how Mendeleev's Periodic Table was different to the earlier attempts to order elements. **[2 marks]**

....

....

....

....

c) Describe how the modern Periodic Table is different to Mendeleev's original Periodic Table. **[3 marks]**

....

....

....

4 Chemical Changes (P1) / Chemical Analysis (P2) • Grade 4–5

A student used electrolysis to investigate the products at the electrodes.

The student used the equipment shown in the diagram.

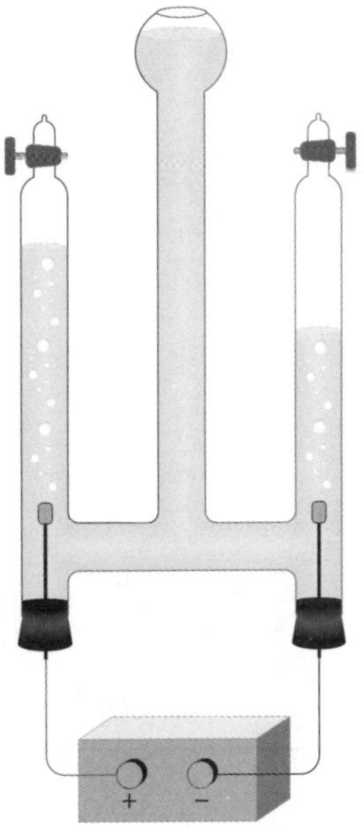

The gaseous products were collected.

In the investigation, samples of chlorine, hydrogen and oxygen gas were collected.

Describe how to test for each gas. **[6 marks]**

Chlorine: ....

....

Hydrogen: ....

....

Oxygen: ....

....

5 Waves P2 • Grade 4–5

A slinky is a long, flexible coil of wire with a diameter of around 6–8 cm.

Describe how it can be used to represent both transverse and longitudinal waves. You may find it useful to include diagrams. **[4 marks]**

Transverse: ....

....

Longitudinal: ....

....

6 Particle Model of Matter P1 • Grade 4–5

Describe how the density of an irregularly shaped insoluble solid can be determined. **[6 marks]**

7 Forces P2 • Grade 4–5

The graph shows changes in the velocity of a racing car.

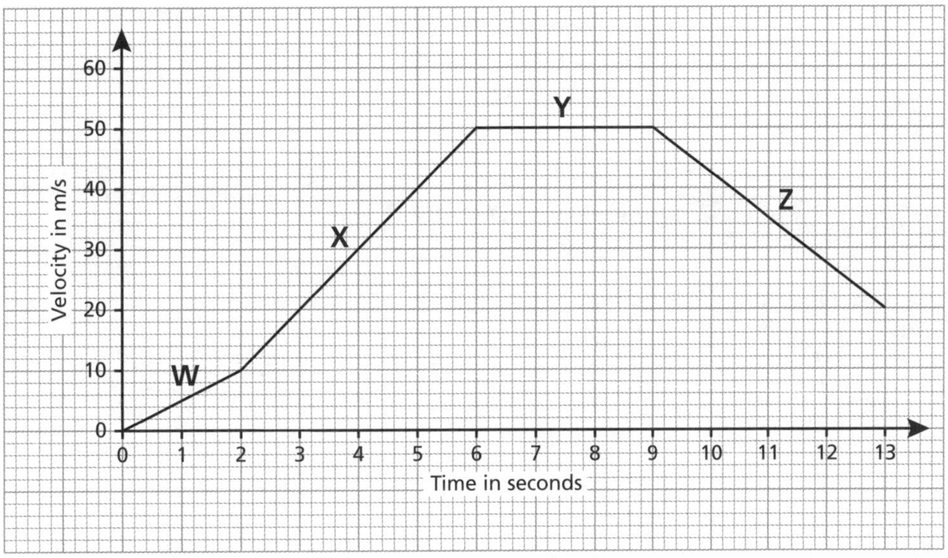

Describe the motion of the car in the section marked Z. **[1 mark]**

8 Cell Biology P1 • Grade 6–7

Stem cells are undifferentiated cells.

Describe what happens to a cell when it differentiates. **[2 marks]**

9 Inheritance, Variation and Evolution P2 • Grade 6–7

Describe the structure of a DNA molecule. **[5 marks]**

10 Cell Biology P1 • Grade 6–7

Describe the main processes occurring during the cell cycle. **[5 marks]**

11 Using Resources P2 • Grade 6–7

Malachite is a copper ore that is becoming scarce.

Bioleaching is a new way of extracting copper from low-grade ores.

Describe how copper is extracted from low-grade ores by bioleaching. **[4 marks]**

12 Bonding, Structure, and the Properties of Matter P1 • Grade 6–7

Silica is also called silicon dioxide (SiO_2). The figure is a diagram of a crystal of silica.

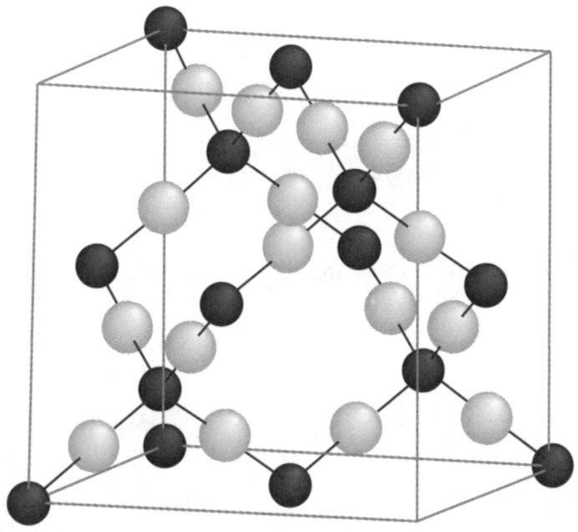

Describe the structure and bonding of silica. **[4 marks]**

....

....

....

....

13 Electricity P1 • Grade 6–7

Describe how the resistance of a resistor can be determined using an ammeter and a voltmeter. Suggest what other equipment you would need to use. You may find it useful to include a diagram. **[6 marks]**

....

....

....

....

....

....

....

....

....

....

....

....

....

14 Forces P2 • Grade 6–7

A group of students make their own weighing device by setting up a spring with a pointer and a scale.

Describe how they could calibrate their device so it can be used to weigh various objects. **[6 marks]**

The diagram shows a potometer that can be used to measure water uptake by a leafy shoot.

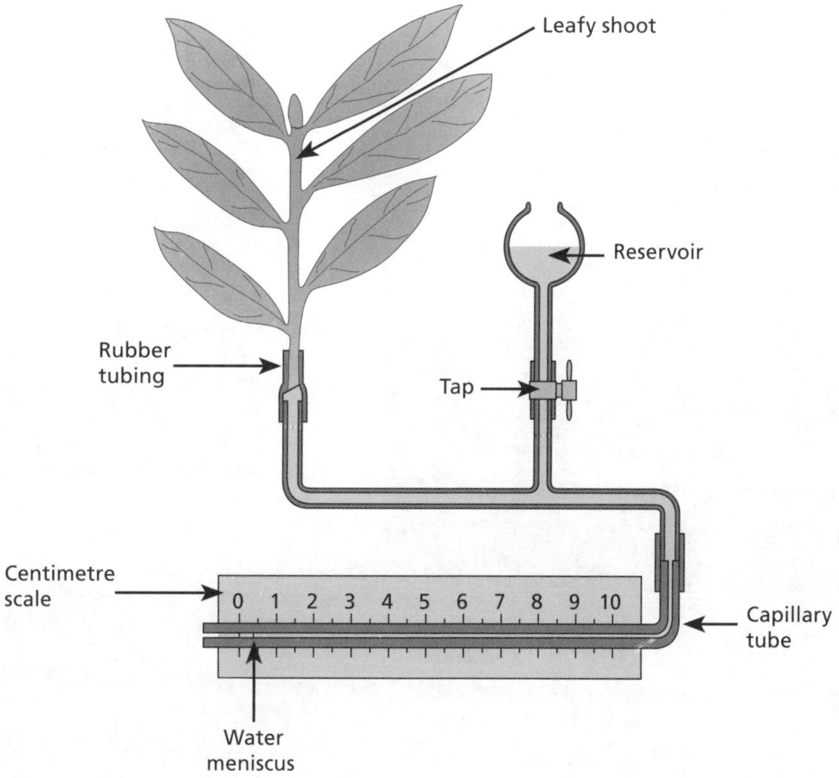

Describe how this apparatus could be used to measure the volume of water taken up by the shoot in cm^3/ hour. **[5 marks]**

Total score: .... / 67

Why/ What/ Which...

Why/What/Which/ Where/When/Who/How

These command words are used for direct questions to prompt short and precise answers.

Worked example and more!

TOP TIP
Even though a good answer may be quite brief, it does need to be relevant.

Example question

1 **Cell Biology P1 • Grade 4–5**

Some students investigate the growth of onions.

They put an onion bulb in a jar of water. The bulb starts to grow roots.

Cells in the root tip are dividing.

Which part of the cell cycle involves cells dividing? **[1 mark]**

Complete the example

2 **Bonding, Structure, and the Properties of Matter P1 / Using Resources P2 • Grade 4–5**

Pure iron and steel can rust. The diagram shows the difference in the structure between iron and steel.

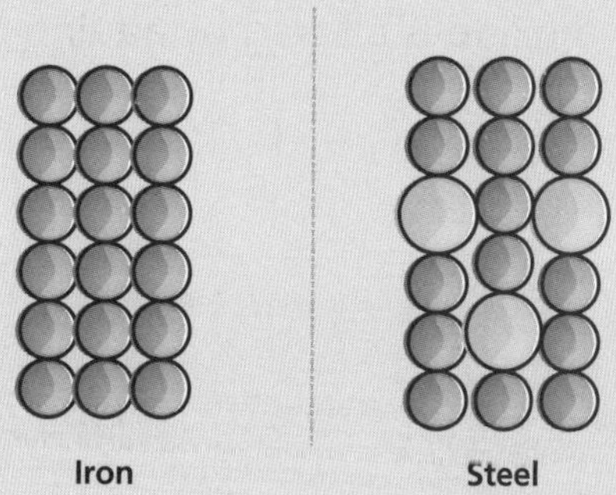

Iron Steel

a) Which of the following words describe steel?

Tick (✓) **two** boxes. **[2 marks]**

This is an AO2 question as you are asked to remember the definition of the key words and apply it to the example you are being given. Note that you are being asked to tick **two** boxes; there will be 1 mark for each correct answer.

Compound ☐

Mixture ☐

Element ☐

Formulation ☐

Aqueous solution ☐

b) Why are alloys harder than pure metals? **[2 marks]**

In pure metals, the layers of .... *easily*

over each other, but in alloys, the different sizes of ....

distort the layers so they can't .... *as easily*.

3 **Forces P2 • Grade 4–5**

What is the difference between speed and velocity? **[2 marks]**

Speed is a .... *quantity and only has* ....

Velocity is a .... *quantity and has* ....

as well as ....

Exam practice questions

39

1 Bioenergetics P1 • Grade 4–5

The diagram shows apparatus used to investigate the effect of carbon dioxide concentration on the rate of photosynthesis in pondweed.

The concentration of carbon dioxide is altered by adding different masses of sodium hydrogen carbonate to the beaker.

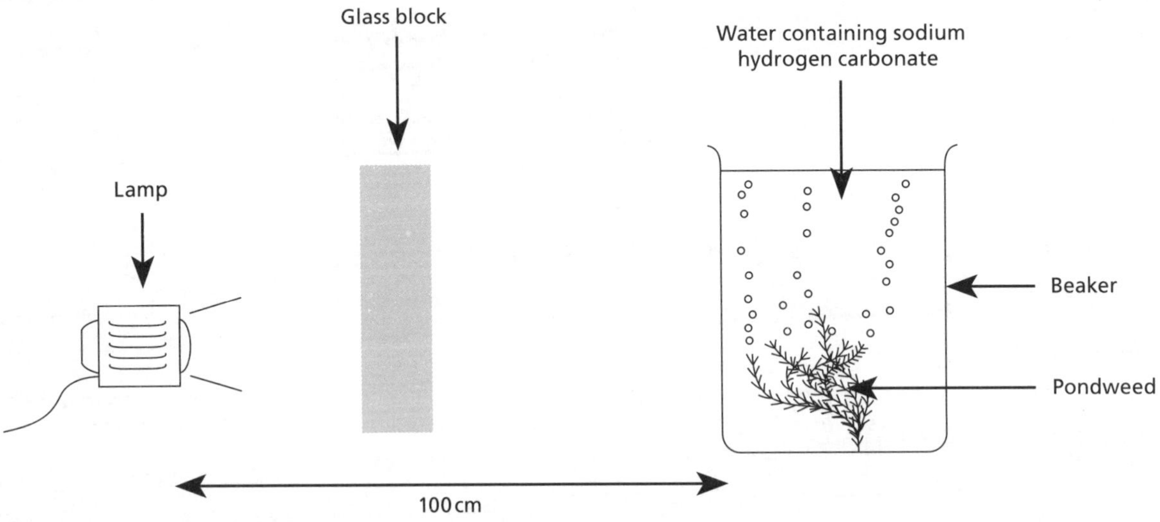

a) What is the function of the glass block in this experiment? **[1 mark]**

....

....

b) What is the dependent variable in this experiment? **[1 mark]**

....

....

2 Organisation P1 • Grade 4–5

The diagram shows a specialised cell.

a) What is the name of this cell? **[1 mark]**

....

b) Why does this cell not have a nucleus? **[1 mark]**

....

....

3 Organic Chemistry P2 / Using Resources P2 • Grade 4–5

Poly(propene) is a polymer used for plastic packaging.

The picture below shows a single-use water bottle made from poly(propene).

a) What is the name of the monomer used to make poly(propene)? **[1 mark]**

Tick (✓) **one** box.

Propane ☐

Propene ☐

Propanol ☐

Propanoic acid ☐

b) How can poly(propene) bottles be recycled into new plastic bottles? **[4 marks]**

....

....

....

....

4 Quantitative Chemistry P1 • Grade 4–5

When calcium carbonate is strongly heated, it decomposes to form calcium oxide and carbon dioxide:

$CaCO_3(s) \rightarrow CaO(s) + CO_2(g)$

a) Why is the total mass of the reactants before the reaction equal to the total mass of the reactants after the reaction? **[1 mark]**

....

b) 10.0 g of calcium carbonate was heated until it had all reacted. 5.6 g of calcium oxide was produced.

Why had the mass of the solid gone down? **[2 marks]**

....

....

5 Electricity P1 • Grade 4–5

The diagram shows part of the National Grid.

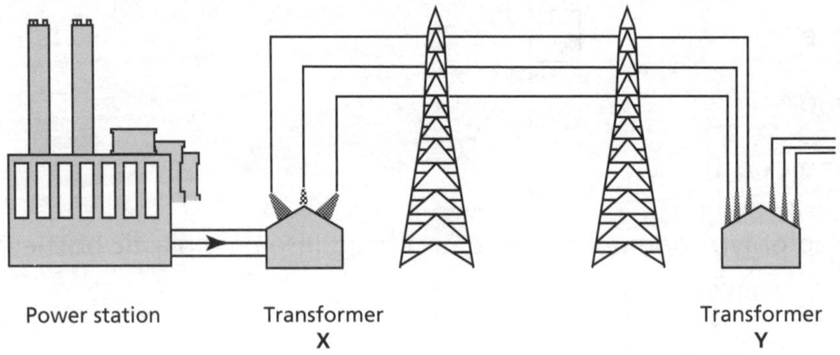

At X, the transformer increases the voltage to a very high value.

At Y, the voltage is reduced to 230 V for use by consumers.

a) What happens to the current as the voltage is increased at X? **[1 mark]**

....

b) Why is electrical energy transmitted at very high voltages? **[1 mark]**

....

c) What name is given to the type of transformer at Y? **[1 mark]**

....

6 Waves P2 • Grade 4–5

Why might central heating radiators in a building be more effective at radiating energy if they were painted matt black? **[2 marks]**

7 Atomic Structure P1 • Grade 4–5

Which type of ionising radiation is most ionising? **[1 mark]**

8 Forces P2 • Grade 4–5

Motion can be displayed on both distance–time graphs and on velocity–time graphs.

a) What does a horizontal straight line on a distance–time graph indicate about the motion of the object? **[1 mark]**

b) What does a horizontal straight line on a velocity–time graph indicate about the motion of an object? **[1 mark]**

9 Organisation P1 • Grade 6–7

The diagram shows a section through a leaf, with different layers labelled A–E.

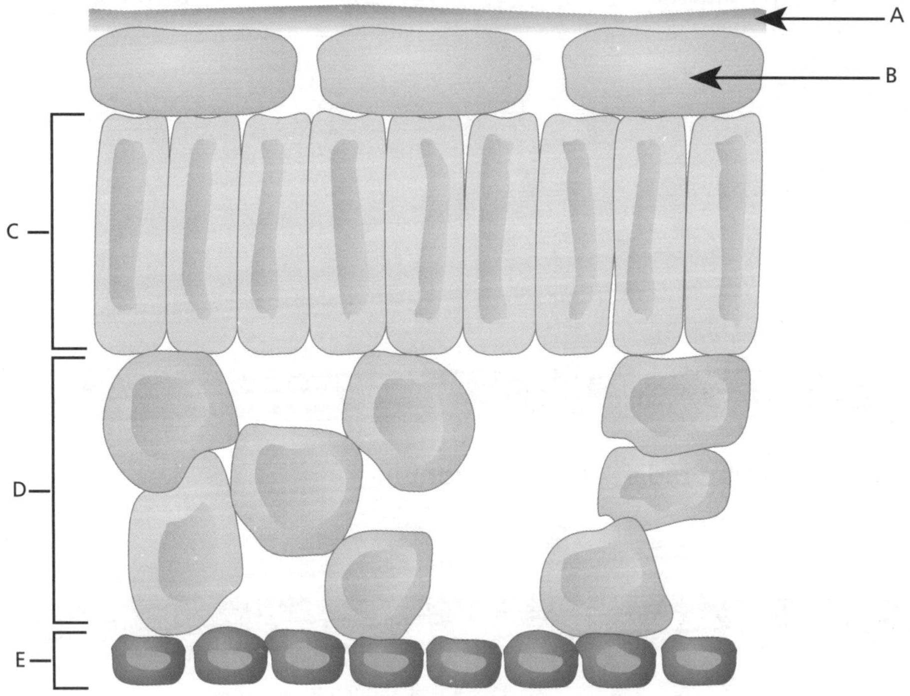

a) Which layer, A, B, C, D, or E, does **not** contain cells? **[1 mark]**

....

b) Which layers contain chloroplasts? **[1 mark]**

....

c) Which layer allows gases to diffuse most easily? **[1 mark]**

....

10 The Rate and Extent of Chemical Change P2 • Grade 6–7

A student wanted to make a pure, dry sample of copper(II) chloride.

They used these steps:

1. React an insoluble salt with hydrochloric acid.
2. Filter off the excess.
3. Crystalise the filtrate.
4. Remove crystals and pat dry with absorbent paper.

a) Which of these insoluble solids can be used to make a copper salt by reacting the solid with dilute hydrochloric acid?

Tick (✓) **one** box. **[1 mark]**

Copper and copper(II) oxide only ☐

Copper and copper(II) carbonate only ☐

Copper(II) oxide and copper(II) carbonate only ☐

Copper, copper(II) oxide and copper(II) carbonate ☐

b) Often the filtrate is gently heated in the crystalising process.

How should the filtrate be gently heated? **[1 mark]**

....

11 The Rate and Extent of Chemical Change P2 • Grade 6–7

A student wanted to investigate the rate of reaction between magnesium metal and hydrochloric acid.

The results of the experiment are shown in the graph below.

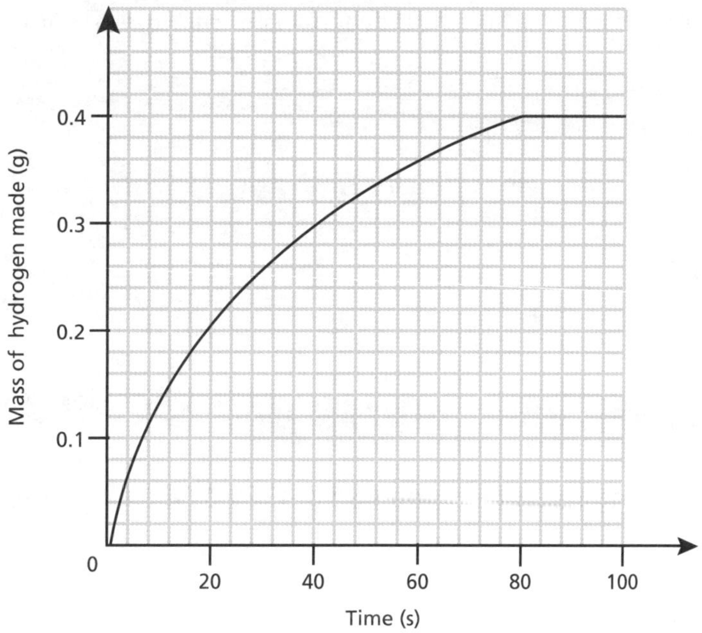

a) What measuring instrument would you use to monitor the dependent variable? **[1 mark]**

....

b) How do the results from the graph above support the conclusion that the reaction stopped at 80 seconds? **[1 mark]**

....

12 Quantitative Chemistry P1 / Chemical Changes P1 / Organic Chemistry P2 • Grade 6–7

This question is about acids.

Hydrogen chloride and ethanoic acid both dissolve in water.

All hydrogen chloride molecules ionise in water.

Approximately 1% of ethanoic acid molecules ionise in water.

a) What is the molecular formula of ethanoic acid? **[1 mark]**

....

b) Which of the following best describes a 0.1 g/dm^3 solution of ethanoic acid?
Tick (✓) **one** box. **[1 mark]**

Is a solution of a strong acid ☐

Is a concentrated solution ☐

Has a pH value of more than 7 ☐

Is an aqueous solution ☐

Is a pure, weak acid ☐

c) How many moles of ethanoic acid are in 1 dm^3 of 1 g/dm^3 solution of ethanoic acid?

Tick (✓) **one** box. **[1 mark]**

0.02 mol ☐

1 mol ☐

4.6 mol ☐

46 mol ☐

13 Waves P2 • Grade 6–7

A ray diagram showing the reflection of a light ray by a plane mirror includes a feature called the normal.

a) What is the position of the normal on the diagram? **[1 mark]**

....

b) How is the normal drawn, to show that it is not a ray? **[1 mark]**

....

c) What is the purpose of the normal? **[1 mark]**

....

....

14 Forces P2 • Grade 6–7

One type of speed camera works by taking two pictures of a car.

The picture shows this type of speed camera.

a) Why are there grid markings on the road in the area where the pictures are taken? **[1 mark]**

....

....

b) Why does the camera need to know the time interval between the two pictures being taken? **[2 marks]**

....

....

....

c) How does the camera calculate the speed of the car? **[1 mark]**

....

....

15 Inheritance, Variation and Evolution P2 • Grade 8–9

All human egg cells contain approximately the same amount of DNA.

However, some human sperm cells contain more DNA than other sperm cells.

What is the reason for this? **[2 marks]**

....

....

....

Total score: .... **/ 39**

Use

Base your answer on the information provided in the question.

Worked example and more!

TOP TIP
In some cases, you might be asked to use your own knowledge and understanding.

Example question

1 **Forces P2 • Grade 8–9**

A lump of rock falls off the edge of a cliff down onto the beach below. The cliff is 25 m high, the mass of the rock is 10 kg and the force acting on the rock due to gravity is 10 N/kg.

Assume that all the energy transferred out of the rock's gravitational potential store is now in its kinetic energy store.

Use the relevant equations and the information provided to calculate the velocity reached by the rock, just before it hits the beach, to two decimal places. **[5 marks]**

Complete the example

2 Atomic Structure and the Periodic Table P1 • Grade 4–5

The table gives some information about atoms.

Particle	Atom	Nucleus
Radius (m)	1×10^{-10}	1×10^{-14}

Name the smallest particle.

Use the table. **[1 mark]**

....

3 Cell Biology P1 • Grade 6–7

Some students use cylinders of potato tissue in an osmosis experiment. They place the cylinders in different concentrations of sugar solution.

After an hour they calculate the percentage change in mass of the cylinders. The graph shows the results.

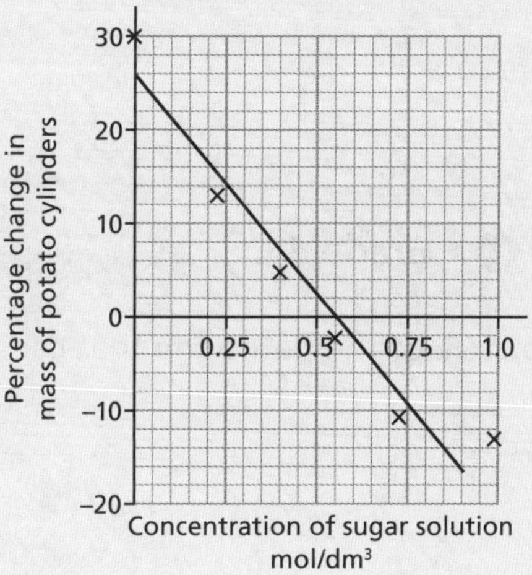

The students conclude that the concentration of the potato tissue is about 0.55 mol/dm³.

Use the graph to explain why they are correct. **[4 marks]**

The students are correct because at 0.55 mol/dm³ the line crosses the .... *and so there is no* .... *in mass. This means that there is no net movement of* .... *. Therefore the inside and outside of the potato cells must have the* ....

....

Exam practice questions

34

1 Infection and Response P1 • Grade 4–5

Smallpox is a disease that killed millions of people. Due to vaccination, the disease has disappeared. The diagrams show how people were vaccinated for smallpox.

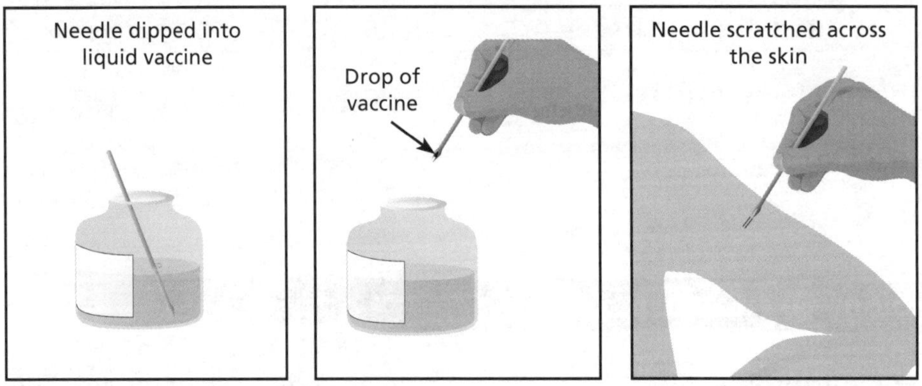

Needle dipped into liquid vaccine
Drop of vaccine
Needle scratched across the skin

Use the diagrams to suggest reasons why this method enabled large numbers of people to be vaccinated very quickly. **[2 marks]**

....

....

....

2 Infection and Response P1 • Grade 4–5

The diagram shows the life cycle of the pathogen that causes malaria.

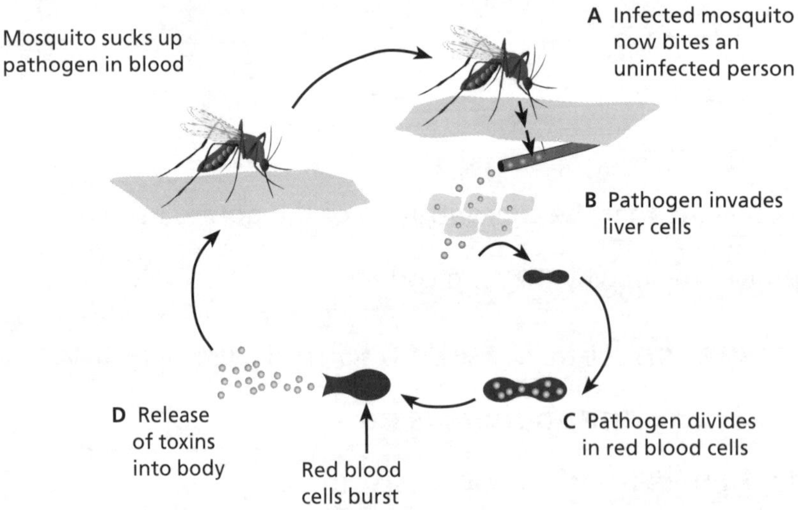

Mosquito sucks up pathogen in blood
A Infected mosquito now bites an uninfected person
B Pathogen invades liver cells
C Pathogen divides in red blood cells
Red blood cells burst
D Release of toxins into body

Use the information in the diagram to explain at which point, A, B, C or D, the person gets a fever. **[2 marks]**

....

....

....

3 Using Resources P2 • Grade 4–5

This question is about alloys.

High carbon steel is an alloy used in construction because it is strong.

The figure below shows a diagram of steel.

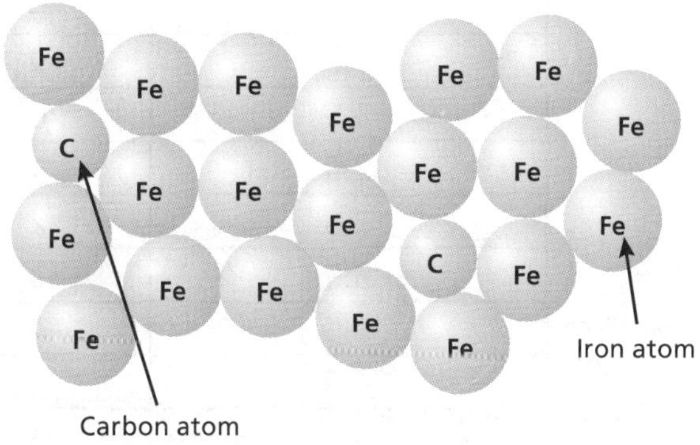

Calculate the ratio of iron to carbon atoms in the sample of steel.

Use the figure above. **[2 marks]**

....

4 Energy P1 • Grade 4–5

The figure shows an energy transfer diagram for an LED light.

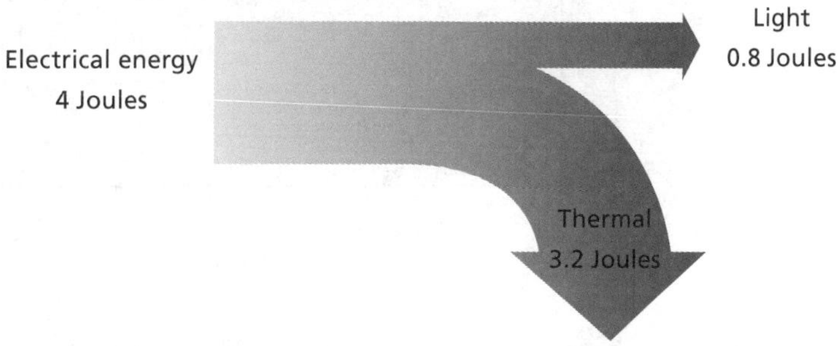

Use the information provided on the diagram to work out:

a) The amount of energy transferred out of the light which is not useful. **[2 marks]**

....

....

b) The efficiency of the light. **[2 marks]**

....

....

....

5 Electricity P1 • Grade 4–5

Use the information in this table to plot a graph, showing the relationship between the potential difference across a diode and the current flowing through it. **[4 marks]**

Potential difference/V	Current/mA
0	0
0.5	0
1.0	0
1.5	0
2.0	1
2.5	2
3.0	3
3.5	4
4.0	5
4.5	6

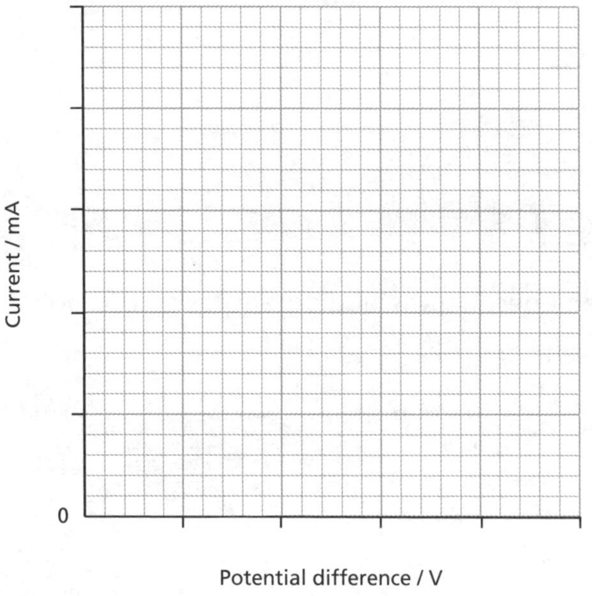

6 Ecology P2 • Grade 6–7

The graph shows how the numbers of hares and lynx varied in a habitat.

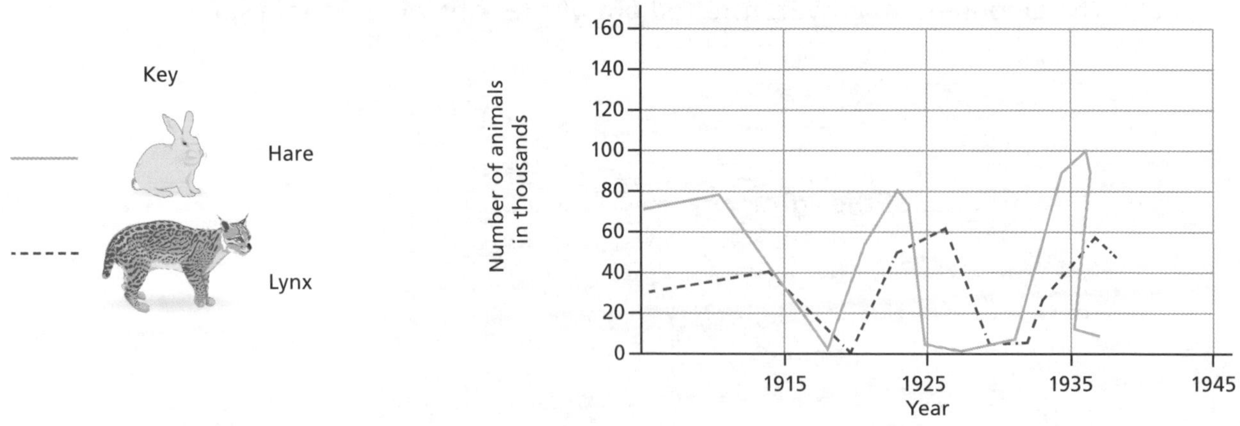

Use the data in the graph to explain how you can tell that the lynx is a predator of the hare. **[3 marks]**

....

....

....

....

7 Atomic Structure P1 • Grade 6–7

a) Use the data in this table to draw a graph, showing the relationship between the level of emissions from a radioactive source and the time passed. **[4 marks]**

Radioactive emissions	100	81	65	52	40	31	24
Time/s	0	20	40	60	80	100	120

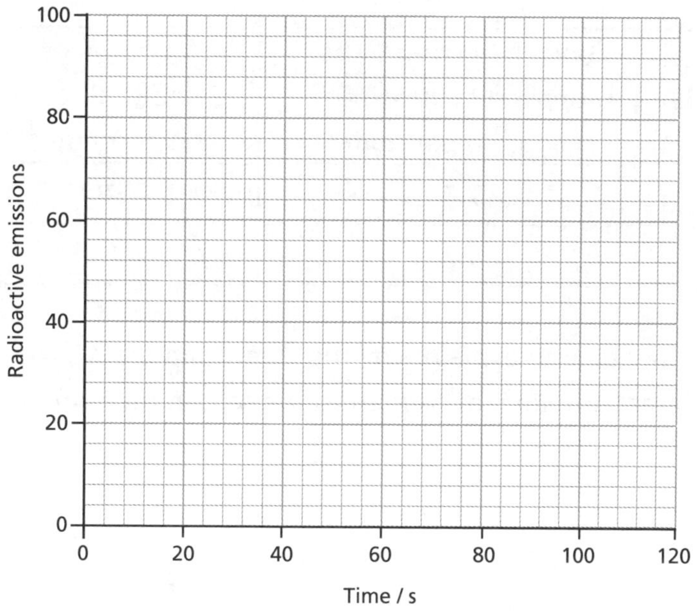

b) Use the graph to calculate the half life of the source. **[3 marks]**

....

8 Forces P2 • Grade 6–7

An apple falls from the bough of a tree by a distance of 2 m before it hits the ground.

Just before it reaches the ground, its velocity is 6 m/s.

Use the following equation to determine the acceleration due to gravity: **[4 marks]**

$v^2 - u^2 = 2as$

9 Cell Biology P1 • Grade 8–9

The table gives some information about oxygen needs and red blood cells in two different mammals.

Mammal	Oxygen needed to be supplied in litres per kilogram per hour	Surface area of one red blood cell in arbitrary units	Volume of one red blood cell in arbitrary units
shrew	7.4	58	24
mouse	1.7	91	52

Use the data in the table to explain why the shrew and mouse red blood cells can supply very different amounts of oxygen to the cells in the two mammals. **[3 marks]**

A student used chromatography to investigate the composition of some fizzy drinks.

The figure below shows the results.

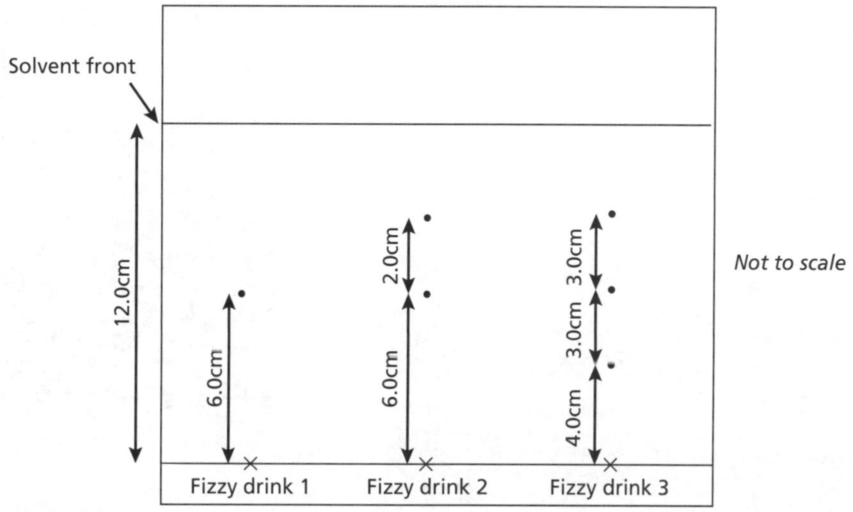

a) Use the figure above to justify the conclusion that fizzy drink 1 is pure. **[1 mark]**

....

....

b) Calculate the R_f value of the common component found in fizzy drinks 1 and 2.

Use the figure above. **[2 marks]**

....

Total score: .... / 34

Draw

Draw lines to connect information, draw either a complete drawing or diagram, or add to one you are given.

Worked example and more!

TOP TIP
Artistic ability is not important, but clarity and accuracy are. Think about the key features you need to include and ensure that these can be understood.

Example question

1 **Particle Model of Matter P1 • Grade 4–5**

Draw a diagram to show how the volume of an irregular shaped object can be determined by immersing it in water. **[3 marks]**

Complete the example

2 Cell Biology P1 • Grade 4–5

The photograph shows a cheek cell taken using a light microscope.

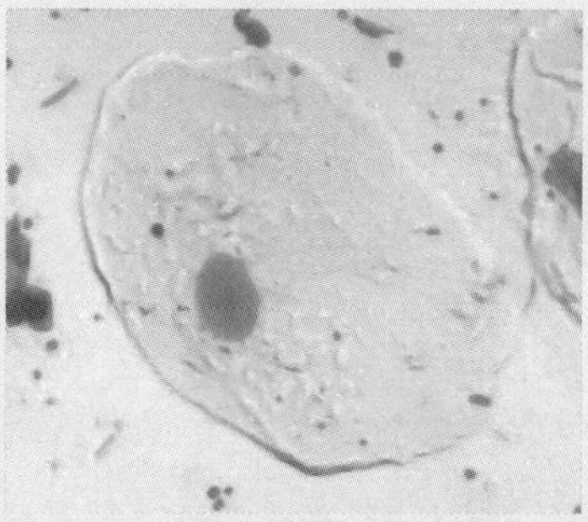

Draw a labelled biological drawing of the cheek cell. **[3 marks]**

Remember that in biological drawings there should be no shading and the lines should be clear and not sketched.

3 Atomic Structure and the Periodic Table P1 • Grade 4–5

Magnesium is a Group 2 metal. Chlorine is a Group 7 non-metal. Magnesium and chlorine can react together to make magnesium chloride.

Draw a dot-and-cross diagram to show what happens when atoms of magnesium and chlorine react to produce magnesium chloride. **[5 marks]**

When a metal and a non-metal react together, an ionic compound is formed. Use square brackets to show each individual ion. Remember that metals lose electrons and become positive ions. Non-metals gain electrons and become negative ions.

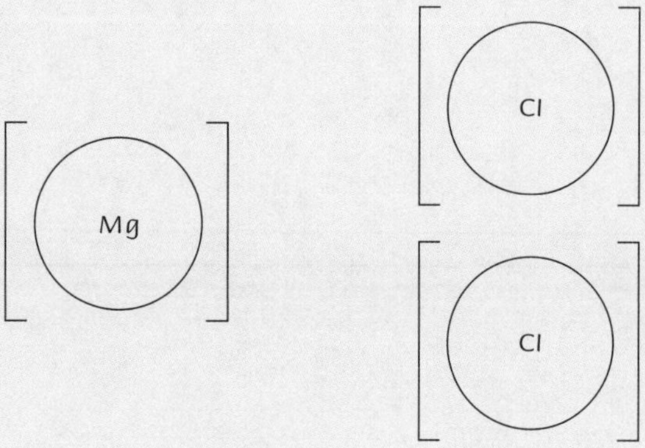

Exam practice questions

37

1 Homeostasis and Response P2 • Grade 4–5

The diagram shows a person touching a drawing pin and taking their hand away.
This is a reflex action.

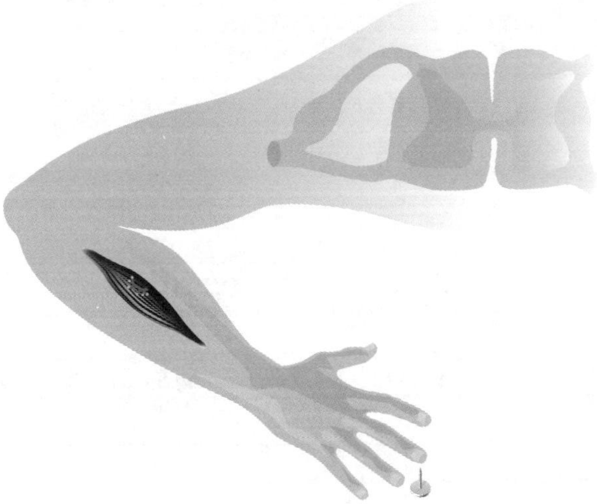

Draw on the diagram the positions of the three types of neurone that are involved in this reflex. Label the neurones. **[3 marks]**

2 Atomic Structure and the Periodic Table P1 / Bonding, Structure, and the Properties of Matter P1 • Grade 4–5

Fluorine is a yellow gas at room temperature.

The proton number of fluorine is 9.

a) Draw the electronic structure of fluorine. **[2 marks]**

b) Fluorine forms molecules at room temperature.

Draw a dot-and-cross diagram for a fluorine molecule.

Show only the outer shell electrons. **[2 marks]**

3 Electricity P1 • Grade 4–5

Some students are investigating the relationship between the length of a piece of copper wire and its resistance.

They have copper wire, connecting wires, ammeter, voltmeter, a ruler and power supply.

Draw a diagram showing how this equipment should be set up to produce data that will allow the resistance of a particular length of wire to be determined. **[4 marks]**

4 Cell Biology P1 • Grade 6–7

A typical bacterial cell is about 2 micrometres long. A relay neurone can be 2 centimetres long.

Draw one line from each length to the correct length in metres expressed in standard form. **[2 marks]**

Length	Expressed in standard form
	2×10^{-2} m
2 micrometres	2×10^{2} m
2 centimetres	2×10^{6} m
	2×10^{-6} m

5 Bonding, Structure, and the Properties of Matter P1 • Grade 6–7

Ionic compounds form between metals and non-metals.

a) Draw the electronic structure of a fluoride ion. Show only the outer shell electrons. **[2 marks]**

b) Potassium metal and chlorine gas can react together to make potassium chloride.

Draw the dot and cross diagram of potassium chloride. Show only the outer shell electrons. **[4 marks]**

6 Waves P2 • Grade 6–7

A group of students are exploring how a ray of light is refracted when it enters a rectangular block of glass from air and again when it leaves the glass and re-enters the air.

They have a ray box lamp which produces a single ray of light, a power pack and a glass block.

Draw a diagram to show how the equipment should be set up to show the path of the ray both into and out of the glass block. **[4 marks]**

7 Forces P2 • Grade 6–7

A teacher has a trolley, a set of masses, a pulley and a set of light gates to measure speed.

Draw and label a diagram to show how these could be set up to investigate how varying the force on an object with constant mass will affect its acceleration. **[4 marks]**

8 Organisation P1 • Grade 8–9

An enzyme called catalase gives off oxygen when mixed with yeast.

The graph shows the total volume of oxygen given off at different times throughout the reaction.

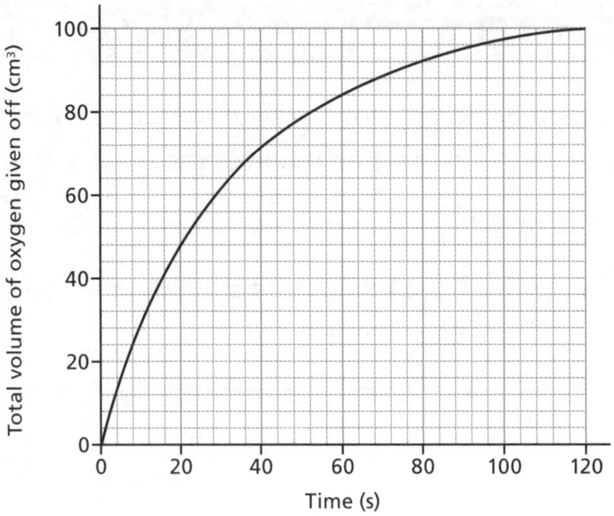

Draw a tangent on the graph at 40 seconds.

Use your tangent to calculate the rate of the reaction at 40 seconds. **[3 marks]**

Rate of reaction = ... cm^3/s

9 Bonding, Structure, and the Properties of Matter P1 • Grade 8–9

Polypropene is a polymer that is widely used to make re-useable shopping bags.

Propene is used to make polypropene.

The figure below shows the structure of propene.

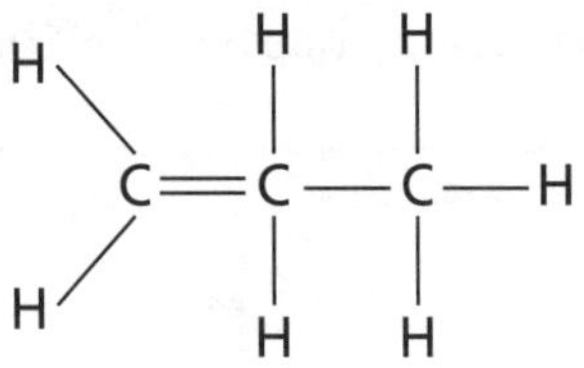

Draw the repeating unit of polypropene. **[4 marks]**

Sherbet sweets contain citric acid and sodium hydrogencarbonate.

When you eat sherbet, the two chemicals react together and cause a decrease in temperature.

Draw the reaction profile for the reaction between citric acid and sodium hydrogencarbonate.

You should label:

- the energy level of the reactants and of the products
- the activation energy
- the overall energy change. **[3 marks]**

Total score: .... / 37

Sketch

Draw approximately: your drawing doesn't need to be accurate but you should include enough information to demonstrate your understanding of the principles.

Worked example and more!

TOP TIP
The difference between draw and sketch is that more accuracy is expected when drawing whereas sketching involves a degree of approximation.

Example question

1 **The Rate and Extent of Chemical Change P2 • Grade 4–5**

Iron can undergo an oxidising reaction in air. The rate of reaction for the rusting of an iron nail can be monitored by measuring the mass change.

The graph shows the rate of reaction for the rusting of an iron nail.

On the figure, sketch the results you would expect if you used iron powder. **[3 marks]**

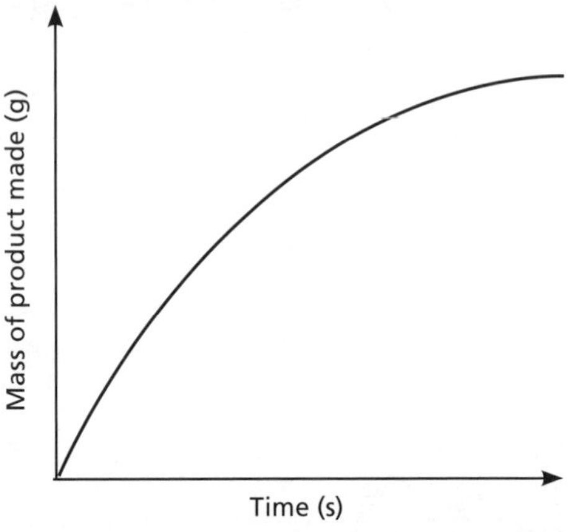

Complete the example

2 Forces P2 • Grade 6–7

A child is swinging to and fro on a swing. Their speed is greatest at the mid-point of the swing and decreases as they get towards either end.

Sketch a distance–time graph to show how their distance from the mid-point varies during one complete swing, starting from the mid-point. **[4 marks]**

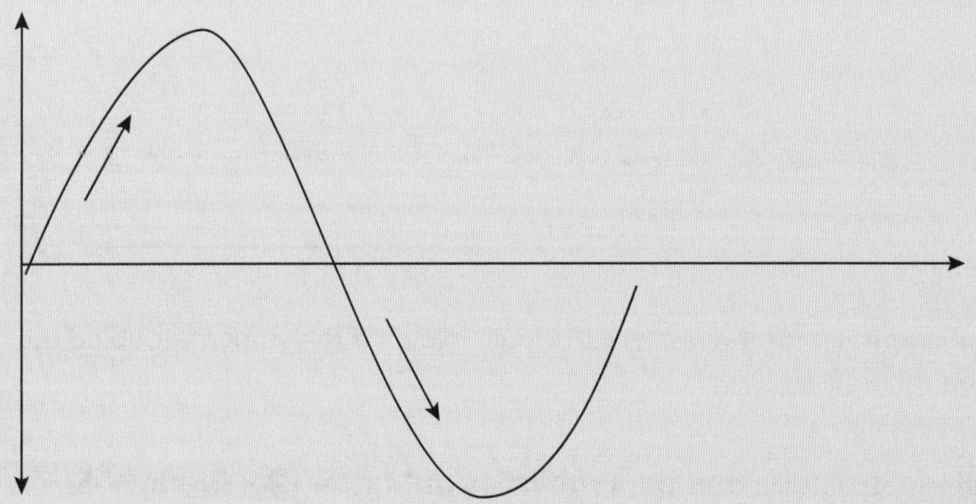

Exam practice questions

24

1 Energy Changes P1 / The Rate and Extent of Chemical Change P2 • Grade 4–5

Zinc can react with hydrochloric acid.

Copper powder can be used as a catalyst to increase the rate of reaction.

The figure below shows the energy level diagram for this reaction without a catalyst.

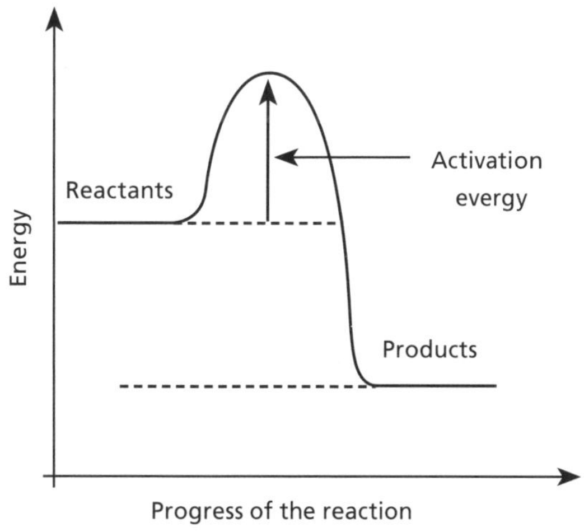

On the figure, sketch the effect of adding a catalyst to this reaction. **[2 marks]**

2 The Rate and Extent of Chemical Change P2 • Grade 4–5

A student investigated the volume of gas produced when large lumps of calcium carbonate reacted with hydrochloric acid.

The figure below shows the results of the experiment.

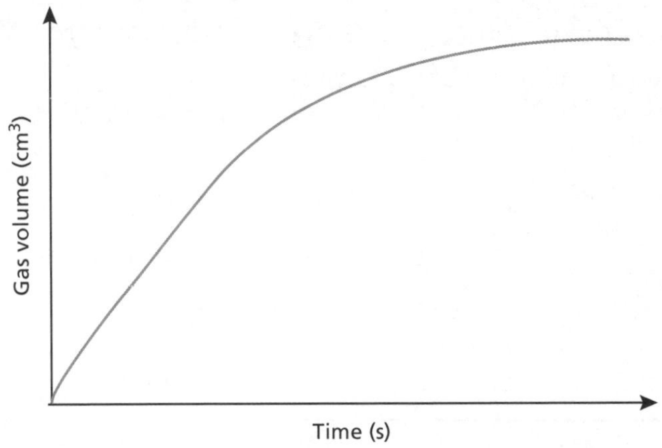

On the figure, sketch the results you would expect if the student doubled the concentration of the acid. **[3 marks]**

3 Bonding, Structure, and the Properties of Matter P1 • Grade 4–5

Sodium chloride (NaCl), is an example of an ionic compound.

Ionic compounds form a lattice made of a giant structure of ions.

Sketch the structure of sodium chloride. You must include at least 5 sodium ions and 5 chloride ions in your sketch. **[3 marks]**

4 Bonding, Structure, and the Properties of Matter P1 • Grade 4–5

All matter is made of particles.

Sketch the particle arrangement for the different states of matter: solid, liquid and gas.

You do not need to draw more than nine particles in each diagram. **[3 marks]**

5 Energy P1 • Grade 4–5

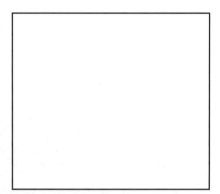

Sketch a graph to show how the temperature of a substance will change if, over a period of time, it is cooling as a liquid, then freezing, and then cooling as a solid. **[3 marks]**

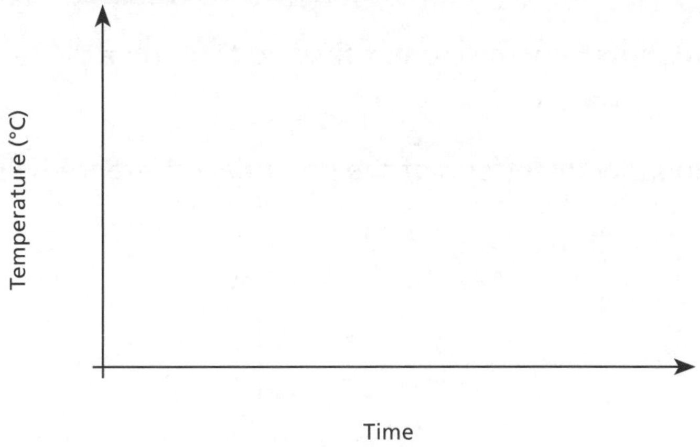

6 Electricity P1 • Grade 4–5

A student investigated the current through an ohmic conductor.

The diagram shows the circuit that the student used.

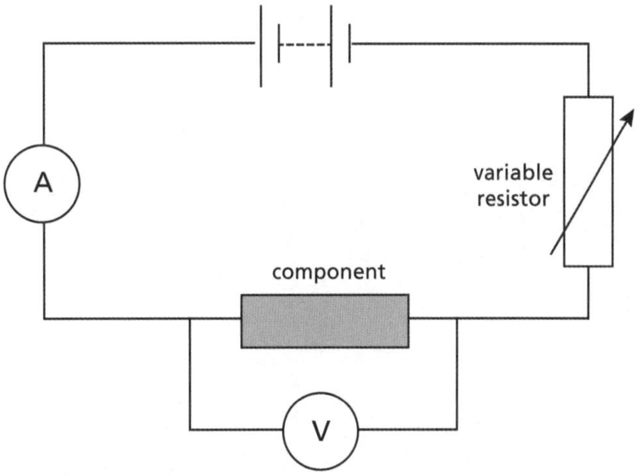

The student discovered that if the temperature remained constant, the resistance was constant as the current changed.

Sketch the graph of the student's results using current and potential difference. **[2 marks]**

7 Electricity P1 • Grade 6–7

Sketch a graph to show how the current flowing through a diode alters as the potential difference across it is varied.

The graph should show the effects of the potential difference being both positive and negative. **[3 marks]**

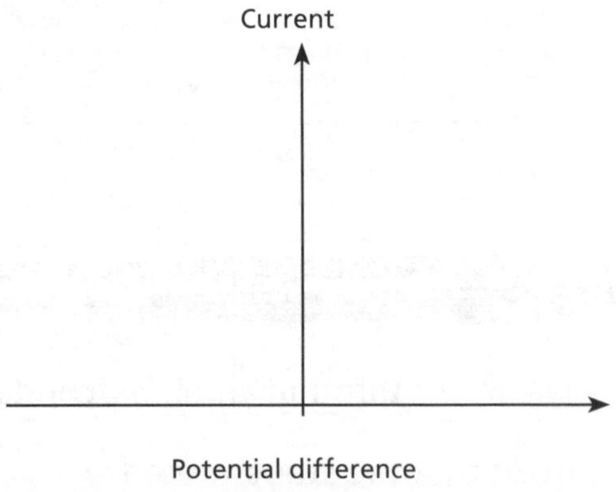

8 Waves P2 • Grade 6–7

This question is about the refraction of waves.

A ripple tank is set up and straight parallel waves are made to travel down the length of the tank. A piece of plastic is put in the tank to make the water in one part shallower so that the waves are refracted.

The diagram below shows the shape of the piece of plastic and the direction of the incoming waves. The diagram shows the view looking down on to the tank from above.

Sketch on the diagram the parallel waves before and after they reach the shallower water. **[3 marks]**

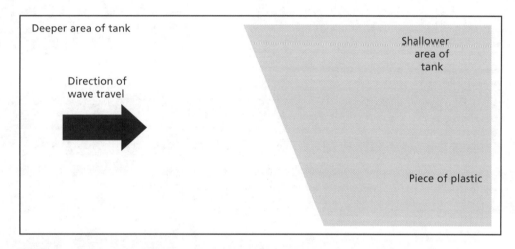

9 Energy Changes P1 • Grade 8–9

Ammonium nitrate is a white solid that dissolves in water.

This change is endothermic.

On the figure, sketch the energy level diagram for this change. **[2 marks]**

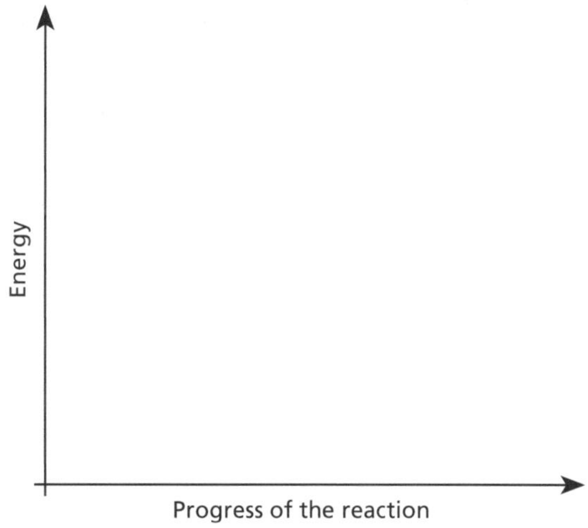

Total score: .... / 24

Label

Add the appropriate names of structures or processes to a diagram.

Worked example and more!

TOP TIP
Make sure you add clear labels and, where required, clear arrows that show where the labels point.

Example question

1 **Energy Changes P1 • Grade 4–5**

The figure shows the energy level diagram for the combustion of methane.

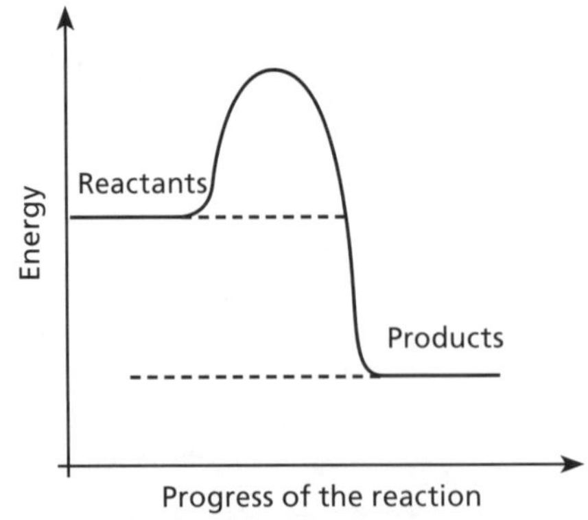

a) Label the activation energy on the figure. **[1 mark]**

b) Label the overall energy change on the figure. **[1 mark]**

Complete the example

2 Waves P2 • Grade 4–5

This diagram shows the glass vessel which is used in a vacuum flask.

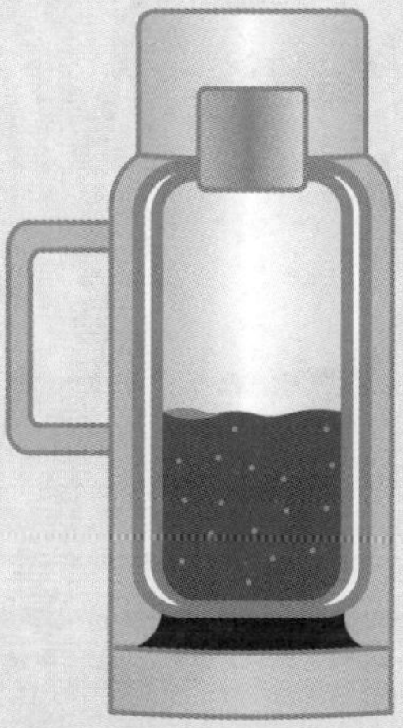

Label the diagram to show:

- Vacuum
- Insulated lid
- Liquid
- Mirrored surface reflecting infrared radiation. **[4 marks]**

3 Homeostasis and Response P2 • Grade 6–7

The graph shows a person's blood glucose level for five hours after eating a meal.

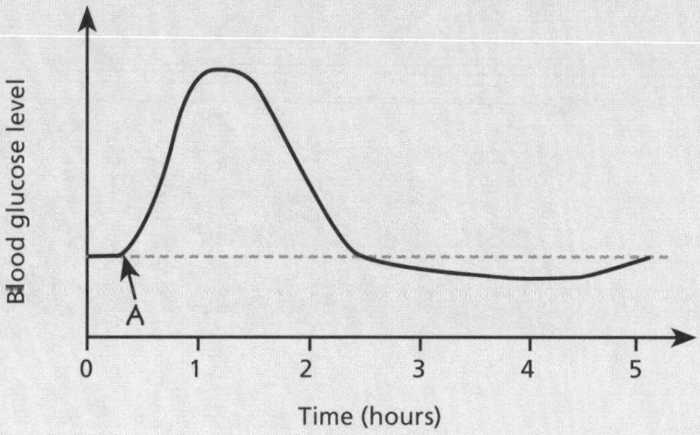

Label the graph with the letters A, B and C to show when these events occurred:

A – The products of digestion were absorbed from the small intestine

B – Increased glucagon starts to affect the liver

C – Increased insulin starts to affect the liver **[3 marks]**

Exam practice questions

20

1 Organisation P1 • Grade 4–5

The diagram shows a section through a human heart.

Label the heart to show the position of:

- the natural pacemaker
- a valve that stops blood passing back into the right atrium from the right ventricle.

[2 marks]

2 Cell Biology P1 • Grade 4–5

The diagram shows details of cells at different stages of the cell cycle.

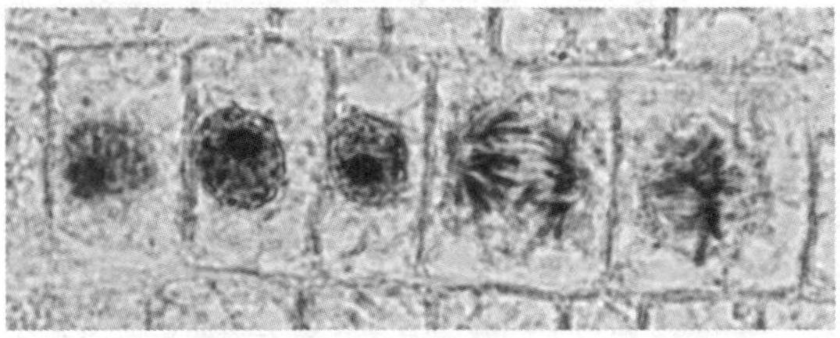

Label the diagram with the letters R, S and T to indicate the cell that is in each of these stages of the cell cycle:

R – a cell that is replicating its DNA and sub-cellular structures

S – a cell that is just starting mitosis

T – a cell that is about to divide **[3 marks]**

3 Forces P2 • Grade 4–5

This diagram shows apparatus set up to explore the relationship between the force applied to a spring and its extension.

Label the diagram to show the:

- spring
- load added
- pointer used to measure length of spring. **[3 marks]**

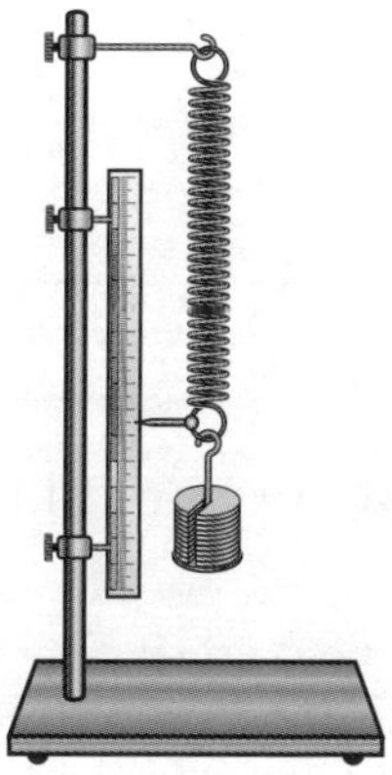

4 Forces P2 • Grade 4–5

This graph shows the results of an experiment in which the load on a spring has been gradually increased and has caused extension.

Label the graph to show the:

- axis showing the independent variable **(A)**
- axis showing the dependent variable **(B)**
- section of the line during which the extension was directly proportional to the load **(C)**
- point at which the elastic limit was exceeded **(D)**. **[4 marks]**

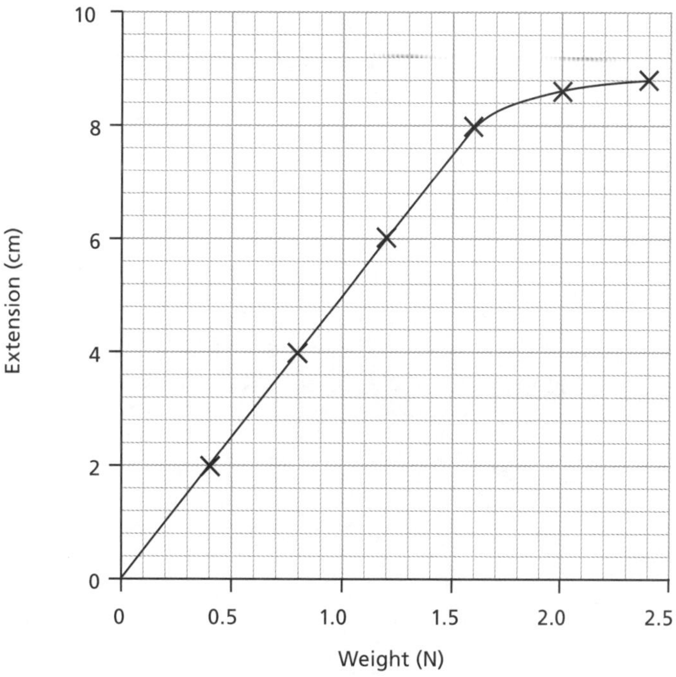

5 Homeostasis and Response P2 • Grade 6–7

The graph shows a person's core body temperature before, during and after some exercise.

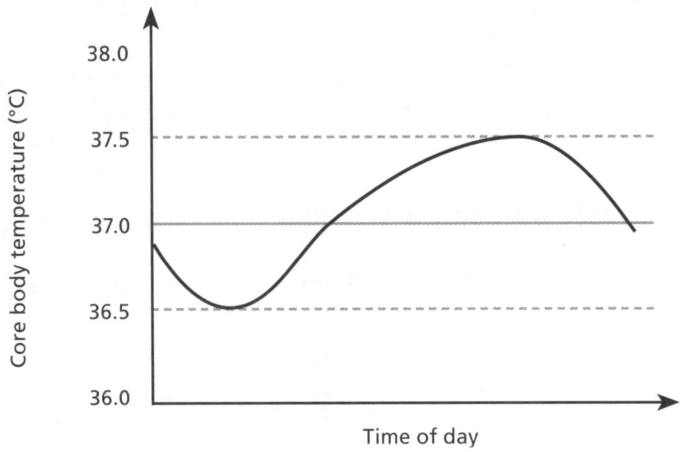

Label the graph with the letter P to show when shivering stopped. **[1 mark]**

6 Electricity P1 • Grade 6–7

This graph shows the relationship between the potential difference placed across a diode and the current flowing through it.

Label the graph to show the:

- point at which the potential difference is zero **(A)**
- point at which the potential difference is just enough to cause a current to flow **(B)**. **[2 marks]**

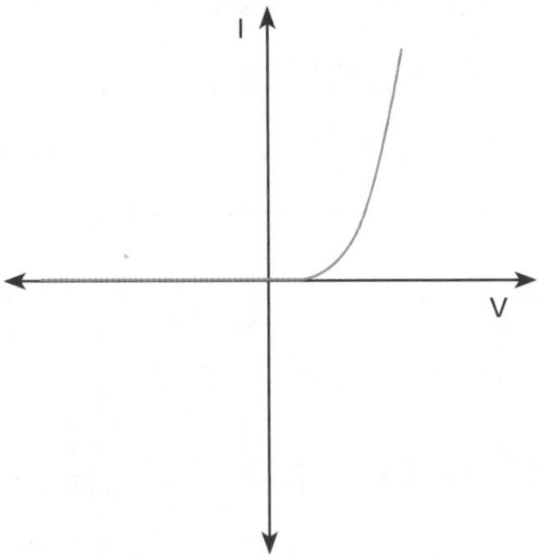

7 Chemical Changes P1 • Grade 8–9

A student investigated the electrolysis of copper(II) sulfate. The student repeated the experiment using different currents.

The mass of the anode was measured at the start. Each experiment was carried out for five minutes. The anode was then dried and the mass measured again.

The figure below is a graph of the results.

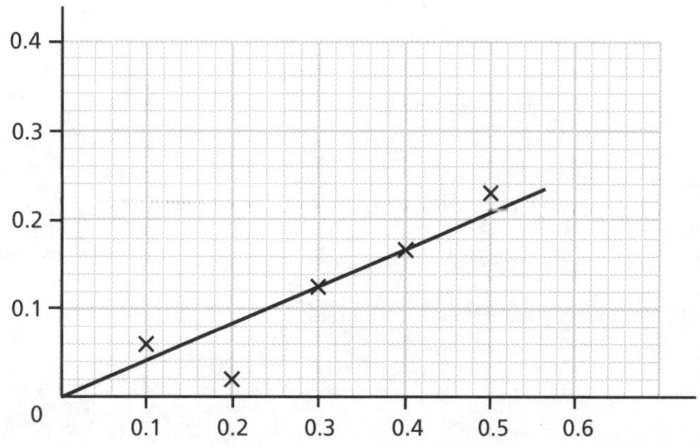

Label the axes. **[2 marks]**

8 Chemistry of the Atmosphere P2 • Grade 8–9

Air is the mixture of gases that make up our atmosphere.

The figure below shows the composition of dry air.

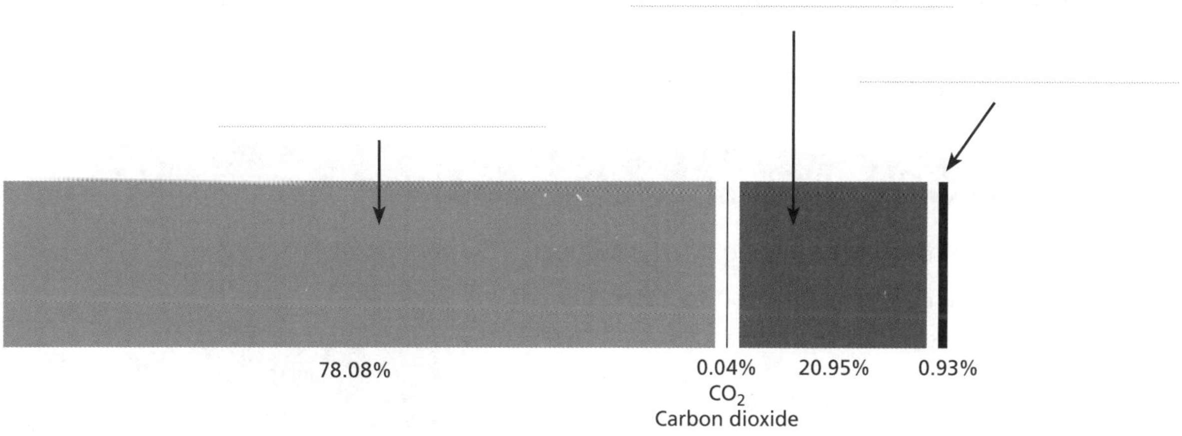

Label the gases on the figure. **[3 marks]**

Total score: .... / 20

Suggest

Apply your knowledge and understanding to a given situation. Do not expect to have learnt the answer.

Worked example and more!

TOP TIP
The examiner wants to see an indication of what is likely to happen: your response needs to be plausible.

Example question

1 **Energy P1 • Grade 4–5**

Two children are playing with a swing. One child gives one push to the child on the swing.

a) Suggest why the swing moves back and forth several times after one push. Use ideas about energy in your answer. **[2 marks]**

b) Suggest why the amplitude of the oscillations of the swing gradually reduce. Use ideas about energy in your answer. **[2 marks]**

Complete the example

2 Inheritance, Variation and Evolution P2 • Grade 4–5

The picture shows seagrass plants growing off the coast of Australia. Scientists have been investigating a large area of the seagrass plants.

The area covers 200 sq km.

They have tested the DNA from a large number of plants.

They found that the DNA from all the plants was identical.

Suggest how the plants started growing in the area and produced enough plants to cover the entire area. **[3 marks]**

A plant may have sexually reproduced and released ....

These were carried to the area and germinated to produce a plant.

This plant must then have used .... *reproduction many*

times as all the plants in the area are .... *identical.*

3 Chemical Changes P1 • Grade 6–7

Lead iodide is an insoluble salt that can be made from a reaction between two soluble salts. The equation for the reaction is:

$Pb(NO_3)_2 + 2NaI \rightarrow PbI_2 + 2NaNO_3$

Suggest how the lead iodide product could be separated from the mixture at the end of the reaction. **[1 mark]**

Think about the different separation techniques.

....

Exam practice questions

26

1 Homeostasis and Response P2 • Grade 4–5

In the 1920s, two scientists called Banting and Best investigated how blood glucose level is controlled.

They removed the pancreas from a dog. The dog could not control the glucose level in its blood.

They then injected an extract from a pancreas into the dog. The dog recovered for a short time.

a) Suggest why the dog recovered, but only for a short time. **[3 marks]**

....

....

....

....

b) Suggest **one** argument for and **one** argument against this type of experiment. **[2 marks]**

For ....

....

Against ....

....

2 The Rate and Extent of Chemical Change P2 • Grade 4–5

Magnesium reacts with hydrochloric acid to make hydrogen gas and a soluble salt.

A student wanted to investigate how the concentration of acid affected the rate of reaction.

Suggest **two** methods that could be used to monitor the rate of reaction. **[2 marks]**

....

....

....

3 Energy P1 • Grade 4–5

A boat was fitted with a solar panel to supply electricity for the lights and radio.

a) Suggest why the energy supplied by the solar panels varies from day to day in the same week. **[1 mark]**

b) Suggest why the amount of electricity generated by the solar panel varies over the course of a year. **[1 mark]**

c) Suggest why fitting a battery to the boat's electrical system makes the system more efficient. **[2 marks]**

4 Bonding, Structure, and the Properties of Matter P1 • Grade 6–7

A construction material is made from a compound made between two non-metals.

The diagram shows the structure of this material. This material has a very high melting point.

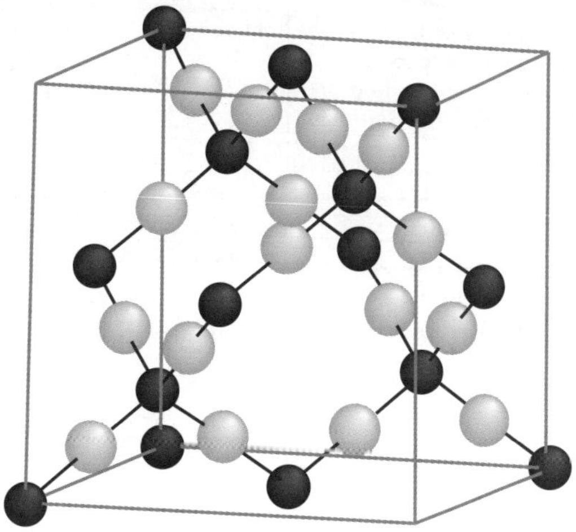

a) Suggest the type of bonding in this material. **[1 mark]**

b) Suggest the structure of this material. **[1 mark]**

5 Particle Model of Matter P1 • Grade 6–7

A car is taking part in a race and is being driven very fast. As it approaches a bend in the circuit, the brake discs start glowing.

a) Suggest why the brake discs are glowing. **[3 marks]**

....

....

....

b) A few minutes later the car is still in the race and travelling quickly but the brake discs are no longer glowing. Suggest why this is. **[2 marks]**

....

....

....

6 Inheritance, Variation and Evolution P2 • Grade 8–9

The timeline shows some important discoveries about sexual reproduction.

Robert Hooke saw plant cells using a microscope with a magnification of 50 times	Antony van Leeuwenhoek saw sperm cells with a microscope that magnified 200 times	Fertilisation was first seen using a microscope	Gregor Mendel discovered that characteristics are controlled by pairs of factors and only one factor is passed on	Edouard van Beneden observed meiosis using a microscope
1665	1670	1800s	1860	1885

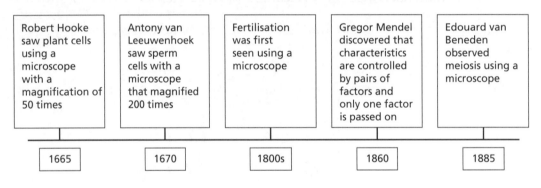

a) Suggest why Hooke could see plant cells in 1665 but sperm cells were not seen until 1670. **[2 marks]**

....

....

....

b) Van Beneden saw meiosis occurring and realised that it produced sex cells with only one chromosome from each pair.

Suggest why he did not realise the importance of this, even though Mendel had carried out his work 25 years earlier. **[2 marks]**

....

....

....

....

7 Energy Changes P2 • Grade 8–9

A student investigates the energy change of a displacement reaction.

This is the method used:

1. Pour 25 cm^3 of copper(II) sulfate solution into a polystyrene cup.
2. Measure the temperature of the copper(II) sulfate solution.
3. Add 2.00 g of zinc powder to the polystyrene cup.
4. Stir the solution.
5. Measure the temperature of the solution every 10 seconds.

The student plotted the results on a graph.

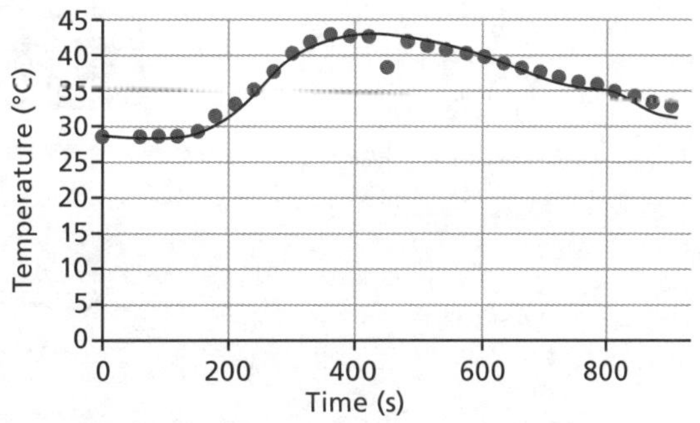

a) Suggest how the colour of the solution would change during the course of the reaction. **[1 mark]**

....

b) Suggest a reason for the anomalous results at 450 s. **[1 mark]**

....

....

8 Forces P2 • Grade 8–9

A team of scientists are investigating the factors that affect the reaction times of drivers. They have selected a varied group of drivers and tested their reactions under the same set of conditions.

Each driver has been tested several times. When the scientists look at the data they can see that there is some variation.

Suggest **two** different reasons for the variation in the reaction times. **[2 marks]**

1 ....

....

2 ....

....

Total score: .... / 26

Explain

Give reasons for something happening or make the relationships between things clear.

Worked example and more!

TOP TIP
Your answer may involve several sentences and the words 'because' or 'therefore' are often needed.

Example question

1 **Cell Biology P1 • Grade 6–7**

Multiple sclerosis is a disorder that affects neurones.

People with the disorder may have difficulty moving their legs.

The diagram shows the effect of multiple sclerosis on one type of neurone.

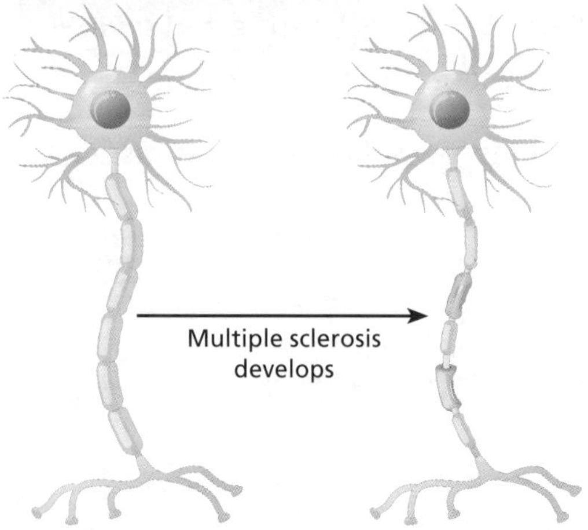

Explain why people with multiple sclerosis may have difficulty moving their legs. **[3 marks]**

Complete the example

2 Bonding, Structure, and the Properties of Matter P1 • Grade 4–5

Carbon nanotubes are like a rolled-up sheet of graphene. The figure below shows a carbon nanotube.

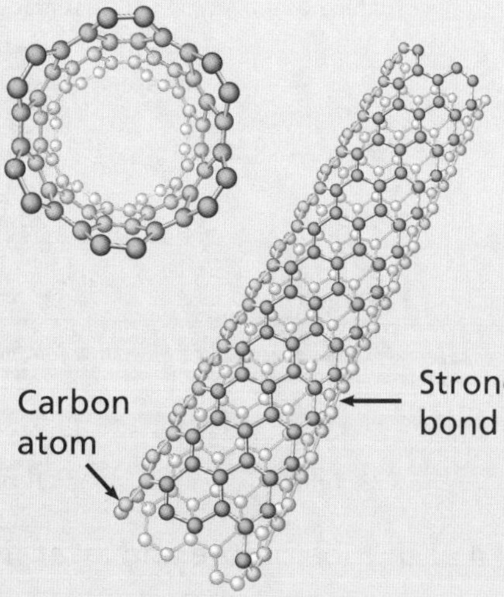

Explain why carbon nanotubes can conduct electricity. **[2 marks]**

Carbon nanotubes contain ....

which are free to ....

and carry ....

3 Electricity P1 • Grade 4–5

A student noticed that when two lamps are connected to a low voltage power supply they are dimmer than if one lamp is connected.

However, the brightness of a single lamp is the same as two lamps connected in a parallel circuit with a low voltage power supply.

Explain these observations. **[6 marks]**

If lamps are connected in series, the potential difference supplied by the .... *will be divided between the lamps so if there are more lamps then each of the lamps receives* .... *and therefore* ....

However, if the lamps are connected in parallel, each of the lamps receives .... *. This means that if more lamps are connected then all of them will receive* .... *and therefore* ....

Exam practice questions

75

1 Organisation P1 • Grade 4–5

A student sets up an experiment about transpiration. They set up four tubes as shown in the diagram.

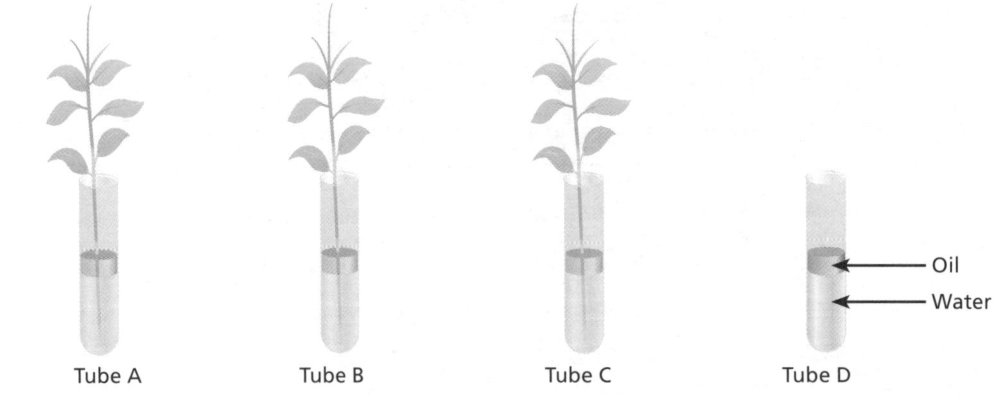

They measure the mass of each tube before and after five days and then calculate the loss in mass.

The table shows the results.

Tube	A	B	C	D
Mass lost in grams	7.0	0.4	6.2	0.0

a) Explain the function of tube **D** in the experiment. **[2 marks]**

b) Explain the difference between the results for tube **B** and tube **C**. **[3 marks]**

2 Cell Biology P1 • Grade 4–5

The picture shows an electron microscope image of *Escherichia coli* (*E.coli*).

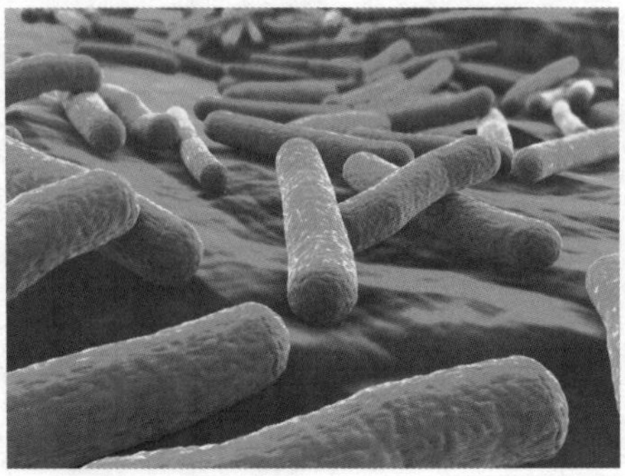

Explain how electron microscopy has increased understanding of sub-cellular structures in *E.coli*. **[4 marks]**

....

....

....

....

3 Atomic Structure and the Periodic Table P1 • Grade 4–5

This question is about groups in the Periodic Table.

a) Explain how the reactivity of Group 1 changes as you go down the group. **[4 marks]**

....

....

....

....

b) Explain how the reactivity of Group 7 changes as you go down the group. **[4 marks]**

....

....

....

....

c) Explain why Group 0 is unreactive. **[1 mark]**

....

....

4 The Rate and Extent of Chemical Change P2 • Grade 4–5

Magnesium metal reacts with hydrochloric acid.

The equation for the reaction is:

magnesium + hydrochloric acid → magnesium chloride + hydrogen

Heating the acid increases the rate of reaction.

Using magnesium powder instead of magnesium ribbon increases the rate of reaction.

a) Explain how increasing the temperature of the acid increases the rate of reaction. **[4 marks]**

b) Explain how using magnesium powder increases the rate of reaction. **[3 marks]**

5 Ecology P2 • Grade 6–7

An animal called the red king crab is increasing in popularity in restaurants.

In the 1960s, these crabs were introduced into the sea around Norway. They have increased in numbers and there is now concern that they might be affecting biodiversity.

a) Explain why the crab might have a large effect on the biodiversity in the sea around Norway. **[3 marks]**

b) Explain why it is important to maintain biodiversity. **[2 marks]**

Electrolysis can be used to extract aluminium from bauxite ore.

The figure below shows a diagram for the process.

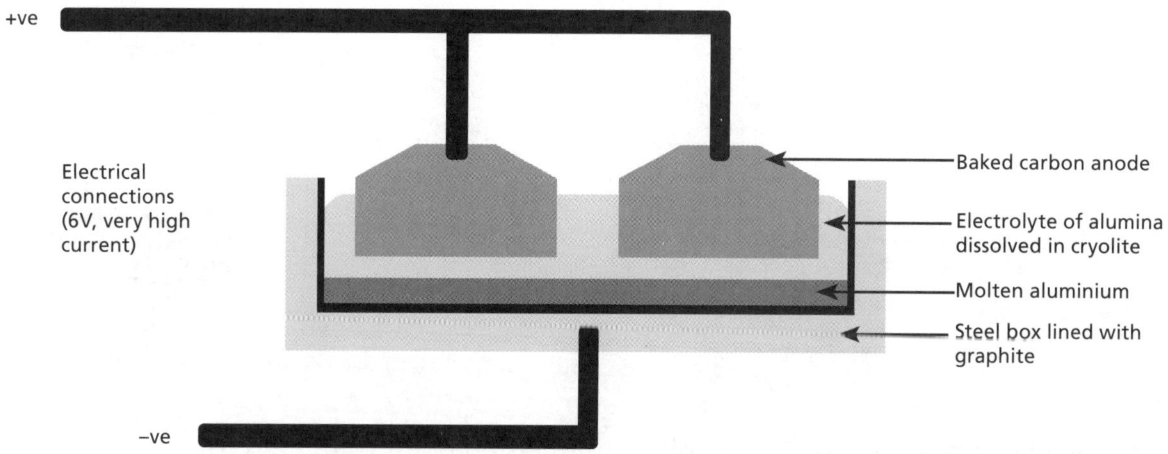

a) Explain why the electrolyte must be molten. **[2 marks]**

....

....

....

b) Explain why cryolite is added to the electrolyte. **[2 marks]**

....

....

....

c) Explain why the positive anode must be continually replaced. **[4 marks]**

....

....

....

....

....

....

7 Bonding, Structure, and the Properties of Matter P1 • Grade 6–7

Carbon is contained in many different substances.

Diamond and methane both contain carbon.

The figure below shows a diagram of diamond and a diagram of methane.

Diamond

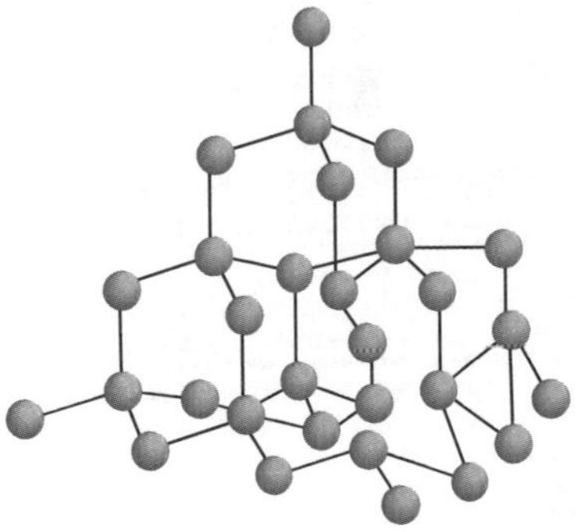

Methane

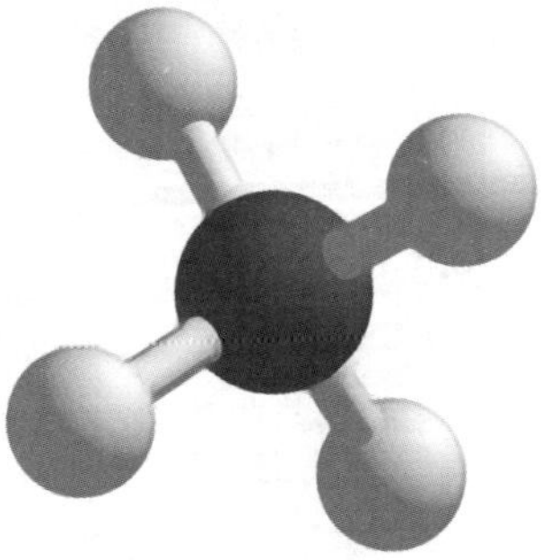

Explain why diamond has a very different melting point compared to methane. **[6 marks]**

....

....

....

....

....

....

....

8 Particle Model of Matter P1 • Grade 6–7

A glass of water has some ice cubes in it as well as the liquid.

The level of water is right up to the rim of the glass and the ice is floating, mainly submerged but with a little showing above the surface of the water.

The glass is left on a table outdoors on a warm day. Gradually the ice melts.

Explain why the water does not overflow. **[4 marks]**

....

....

....

....

....

....

....

9 Energy P1 • Grade 6–7

Water is commonly used as a coolant in internal combustion engines such as the petrol and diesel engines used in cars and other vehicles. It is pumped around the inside of the engine, absorbing heat, and then to a radiator where the heat is transferred to the air.

One of the reasons that water is used is that it is cheap and easily available but another reason is that it has a high specific heat capacity.

Explain why having a high specific heat capacity helps water to be an effective coolant.

[4 marks]

10 Electricity P1 • Grade 6–7

Some students are investigating how changing the potential difference applied to a resistor affects the size of the current flowing through it. Their results are shown in the table.

Potential difference / V	0	1	2	3	4	5	6	7	8
Current flow / mA	0	0.013	0.027	0.038	0.052	0.066	0.078	0.090	0.103

a) Explain how this shows that the resistance of the resistor is relatively constant. Use at least two resistance values in your answer. **[4 marks]**

b) Explain why the calculated resistance of the resistor may vary slightly. **[4 marks]**

11 Homeostasis and Response P2 • Grade 8–9

The diagram represents events happening at a synapse between a sensory and a relay neurone.

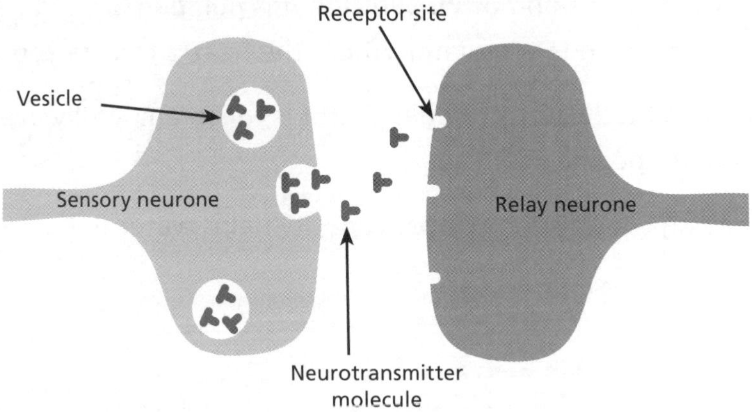

a) Explain how an impulse reaching the end of the sensory neurone produces an impulse in the relay neurone. **[3 marks]**

b) Explain why nerve impulses can only pass one way across a synapse.

Use information from the diagram in your answer. **[3 marks]**

12 Quantitative Chemistry P1 / Chemical Changes P1 • Grade 8–9

Hydrogen chloride gas can dissolve in water to make hydrochloric acid.

Solution A is made by dissolving 36.5 g of hydrogen chloride gas in 1 dm^3 of pure water.

Solution B is made by dissolving 18.25 g of hydrogen chloride gas in 250 cm^3 of pure water.

a) Explain why hydrochloric acid is a strong acid. **[2 marks]**

b) Explain which solution is the most concentrated. **[3 marks]**

13 Energy P1 • Grade 8–9

Some students carry out an experiment to measure the amount of energy stored in a small piece of wood.

They light the wood and hold it underneath a test tube of water. There is a thermometer in the water. The water starts off at room temperature but increases as the burning wood is held underneath it.

The students record the temperature increase of the water and have measured its mass. Using the accepted value for the specific heat capacity of water, they calculate the energy transferred into the water and suggest that this must be equivalent to the energy released by the wood.

Explain why their calculated value is likely to be significantly lower than the actual value. **[4 marks]**

Total score: / 75

Show

Provide evidence to reach a conclusion. This usually involves using mathematics to show that a statement or result is correct.

Worked example and more!

TOP TIP
Make sure you include all the steps leading to the conclusion.

Example question

1 **Chemical Changes P1 / Quantitative Chemistry P1 • Grade 8–9**

Ethanol (C_2H_5OH) is an important chemical used as a solvent and as a fuel.

Show that the percentage composition of carbon in ethanol is 52%.

A_r H = 1; C=12; O=16 **[4 marks]**

Complete the example

2 Infection and Response P1 • Grade 4–5

Scientists can try to work out how safe drugs are by calculating their therapeutic ratio.

The therapeutic ratio is worked out using this formula:

$$\textbf{Therapeutic ratio} = \frac{\textbf{Dangerous dose}}{\textbf{Smallest dose needed to have an effect}}$$

The table shows data for three drugs, **A, B** and **C**.

Drug	Dangerous dose in mg	Smallest dose to have an effect in mg
A	100 000	10 000
B	75	15
C	64	8

The therapeutic ratio can tell a scientist how likely it is for a person to accidentally take a dangerous dose of the drug.

Show that drug **A** would be the safest drug to use. **[2 marks]**

The therapeutic ratio for drug **A** *is ...., for drug* **B** *it is*

.... and for drug **C** *it is ....*

Therefore, taking drug **A** *would be safest, as it has the ....*

ratio so people would be less likely to take a dangerous dose.

3 Electricity P1 • Grade 4–5

Show that when a lamp with a resistance of 300 Ω is connected to a power supply with a potential difference of 12 V that the current flowing through the lamp will be 0.04 A. **[3 marks]**

V = I x R, so I = V ÷ R

Exam practice questions

36

1 Homeostasis and Response P2 • Grade 4–5

Before IVF fertility treatment, patients have their FSH level measured.

The graph shows information about the FSH levels of patients who then had IVF treatment.

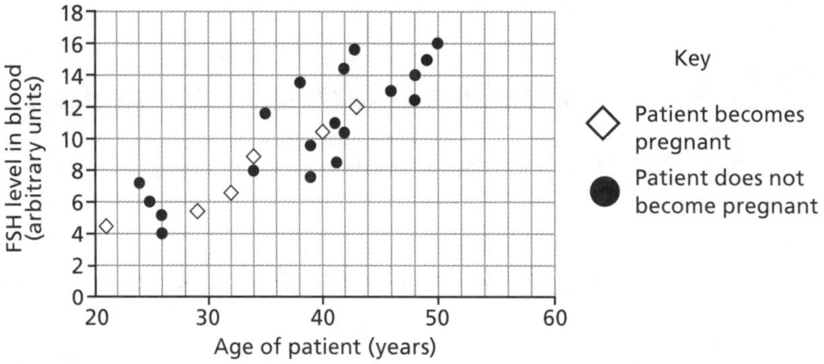

Show that 24% of women who had the IVF treatment became pregnant. **[2 marks]**

....

....

2 Organisation P1 • Grade 4–5

People were tested for three risk factors for heart disease. They were tested for:

- high blood pressure
- high blood cholesterol
- diabetes.

One million people had at least one of these conditions.

The pie chart shows the results for these one million people.

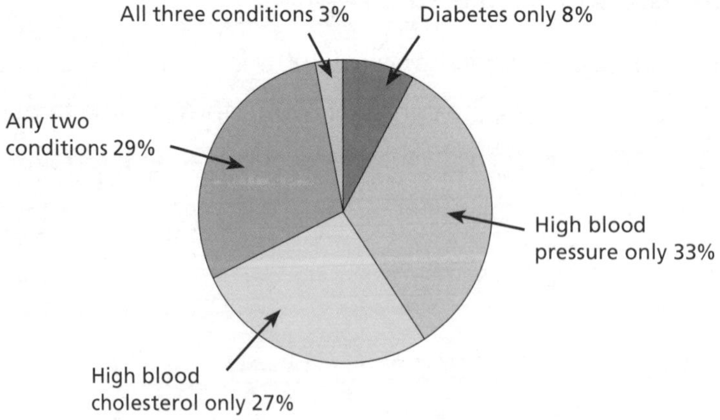

Show that **at least** 360 000 people have high blood pressure. **[2 marks]**

....

....

3 Quantitative Chemistry P1 • Grade 4–5

A student used electrolysis to extract copper metal from copper(II) sulfate solution.

The student calculated that they could obtain a maximum of 63.5 g of copper.
The student collected 15.8 g.

Show that the student obtained a 25% yield. **[3 marks]**

4 Quantitative Chemistry P1 / Chemical Changes P1 • Grade 4–5

Zinc carbonate can undergo thermal decomposition.

The equation for the reaction is:

$ZnCO_3 \rightarrow ZnO + CO_2$

125 g of zinc carbonate was used and the reaction was completed.

Show that 44 g of carbon dioxide was released.

Relative atomic masses (A_r): C = 12 O = 16 Zn = 65 **[2 marks]**

5 Energy P1 • Grade 4–5

An electric motor is supplied with 500 J of energy as electricity.

125 J is transferred out of the motor as kinetic energy, 325 J as heat and 50 J as sound.

Show that the efficiency of the motor is 25%. **[3 marks]**

6 Quantitative Chemistry P1 / Chemical Changes P1 • Grade 6–7

The thermite reaction is used to weld railway tracks together. The figure below shows a diagram of the process.

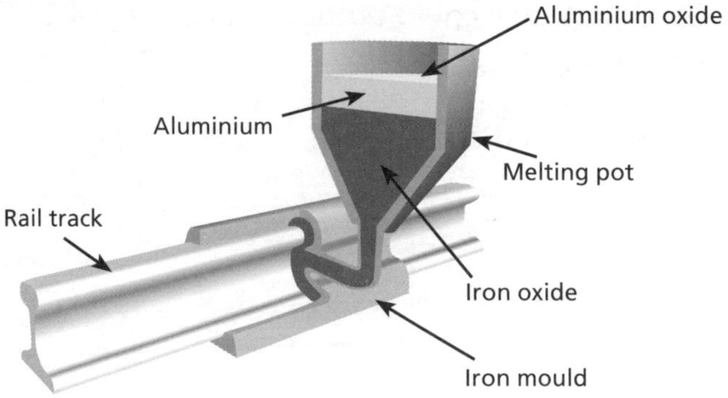

The equation for the reaction is:

$2Al + Fe_2O_3 \rightarrow 2Fe + Al_2O_3$

A mixture of 0.5 kg of aluminium with 1.5 kg of iron(II) oxide was used.

Show that aluminium is the limiting reagent.

Relative atomic masses (A_r): O = 16 Al = 27 Fe = 56 **[5 marks]**

7 Particle Model of Matter P1 • Grade 6–7

A rectangular concrete block measures 10 cm × 20 cm × 30 cm and has a mass of 13.5 kg.
Gravitational field strength = 10 N/kg

a) Show that the density of concrete is 2250 kg/m^3. **[4 marks]**

b) The block was placed with its largest face in contact with the ground. It is now moved so that its smallest face is in contact with the ground.

Show that the pressure exerted on the ground is now three times greater. **[4 marks]**

8 Electricity P1 • Grade 6–7

A 10 W lamp is left on continuously.

Show that every day it transfers 864 kJ of energy. **[4 marks]**

9 Particle Model of Matter P1 • Grade 6–7

An ice cube with a 2 cm side has a mass of 7.36 g.

Show that it will float in water (density of 1 g/cm^3) and sink in methanol (density of 0.79 g/cm^3). **[4 marks]**

10 Inheritance, Variation and Evolution P2 • Grade 8–9

The diagram shows part of a family tree for the condition nanophthalmos.
This is a genetically controlled eye condition.

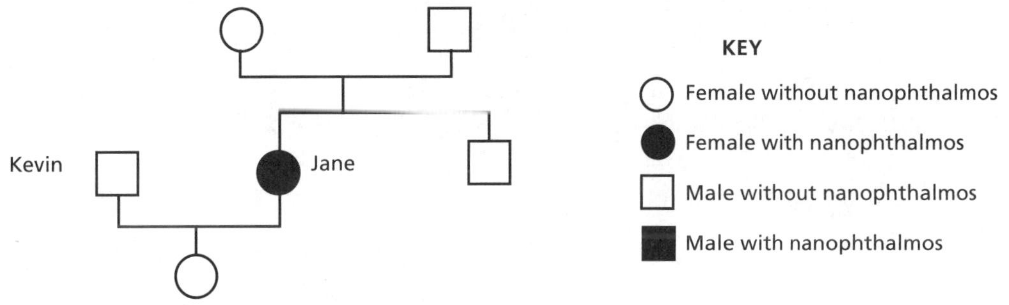

Kevin and Jane are expecting another child.

Show that the probability of the child being a boy with nanophthalmos is 0.125 ($\frac{1}{8}$). **[3 marks]**

Total score: .... / 36

Determine

Use the given data or information to obtain your answer.

Worked example and more!

TOP TIP
Data just means information. It might be in the question rubric or in tables, graphs or charts. Use any data that you need to help you answer the question.

Example question

1 **Energy (P1) • Grade 6–7**

A toy rocket is fired vertically up into the air. When it reaches the highest point of its journey it has 1000 J of energy. Its mass is 0.5 kg and the gravitational attraction of the Earth is 10 N/kg.

Determine the height the rocket reached. **[3 marks]**

Complete the example

2 Ecology P2 • Grade 4–5

Lichens often grow on gravestones. They are very sensitive to acidic gases in the air and so they cannot survive in polluted areas. They can therefore be used as an indicator of pollution.

A scientist is investigating lichens growing in three towns, **P**, **Q** and **R**.
Here are their results.

	Town P	Town Q	Town R
Total number of gravestones looked at	120	100	64
Number of gravestones with lichens	20	20	16

Determine which town is the most polluted. Explain how you worked out your answer. **[3 marks]**

The percentage of gravestones with lichens in town P is .... %, in town Q it is .... % and in town R it is .... %. Therefore, town .... contains the most pollution as lichens are more likely to ....

3 Chemical Analysis P2 • Grade 8–9

A student used chromatography to analyse the colouring in fizzy drinks. The figure shows the chromatogram the student produced.

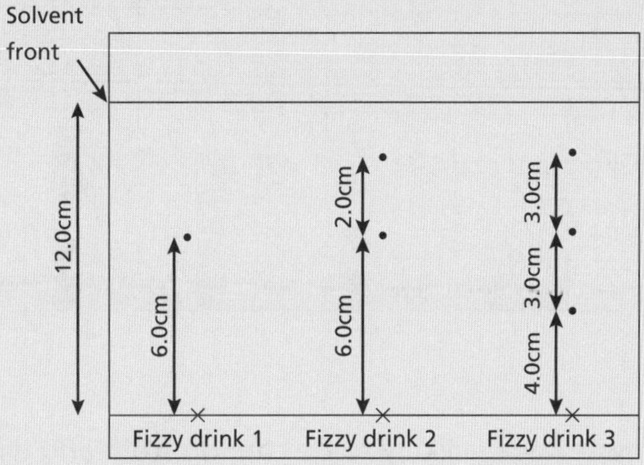

Determine the R_f value of the colouring that was common to fizzy drinks 1 and 2. **[3 marks]**

The colour common in both drinks moved ....

R_f = ...

Exam practice questions

47

1 Ecology P2 • Grade 4–5

Sewage can pollute seas and rivers if it is not treated. Scientists think that sewage is leaking into the sea near a beach.

The diagram shows the area next to the sea.

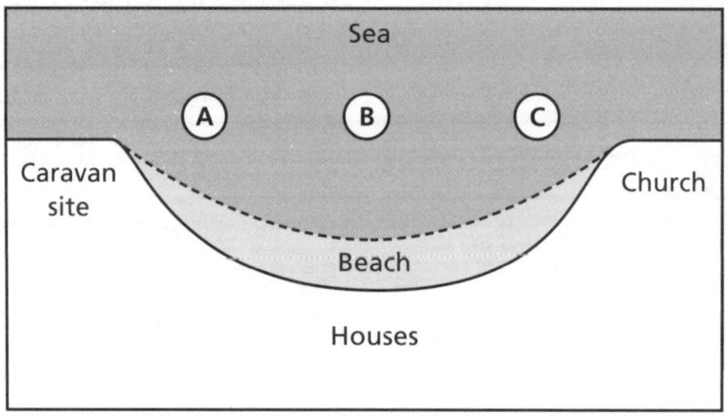

The scientists measure the number of human gut bacteria in the sea at three points, **A**, **B**, and **C**, throughout the summer.

They will have to stop people swimming in the sea if levels of bacteria rise above 1000 in 100 cm^3 of sea water anywhere along the beach.

The graph shows their results.

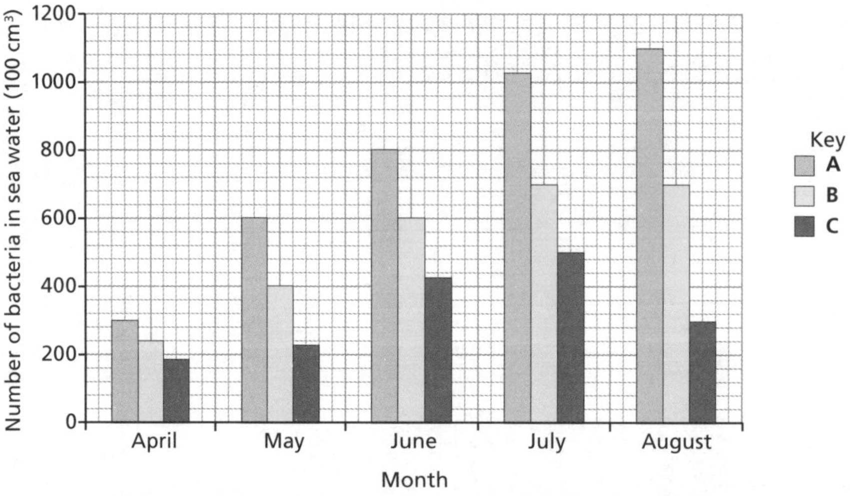

Determine where the sewage is likely to be coming from and when the beach will have to be closed to swimmers. **[2 marks]**

....

....

2 The Rate and Extent of Chemical Change P2 • Grade 4–5

A student monitored the rate of reaction between hydrochloric acid and magnesium ribbon.

The figure below is a graph of the results.

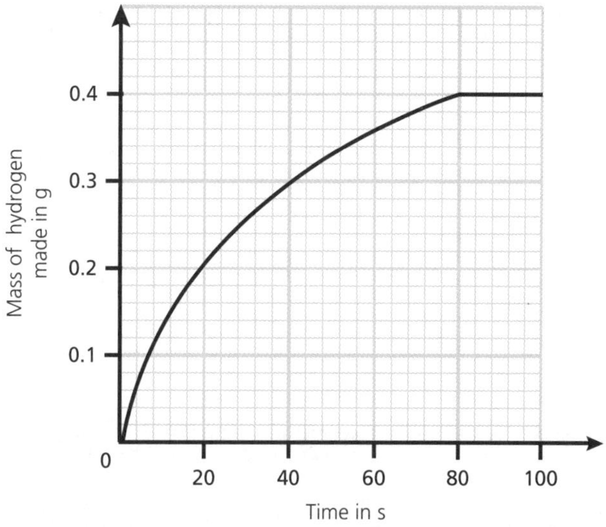

a) Determine the mean rate of reaction in the first 20 seconds. **[3 marks]**

....

....

....

b) Determine when the reaction stopped. **[2 marks]**

....

....

3 Energy Changes P1 • Grade 4–5

A student investigates the reactivity of metals with nitric acid.

This is the method used:

1. Measure 20 cm^3 of nitric acid into a polystyrene cup.
2. Measure the temperature of the nitric acid.
3. Add one spatula of metal powder to the nitric acid and stir.
4. Measure the highest temperature the mixture reaches.
5. Calculate the temperature increase for the reaction.
6. Repeat steps 1 to 5 three more times and take an average.
7. Repeat steps 1 to 6 with different metals.

The table shows the results of the experiment.

Metal	Temperature increase in °C				Mean temperature increase in °C
	Trial 1	Trial 2	Trial 3	Trial 4	
Cobalt	6	7	5	9	7
Calcium	54	50	53	55	53
Copper	0	0	0	0	0

a) Determine the independent variable in this experiment. **[1 mark]**

....

b) Determine the unit of the dependent variable in this experiment. **[1 mark]**

....

c) Determine the order of reactivity for the metals cobalt, calcium and copper. **[1 mark]**

most reactive ....

....

least reactive ....

4 Chemical Changes P1 • Grade 4–5

Sodium chloride (NaCl) and potassium nitrate (KNO_3) are both salts.

The graph shows the maximum mass of each salt that can dissolve in 100 cm³ of water at different temperatures.

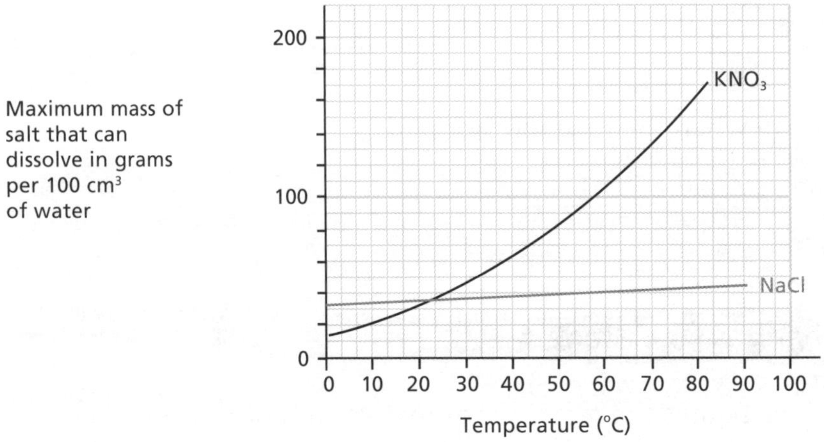

a) Determine the temperature when both salts have the same maximum mass dissolved in 100 cm³ of water. **[1 mark]**

....

b) A student adds potassium nitrate to water at 80°C until no more dissolves.

The student cools 100 cm³ of this solution of potassium nitrate from 80°C to 50°C to produce crystals of potassium nitrate.

Determine the mass of potassium nitrate that crystallises on cooling 100 cm³ of this solution from 80°C to 50°C. **[3 marks]**

....

....

....

Mass = ... g

5 Energy P1 • Grade 4–5

Determine the efficiency of an engine which has a useful energy output of 250 J for every 1 kJ of input energy. **[4 marks]**

....

....

....

6 Inheritance, Variation and Evolution P2 • Grade 6–7

The diagram shows a family tree for a genetic condition called galactosaemia. Galactosaemia is caused by a recessive allele.

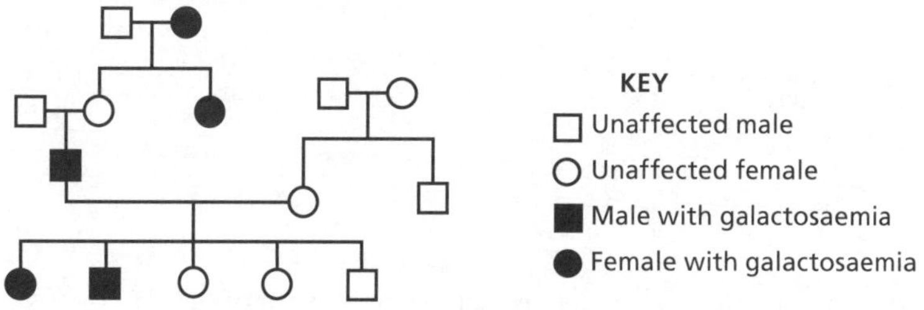

Determine how many of the people in the family tree are:

a) Homozygous recessive for the galactosaemia gene. .... **[1 mark]**

b) Definitely heterozygous for the galactosaemia gene. .... **[1 mark]**

7 Chemistry of the Atmosphere P2 / Quantitative Chemistry P1 • Grade 6–7

A teacher investigated the reaction of iron with oxygen. The reaction went to completion and there were no limiting reactants.

The word equation for the reaction is:

iron + oxygen → iron oxide

The teacher measured the mass of:

- the glass tube
- the glass tube and iron before the reaction
- the glass tube and iron oxide after the reaction.

The table shows the teacher's results.

	Mass in g
Glass tube	50.00
Glass tube and iron	106.00
Glass tube and iron oxide	130.00

Determine the balanced equation for the reaction.

Relative atomic masses (A_r): O = 16 Fe = 56 **[6 marks]**

....

....

....

....

....

8 Electricity P1 • Grade 6–7

A current of 16 mA flows through a 10 Ω resistor.

a) Determine the potential difference across the resistor. **[4 marks]**

....

....

....

b) Determine the power loss due to the current flow through the resistor. **[4 marks]**

....

....

....

9 Electricity P1 • Grade 6–7

A fuse has a rating in amps. If a current greater than the rating flows then the fuse will blow. Fuses are available as 1 A, 3 A, 5 A and 13 A.

A drill has a power rating of 0.96 kW and runs on a 240 V mains supply.

Determine the lowest fuse rating that will allow the normal operating current of the drill to flow. **[5 marks]**

....

....

....

....

10 Homeostasis and Response P2 • Grade 8–9

The small intestine can be thought of as a cylinder and the total internal surface area calculated using this formula:

Surface area = $\pi r^2 l$ (where r is the radius, l is the length and π = 3.14)

The length of the small intestine is 500 cm long. It has a diameter of 2 cm.

a) Determine the internal surface area of the small intestine using the formula. **[2 marks]**

Surface area = ... cm^3

b) The small intestine has folds, villi and microvilli.

- Folds increase the surface area 10 times.
- Villi further increase the surface area 20 times.
- Microvilli further increase the surface area by 6 times.

Determine the actual surface area of the small intestine. **[2 marks]**

Actual surface area = ... cm^3

11 Homeostasis and Response P2 • Grade 8–9

The graph shows the blood glucose concentration and the blood insulin concentration of a person. The readings are taken after they have eaten some glucose.

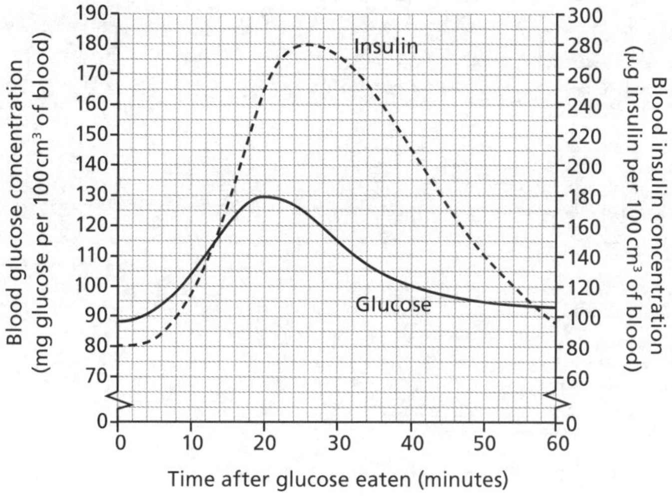

a) Determine the time it takes for the blood insulin level to start to increase after the person eats glucose. **[1 mark]**

Time = ... minutes

b) The blood glucose concentration increases by 40% between eating the glucose and reaching the maximum glucose concentration.

Determine the percentage increase of insulin concentration between eating the glucose and reaching the maximum insulin concentration. **[3 marks]**

Percentage increase = ... %

Total score: .... / 47

Calculate

Use the number values given in the question to work out the answer.

Worked example and more!

TOP TIP
You will often need to use an equation: this may be given or you may need to recall it.

Example question

1 **Forces P2 • Grade 4–5**

Calculate the acceleration of a train that speeds up from rest to 50 m/s in 10 seconds. **[4 marks]**

Complete the example

2 Cell Biology P1 • Grade 4–5

Some students investigate the effect of the surface area : volume ratio on the rate of diffusion.

They use gelatine cubes stained red with a pH indicator solution.
They put different sized cubes into three different test tubes of hydrochloric acid.
They then time how long it takes for the cubes to completely change colour.

The table shows the results.

Length of each side of cube (mm)	Surface area : volume ratio	Time to completely change colour in seconds	Rate = $\frac{1}{\text{Time}}$
2	....	36	....
4	1.5 : 1	60	0.017
6	1 : 1	160	0.0063

a) Calculate the surface area : volume ratio for the cube with sides 2 mm. **[3 marks]**

Surface area = 24

Volume = 8

Ratio = ...

b) Calculate the rate for the cube with sides 2 mm.
Give your answer to 2 significant figures. **[2 marks]**

1 ÷ 36 =

Rate = ... /second

3 Atomic Structure and the Periodic Table P1 • Grade 6–7

Chlorine has two stable isotopes.

The table shows the composition of a sample of chlorine gas.

Chlorine isotope	$^{35}_{17}Cl$	$^{37}_{17}Cl$
Composition (%)	75	25

Calculate the relative atomic mass of chlorine. **[2 marks]**

$$\frac{(35 \times 75) + (37 \times 25)}{} =$$

....

....

Exam practice questions

46

1 Cell Biology P1 • Grade 4–5

The table shows the size of different biological structures.

Type of cell	Diameter/length
Cheek cell	70 μm
Red blood cell	7 μm
Salmonella bacterium	1 μm
HIV virus	100 nm

a) Calculate how many times larger a salmonella bacterium is compared to an HIV virus. **[2 marks]**

Answer = ... times

b) Calculate the number of orders of magnitude between the size of a cheek cell and a red blood cell. **[1 mark]**

Numbers of magnitude difference = ...

2 The Rate and Extent of Chemical Change P2 • Grade 4–5

A student investigated the rate of reaction between magnesium ribbon and hydrochloric acid.

The figure below shows the equipment used to monitor the reaction.

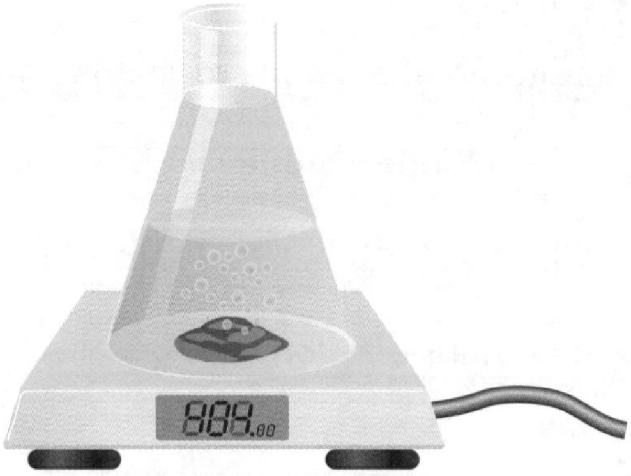

The starting mass was 404.80 g.

The reaction finished after 90 seconds with the final mass reading 403.65 g.

Calculate the mean rate of reaction.

Give your answer to 3 significant figures. Choose the unit from the box. **[4 marks]**

g	s/g	g/dm^3	mol/dm^3	g/s

....

....

....

3 Forces P2 • Grade 4–5

Calculate the kinetic energy of a 15000 kg bus travelling at 10 m/s. **[4 marks]**

....

....

....

Kinetic energy = ...

4 Cell Biology P1 • Grade 6–7

The diagram shows the range in length of different biological structures.

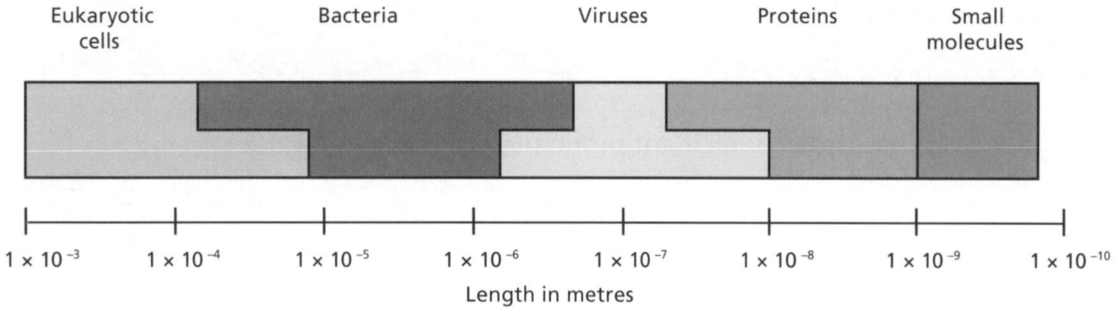

Scientists have seen a new structure under a microscope.

They have measured the length as 5 μm.

Calculate this length in metres and use the diagram to identify the type of structure. **[2 marks]**

....

....

5 Infection and Response P1 • Grade 6–7

Doctors test three antibiotics, A, B and C, to find out which to use to kill a type of bacteria.

They put a disc soaked in the antibiotic on agar that has the bacteria growing on the surface.

The diagram shows the results using antibiotic **C**.

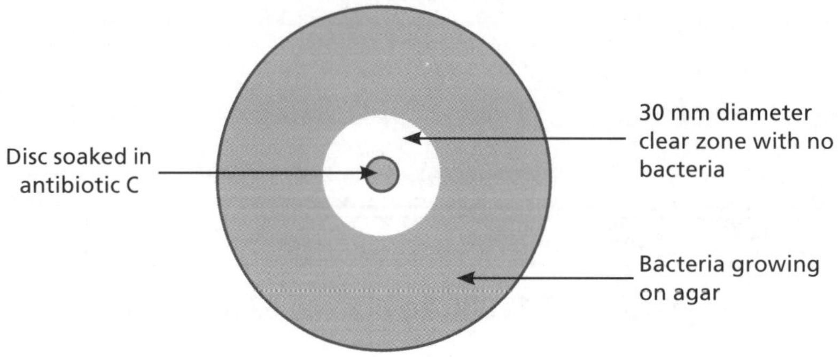

The table shows the area of the clear zone for antibiotics **A** and **B**.

Antibiotic	Area of clear zone (including disc) in mm^2
A	750
B	650

Calculate the area of the clear zone for antibiotic C.

Use the formula: $\mathbf{A} = \pi \mathbf{r}^2$

Use your result to explain which antibiotic the doctors should use.

[3 marks]

6 Particle Model of Matter P1 • Grade 6–7

The specific latent heat of fusion of water is 334 000 J/kg.

If there was 500 g of ice in the system at the start, calculate how much energy is needed to completely melt the ice once it has reached 0°C. **[2 marks]**

7 Quantitative Chemistry P1 • Grade 6–7

Ammonia, NH_3, is produced from nitrogen and hydrogen.

Relative atomic masses (A_r): N = 14, H = 1

a) Calculate the mass of 1.00 mole of ammonia, NH_3. **[1 mark]**

....

....

b) Calculate the mass of 0.5 moles of ammonia, NH_3. **[1 mark]**

....

....

8 Quantitative Chemistry P1 / Using Resources P2 • Grade 6–7

Ammonia, NH_3, is made in the Haber process.

Ammonia can be used to make nitrogen-based fertilisers, which are important for reliable food production.

a) Calculate the relative formula mass of ammonia.

Relative atomic masses (A_r): H = 1 N = 14 **[1 mark]**

....

....

b) Calculate the percentage composition of nitrogen in one molecule of ammonia. **[2 marks]**

....

....

.... %

9 Particle Model of Matter P1 / Energy P1 • Grade 6–7

A student is investigating the transfer of thermal energy from hot water to cold steel.

The student suspends a block of steel at room temperature from a thread and lowers it into hot water.

a) The steel block measures 5 cm × 5 cm × 5 cm and its density is 7.85 g/cm^3.

Calculate the mass of the block in kilograms (kg). **[3 marks]**

....

....

....

Mass of the block = ... kg

b) The specific heat capacity of steel is 502 J/kg °C.

It is at 15°C and rises to 35°C when placed in the water.

Calculate the amount of energy transferred into it.

Use the equation: $\Delta E = m \times c \times (T_2 - T_1)$ **[3 marks]**

....

....

....

Amount of energy transferred = ...

10 Electricity P1 • Grade 6–7

A step-up transformer has a potential difference of 1000 V ac placed across the terminals of the primary coil; a current of 5 A flows through it.

This causes the secondary coil to have 10 000 V ac across its terminals and a current of 0.48 A flowing through it.

Calculate the efficiency of the transformer. **[4 marks]**

....

....

....

Efficiency = ...

11 Homeostasis and Response P2 • Grade 8–9

At a synapse in the brain, a neurotransmitter diffuses between two neurones.

The diffusion distance is 30 nm and it takes 1.8×10^{-7} seconds.

Calculate the speed of diffusion of the neurotransmitter.

Use this formula and give your answer in metres per second. **[3 marks]**

$$\text{speed} = \frac{\text{distance}}{\text{time}}$$

....

....

....

Speed = ...

12 Quantitative Chemistry P1 • Grade 8–9

A student made a standard solution of hydrochloric acid, HCl.

The student used 1.825 g of hydrochloric acid and 500 cm^3 of pure water.

a) Calculate the number of moles of hydrochloric acid the student used. **[3 marks]**

....

....

....

.... mol

b) Calculate the concentration of hydrochloric acid in g/dm^3. **[3 marks]**

....

....

....

.... g/dm^3

13 Energy P1 • Grade 8–9

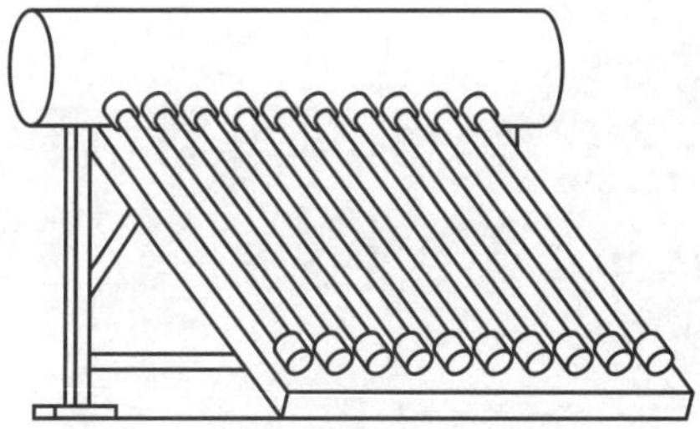

This solar-powered water heater consists of tubes filled with water.

Energy is absorbed by the water, causing its temperature to increase.

The specific heat capacity of water is 4200 J/kg°C.

The system causes the water temperature to rise from 15°C to 40°C as a result of 5 MJ being transferred to the water.

Calculate the mass of water in the system to 3 significant figures.

Use the equation: $\Delta E = m \times c \times (T_2 - T_1)$ **[4 marks]**

....

....

....

....

Mass of water = ...

Total score: .... / 46

Balance

Balance a chemical equation.

Worked example and more!

TOP TIP
Remember there are the same number and type of atoms at the start of the reaction as at the end of the reaction.

Example question

1 **Atomic Structure and the Periodic Table P1 • Grade 7–8**

A student investigated the displacement reaction between potassium iodide solution and chlorine water.

Balance the ionic equation for this reaction. **[1 mark]**

$$\ldots\ldots I^{-}\,(aq) + \ldots\ldots Cl_2\,(aq) \rightarrow \ldots\ldots Cl^{-}\,(aq) + \ldots\ldots I_2\,(aq)$$

Complete the example

2 **Using Resources P2 • Grade 4–5**

The Haber process is used to manufacture ammonia. Ammonia can be used to make nitrogen-based fertilisers.

Balance the equation for the Haber process.

$N_2 + 3H_2 \rightleftharpoons$ .... NH_3 **[1 mark]**

Exam practice questions

6

1 **Organic Chemistry P2 • Grade 4–5**

Ethanol can be used as a fuel.

Balance the symbol equation for the complete combustion of ethanol.

C_2H_5OH + ... O_2 → .... CO_2 + ... H_2O **[1 mark]**

2 **Chemical Changes P1 • Grade 4–5**

Sodium carbonate can react with hydrochloric acid to make a soluble salt, a gas and water.

Balance the equation for this reaction.

.... Na_2CO_3 + ... HCl → .... NaCl + ... CO_2 + ... H_2O **[1 mark]**

3 **Chemical Changes P1 • Grade 6–7**

A student investigated the electrolysis of copper(II) chloride solution.

a) Balance the half equation for the reaction at the anode.

.... Cl^- → .... Cl_2 + ... e^- **[1 mark]**

b) Balance the half equation for the reaction at the cathode.

.... Cu^{2+} + ... e^- → .... Cu **[1 mark]**

4 **Chemical Changes P1 • Grade 8–9**

A student investigated the electrolysis of copper(II) sulfate solution.

Balance the half equation for the reaction at the anode.

.... OH^- → .... O_2 + ... H_2O + ... e^- **[2 marks]**

Total score: .... **/ 6**

Measure

Find an item of data from a diagram or photograph. You will probably need to use the measurement to calculate another quantity.

Worked example and more!

TOP TIP
You often have to use your measurement to work out something else, so read the question carefully.

Example question

1 **Cell Biology P1 • Grade 6–7**

The electron micrograph shows a mitochondrion.

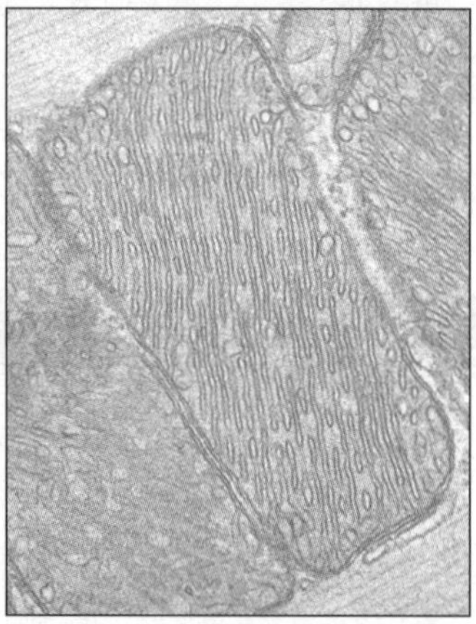

The magnification of this image is ×25 000.

Measure the image length of the mitochondrion and calculate the actual length.

Give your answer in micrometres. **[2 marks]**

Complete the example

2 Organisation P1 • Grade 4–5

The micrograph shows human blood cells.

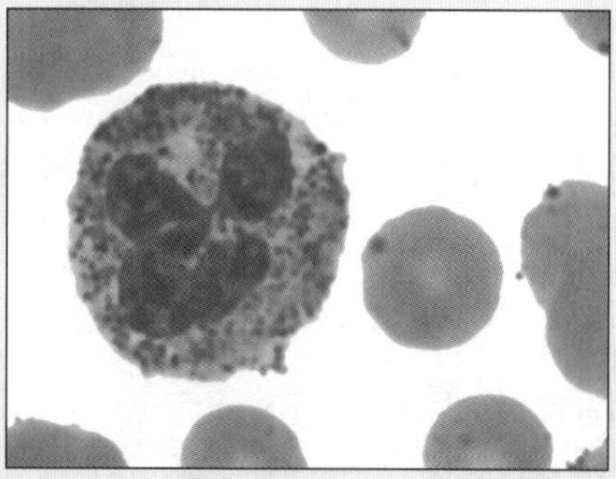

Measure the diameter of the white blood cell and a red blood cell.
Use your measurements to find this ratio:

diameter of a white blood cell : diameter of a red blood cell

Give your answer in the form *n* : 1. **[3 marks]**

White blood cell = 26 mm and red blood cell = ...

Ratio = ... : 1

3 Energy • Grade 4–5

A student wanted to know the specific heat capacity of a metal block.

The picture shows the student measuring the mass of the metal block.

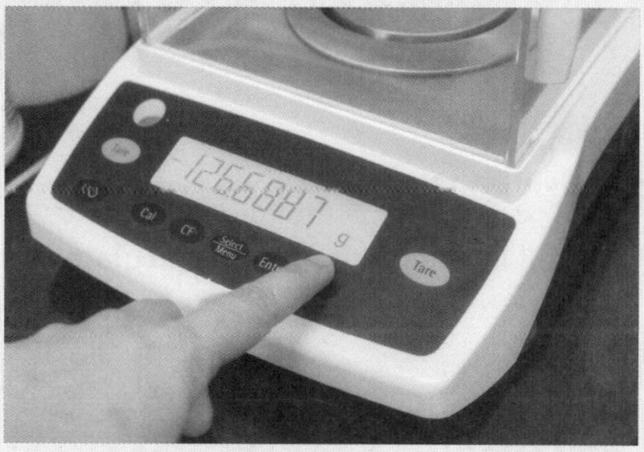

Measure the mass of the metal block in the picture.

Give your answer in kilograms. Give your answer to 2 significant figures. **[3 marks]**

The value on the balance = ... *g*

.... ÷ 1000 = ... *kg*

= .... *kg*

The balance has a reading in grams. You get one mark for correctly noting this value. You then need to convert this into kilograms by dividing by 1000 to gain you another mark.

Exam practice questions

19

1 **Organisation P1 • Grade 4–5**

The photograph shows a stomatal pore on the underside of a leaf.

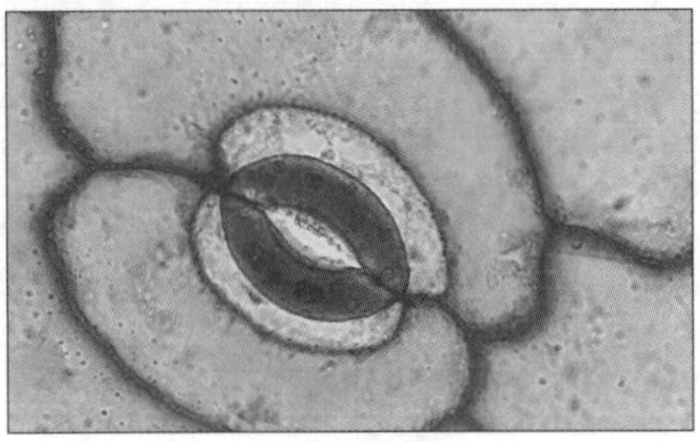

The actual width of the pore is 100 micrometres.

Measure the width of the pore on the image and calculate the magnification of the photograph.

[3 marks]

....

....

Magnification = × ....

2 **Cell Biology P1 • Grade 4–5**

The diagram shows a palisade cell.

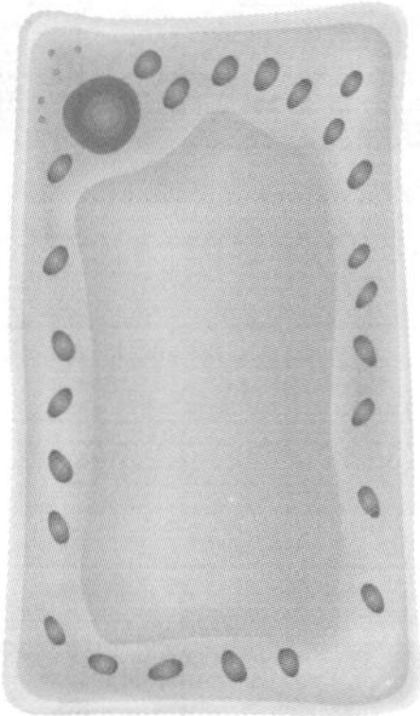

The actual height of the cell is 0.1 mm.

Measure the height of the cell in the diagram and calculate the magnification of the image. **[2 marks]**

....

....

3 **Cell Biology P1 • Grade 4–5**

A student wants to study cells dividing by mitosis.

They use cells from the tip of a plant root. They stain the cells with a dye and look at them under a microscope.

The image shows the photograph that the student takes.

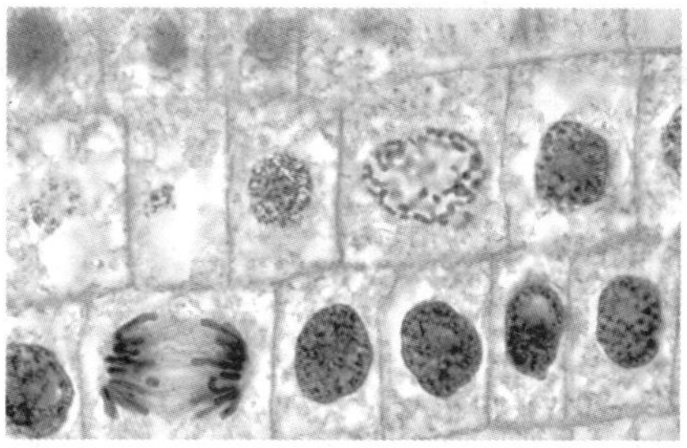

Measure the width of the cell in the photograph and calculate the magnification of the photograph. **[2 marks]**

....

....

4 Cell Biology P1 • Grade 6–7

In an osmosis investigation, some students put 30 mm potato cylinders in different concentrations of sucrose solution.

After an hour they remeasured the length of the cylinders and worked out the increase or decrease in length.

The graph shows their results.

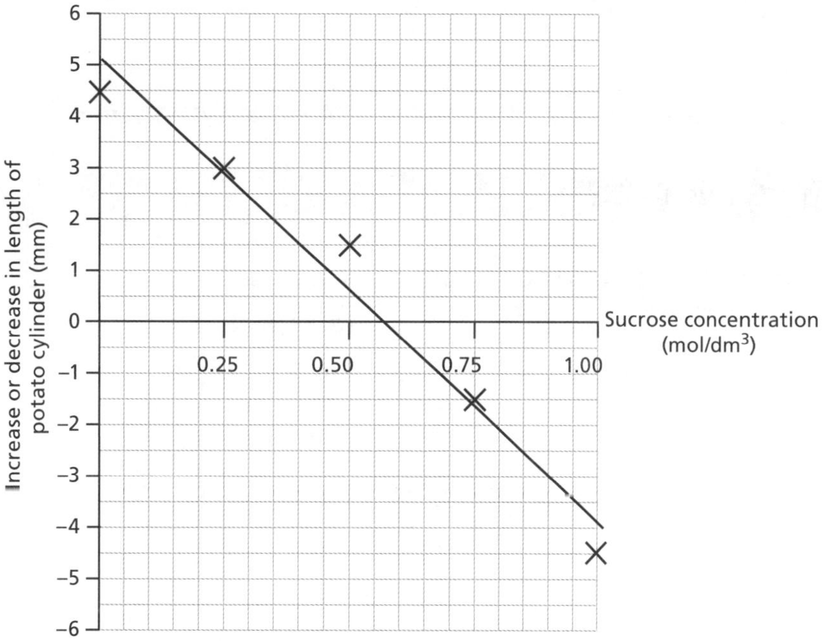

The result of this potato cylinder has not been plotted on the graph.

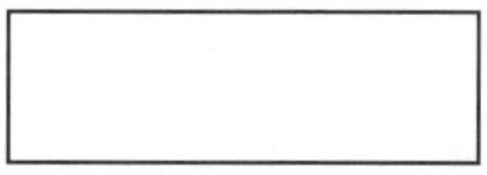

Measure the length of this potato cylinder and use the graph to find out the concentration of the solution that it was soaked in. **[3 marks]**

....

Concentration = ... mol/dm^3

5 Cell Biology P1 • Grade 6–7

The diagram shows a section through an animal cell.

The magnification of the **diagram** is ×200.

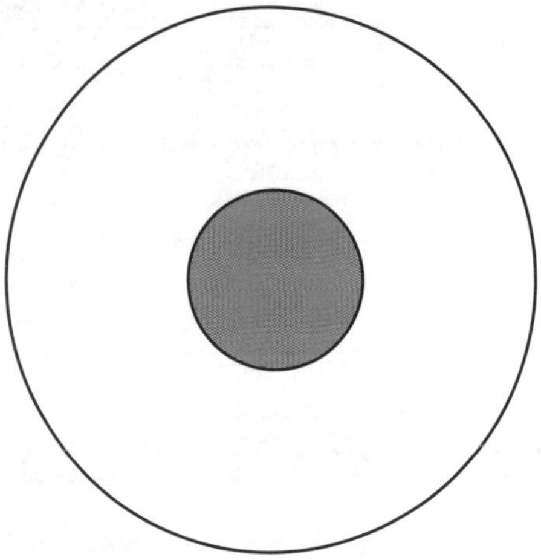

Measure the diameter of the cell and the diameter of the nucleus. Use these measurements to calculate the area of the cytoplasm in the section. Use the formula: **A** = πr^2

Give your answer in mm^2 ($\pi = 3.14$).

[3 marks]

....

....

Area of cytoplasm = ... mm^2

6 Energy P1 • Grade 6–7

This is an image of crystals as seen under a microscope.

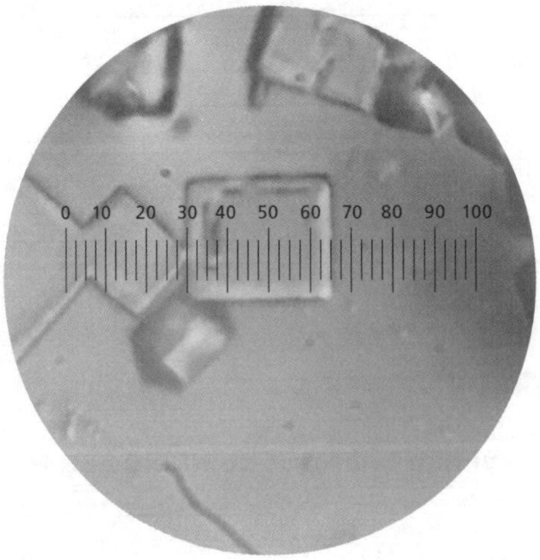

Look at the crystal with its straight left hand edge under the 30 mark. A scale is shown across the top of the image.

The scale measures in μm.

Measure the length of the crystal under the scale from left to right. **[2 marks]**

....

Waves P2 • Grade 8–9

This image shows a wave on a screen.

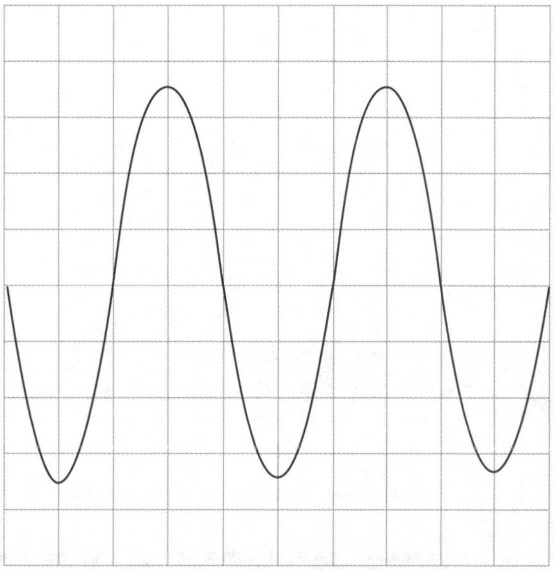

The wave represents the electrical output from a microphone and it is an ac signal, with positive and negative values of voltage. It shows how an electrical signal changes with time.

The screen has a 1 cm grid on it.

The x-axis shows time and the scale is 5 ms/cm.

The y-axis shows voltage and the scale is 5 V/cm.

a) Measure the peak voltage. ....

b) Measure the period of the wave. ....

[4 marks]

Plan

Write a method for carrying out an investigation. This will usually cover one of the required practicals from the specification.

Worked example and more!

TOP TIP
The question may give you hints on what to include in your method or give suggested apparatus.

Example question

1 **Organisation P1 • Grade 4–5**

A person wants to know if sugars or proteins are present in a type of biscuit.

Plan a method that could be used to find out if sugars or proteins are in the biscuits. **[6 marks]**

Complete the example

2 **Chemical Changes P1 • Grade 4–5**

A student is given three metals, 1, 2 and 3, to identify. The metals are calcium, zinc and silver.

Plan an investigation to identify the three metals by comparing their reactions with dilute nitric acid.

Your plan should give valid results. **[4 marks]**

Add the same mass and .... of metals to the same .... and concentration of (dilute) nitric acid.

Observe the temperature change or the number of ....

Determine conclusion:

- *Silver has no reaction.*
- *Zinc has some bubbles and .... in temperature.*
- *Calcium has .... and the .... in temperature.*

3 **Energy P1 • Grade 6–7**

You are provided with a block of a metal and are told its mass.

The block has two holes in it, one to take a small electrical heater and the other to take a thermometer.

A heater is supplied with a power supply, ammeter, voltmeter and wires.

As well as the thermometer, you have an insulated cover for the block and a timer.

Plan how the specific heat capacity of the metal could be determined. **[6 marks]**

- *Measure the ....*
- *Set the block up with ....*
- *Connect the heater to ....*
- *After a set period of time, ...*
- *Calculate the amount of energy transferred to the heater using ....*

- *This can then be equated to* ....

....

....

Exam practice questions

54

1 **Bioenergetics P1 • Grade 4–5**

Pondweed is a water plant that can be used to investigate the rate of photosynthesis.

Plan an experiment to investigate how the rate of photosynthesis varies with light intensity. Use this equipment in your investigation. **[6 marks]**

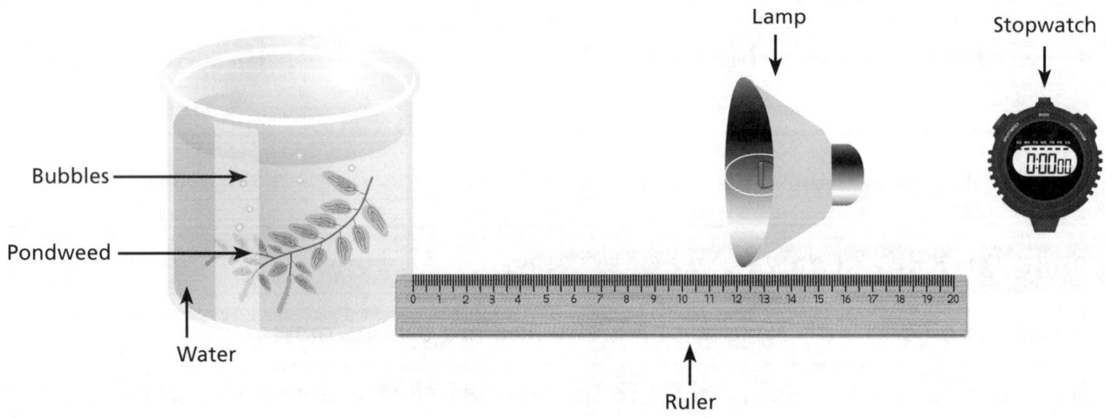

....

....

....

....

....

....

....

....

....

....

....

....

2 Chemical Changes P1 • Grade 4–5

Plan a method for making pure dry crystals of copper(II) sulfate crystals from copper(II) oxide and dilute sulfuric acid.

In your method you should name the apparatus you will use.

You do not need to mention safety. **[6 marks]**

3 Particle Model of Matter P1 • Grade 4–5

Plan a valid investigation to determine the density of an irregularly shaped small rock.

In your method you should name the apparatus you will use.

You do not need to mention safety. **[6 marks]**

4 Electricity P1 • Grade 4–5

Plan an investigation to determine the relationship between length of wire and resistance.

In your method you should name the apparatus you will use.

You do not need to mention safety. **[6 marks]**

5 Homeostasis and Response P2 • Grade 6–7

Reaction time in humans is usually between 0.2 s and 0.9 s. A student wanted to find out whether using the right or left hand of a person would affect their reaction time.

Plan a method for the student's investigation.

Include details of the test you would use for reaction time. **[6 marks]**

6 Ecology P2 • Grade 6–7

The photograph shows a grassy playing field.

On the grassy playing field:

- there are daisy and buttercup plants
- one area of the soil is usually dry
- another area of the soil is usually wet.

Plan an investigation to find out the effect of water in the soil on the number of daisy plants growing in each area. **[6 marks]**

7 Chemical Changes P1 • Grade 6–7

A student was investigating the electrolysis of solutions.

They noticed effervescence at the electrodes and collected the gases into test tubes and put a stopper on them.

Plan an investigation to identify the gases that were collected.

You do not need to mention safety. **[6 marks]**

8 Using Resources P2 / Quantitative Chemistry P1 • Grade 6–7

A student wanted to investigate the concentration of salts in sea water.

Plan an investigation to calculate the concentration of salts in a sample of sea water.

You do not need to mention safety. **[6 marks]**

9 Forces P2 • Grade 6–7

Plan an experiment that will show that the extension of a spring is directly proportional to the load applied to it as long as the elastic limit is not exceeded. **[6 marks]**

Total score: .... / 54

Design

Set out how an investigation could be carried out to test a hypothesis. Often this will relate to an experiment or some other type of practical procedure.

Worked example and more!

TOP TIP
Write in a logical sequence and ensure your design would yield useful evidence if it was carried out.

Example question

1 **Ecology P2 • Grade 4–5**

Two students are on their school football pitch.

One student says that there are more dandelion weeds in the two penalty areas than on the rest of the pitch.

Design an experiment to test this observation. **[6 marks]**

Complete the example

2 **Forces P2 • Grade 4–5**

The photograph shows the equipment that a student used to investigate how the extension of a spring varied with the force acting on the spring.

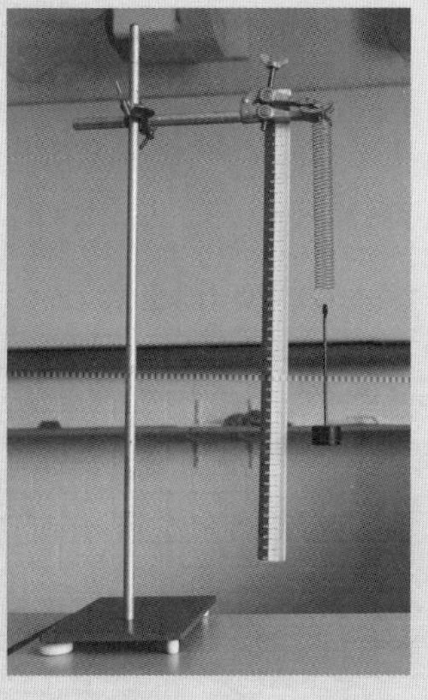

Design an experiment to show the relationship between force and extension of a spring.

You do not need to include safety information.

Give the expected result. **[6 marks]**

Measure the .... of the spring with a ruler.

Then, ...

....

....

Calculate ....

....

....

Repeat the measurements by adding ....

....

....

Plot ....

....

....

The line of best fit should be ....

Exam practice questions

34

1 Particle Model of Matter P1 • Grade 4–5

This bolt is around 5 cm long and is made from metal.

Design a procedure that could be used to find its density, indicating the equipment to use, the measurements to take and the calculations to be carried out. **[6 marks]**

2 Organisation P1 • Grade 6–7

A student looks up amylase on the internet.

They read that amylase produced by fungi often has a lower optimum pH than amylase from bacteria.

Design an experiment to test this hypothesis. **[6 marks]**

3 Cell Biology P1 • Grade 6–7

Two students are talking about potatoes and sweet potatoes.

One says that because of their name, sweet potatoes must contain more sugar than normal potatoes.

Design an osmosis experiment to test the hypothesis that sweet potatoes contain more sugar than normal potatoes. **[6 marks]**

4 Electricity P1 • Grade 6–7

A power generating system consists of a generator that produces 10 000 V, power lines that distribute electricity at 50 000 V and a local supply network that runs at 100 V.

Design step-up and step-down transformers to connect these parts of the system, indicating the number of turns on each coil. None of the coils are to have fewer than 20 turns. **[4 marks]**

5 Energy P1 • Grade 6–7

A scientist is trying to determine the specific latent heat of ice.

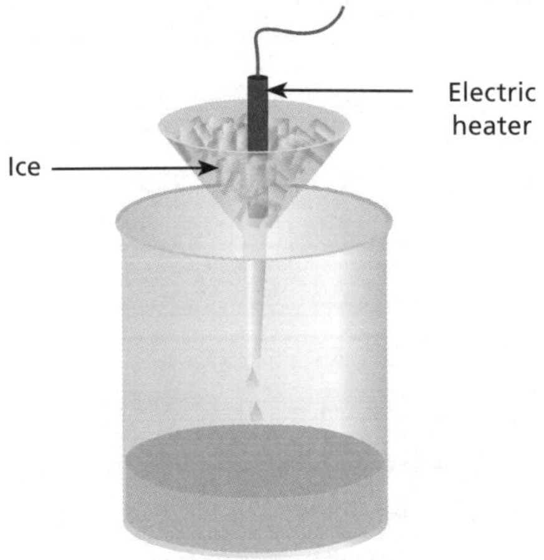

They set up a small electrical heater in the neck of a funnel and load the funnel with small pieces of ice.

As the pieces close to the heater are heated, they melt and run through the funnel, so that more ice descends and takes its place.

Design a procedure using this equipment that will enable them to determine a value for the specific latent heat of ice, indicating the measurements and readings they will need to take.

Use the equation: $\Delta E = m \times l$ **[6 marks]**

6 Cell Biology P1 • Grade 8–9

Vitamin C is important in the diet for building connective tissue.

Orange juice contains vitamin C.

When vitamin C is added to a blue chemical called DCPIP it reacts to produce a colourless chemical.

A student reads that heat can destroy vitamin C.

Design an experiment to test this hypothesis. **[6 marks]**

Total score: .... / 34

Plot

Construct a graph on a printed grid using data given in the question.

Worked example and more!

Example question

1 **Forces P2 • Grade 6–7**

A parachutist has jumped out of an aircraft and is in free fall. They have not yet opened their parachute. The table shows their speed every second.

Plot a graph displaying this data and include a line of best fit. **[4 marks]**

Time / s	0	1	2	3	4	5	6	7	8	9	10	11	12	13	14
Speed / m/s	0	9	17	25	32	37	41	44	45	46	48	49	49	50	50

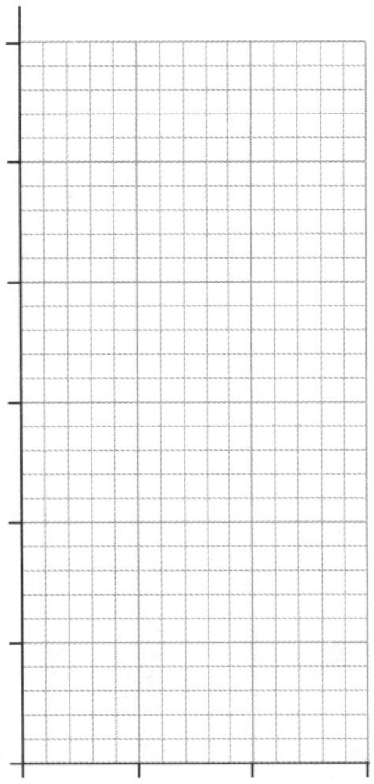

TOP TIP
If you are asked to draw a line of best fit, this could be a smooth curve or one straight line.

Complete the example

2 Homeostasis and Response P2 • Grade 4–5

An athlete is running a long-distance race.

The table shows the concentration of glycogen in the athlete's liver at different times during the race.

Time in minutes	Glycogen concentration in mmol per kg
0	95
20	80
40	65
80	40
120	20
160	10

Plot the results of the experiment on the grid and include a line of best fit. **[3 marks]**

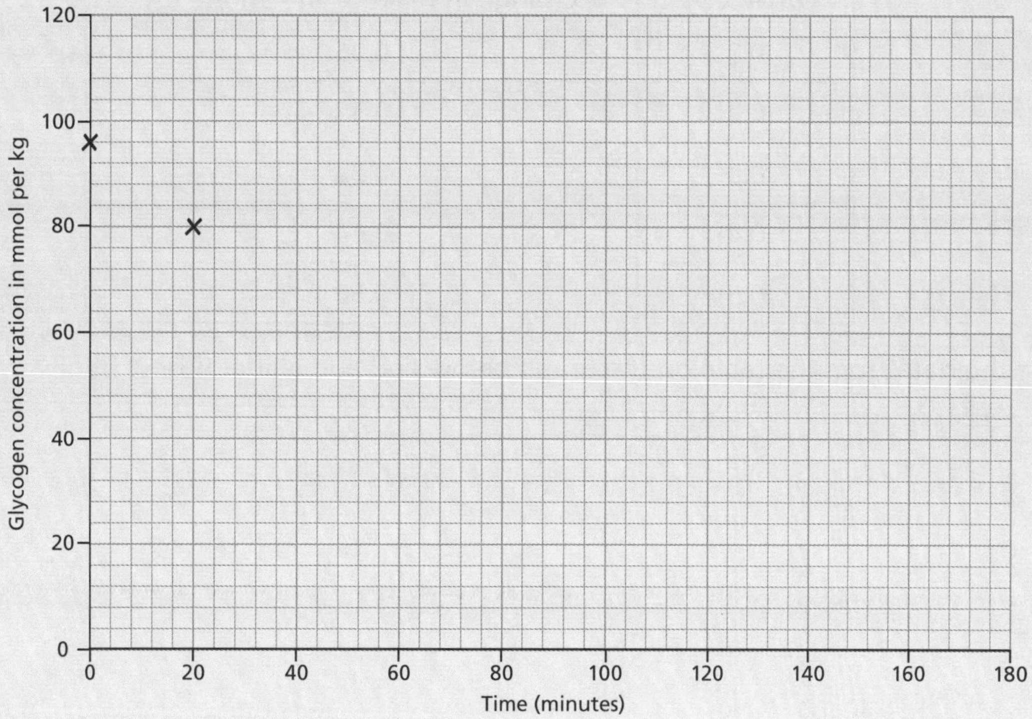

3 Chemical Changes P1 • Grade 8–9

A student is investigating how current affects the mass of the anode in solution electrolysis.

The figure shows the equipment that the student uses.

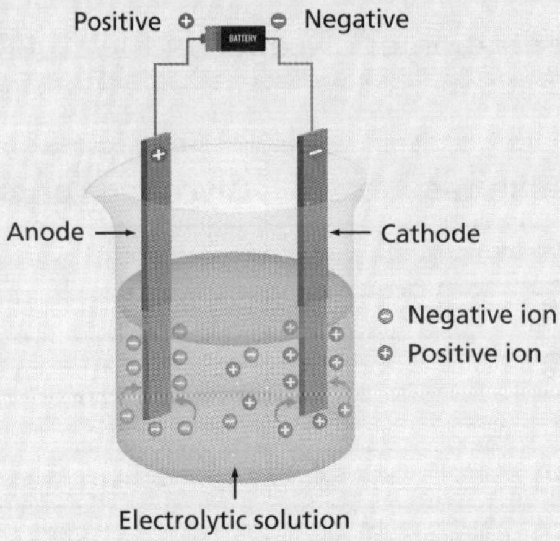

The table shows the student's results.

Current (A)	Change in mass of the anode (g)
0.1	0.06
0.2	0.58
0.3	0.32
0.4	0.44
0.5	0.58

Plot the data from the table on the graph below and add a line of best fit. **[2 marks]**

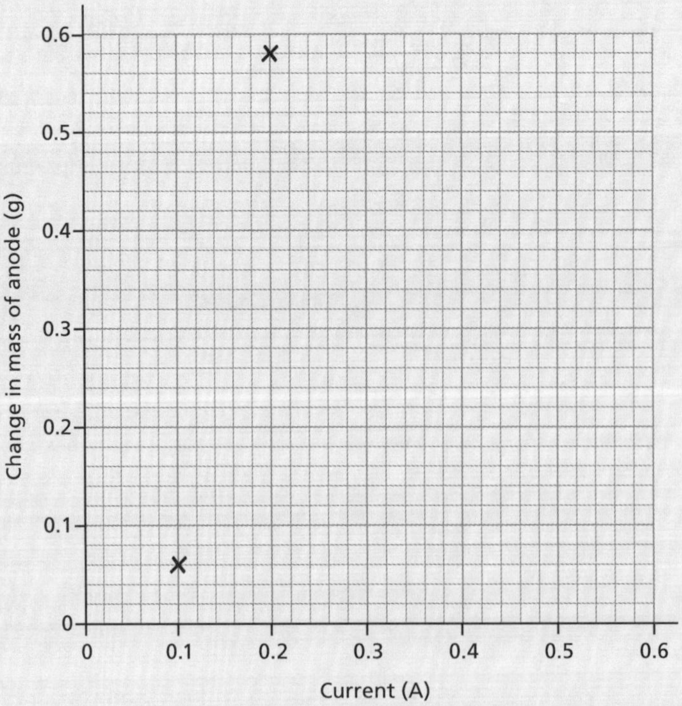

Exam practice questions

35

Ecology P2 • Grade 4–5

Some students investigate plants growing near a tree.

They use a quadrat to measure the percentage of ground covered by plants at different distances from the tree.

The table shows their results.

Distance from the tree in metres	Percentage of ground covered by plants
1	10
2	14
3	18
4	26
5	42
6	52
7	62

Plot these results on the grid.

Include a line of best fit. **[4 marks]**

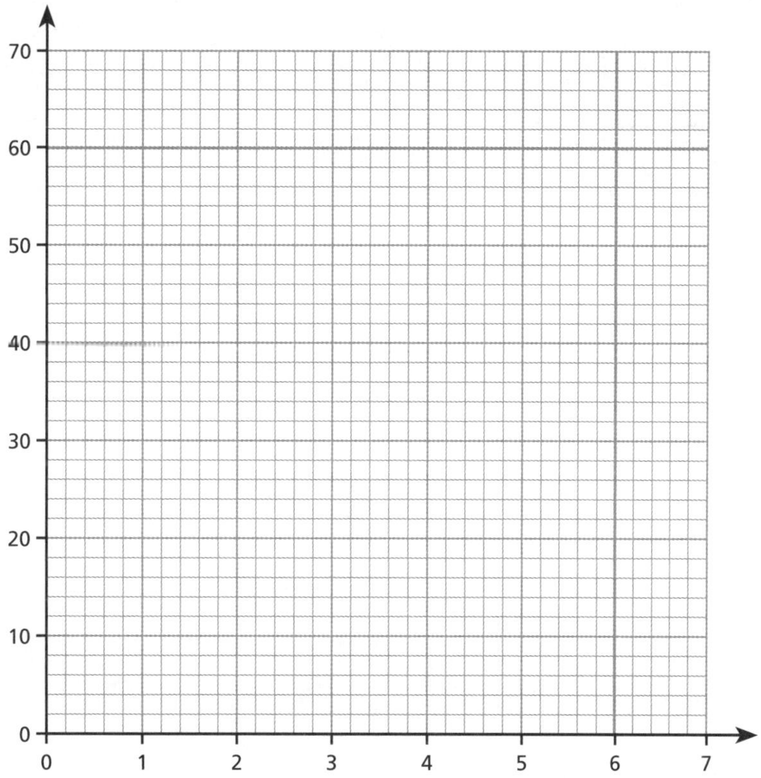

2 Cell Biology P1 • Grade 4–5

Duckweed is a small floating plant found in ponds.

It reproduces quite quickly to produce large populations.

A student decides to investigate duckweed by growing some in a beaker of water.

They count the number of duckweed plants at regular intervals.

The table shows the student's results.

Day	1	4	8	10	15	19	20	23	26	30
Number of Plants	1	2	3	4	15	28	28	28	29	29

Plot a graph of the results to show how the population changed over time. **[3 marks]**

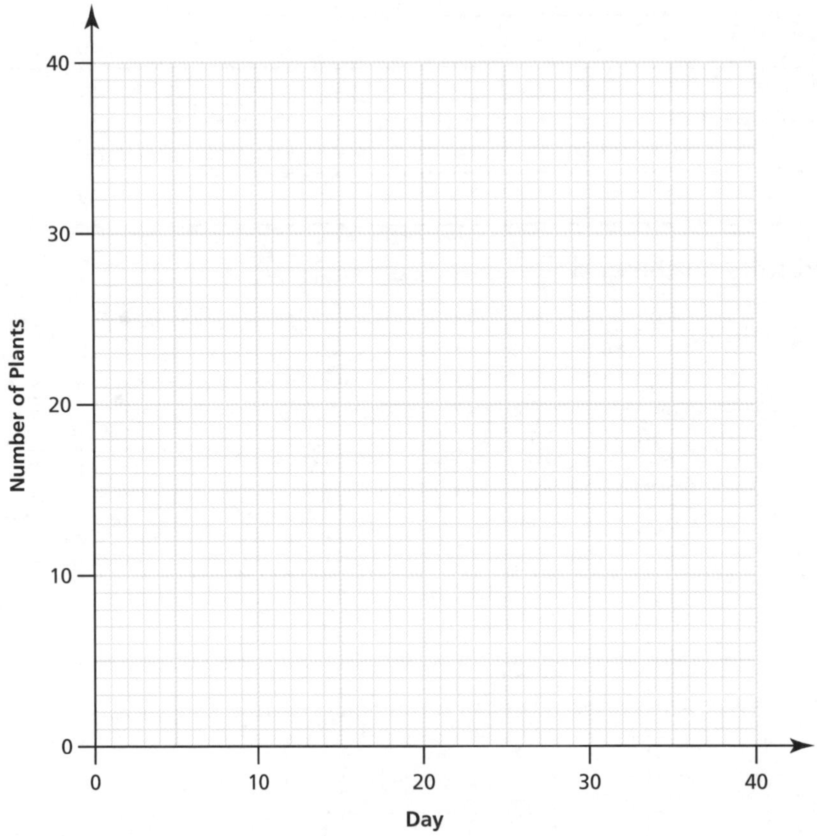

3 Inheritance, Variation and Evolution P2 • Grade 4–5

Bacteria can evolve quickly because they reproduce at such a fast rate.

Some bacteria have evolved to become resistant to antibiotics. MRSA is a bacteria that has evolved to become resistant to the antibiotic methicillin.

The graph shows how the number of cases of MRSA blood infections changed over seven years.

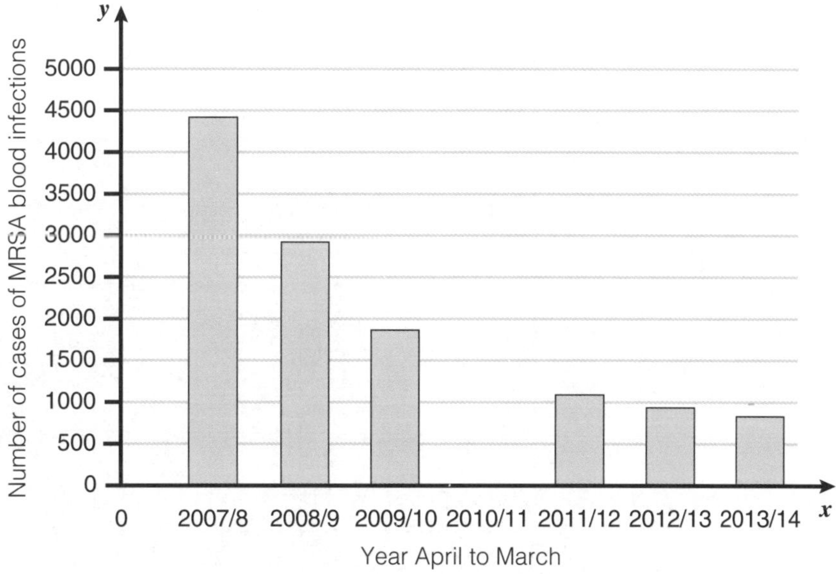

In the year 2010/11, there were 1480 cases of MRSA blood infections.

Plot this result on the graph above. **[1 mark]**

4 The Rate and Extent of Chemical Change P2 • Grade 4–5

Magnesium reacts with dilute hydrochloric acid to form hydrogen gas.

A student is investigating how the mass changes during the reaction.

The student uses the equipment shown in the figure. The table shows the student's results.

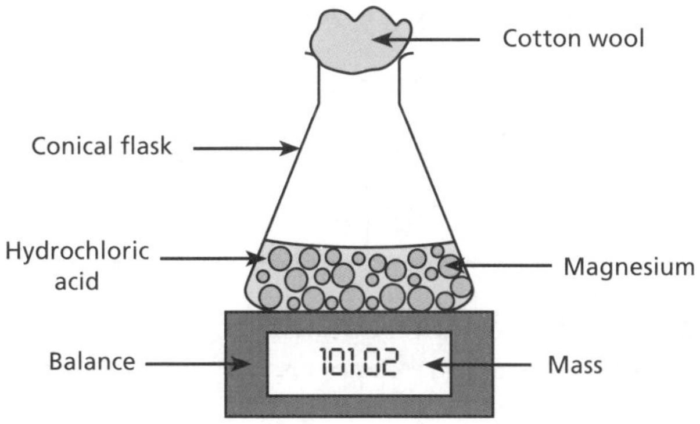

Time (s)	Mass (g)
0	200
20	188
40	176
60	168
80	161
100	155
120	151

Plot the data from the table on the graph below. **[2 marks]**

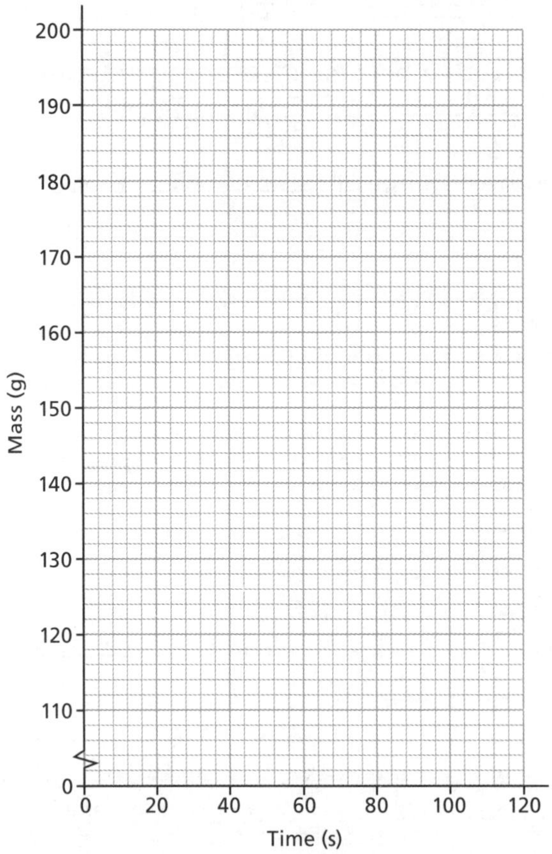

5 Electricity P1 • Grade 6–7

Some students are investigating the resistance of a filament bulb in the diagram shown.

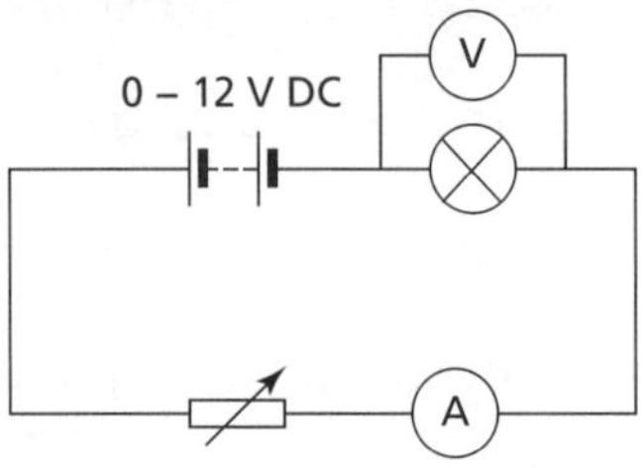

They set up the circuit as shown in the diagram. Their results are shown in the table.

Potential difference/V	–12	–10	–8	–6	–4	–2	0	2	4	6	8	10	12
Current/A	–0.50	–0.47	–0.41	–0.34	–0.24	–0.13	0.00	0.14	0.25	0.34	0.41	0.46	0.50

Use the data in the table to plot a graph of potential difference against current.

Plot the points and add a line of best fit. **[5 marks]**

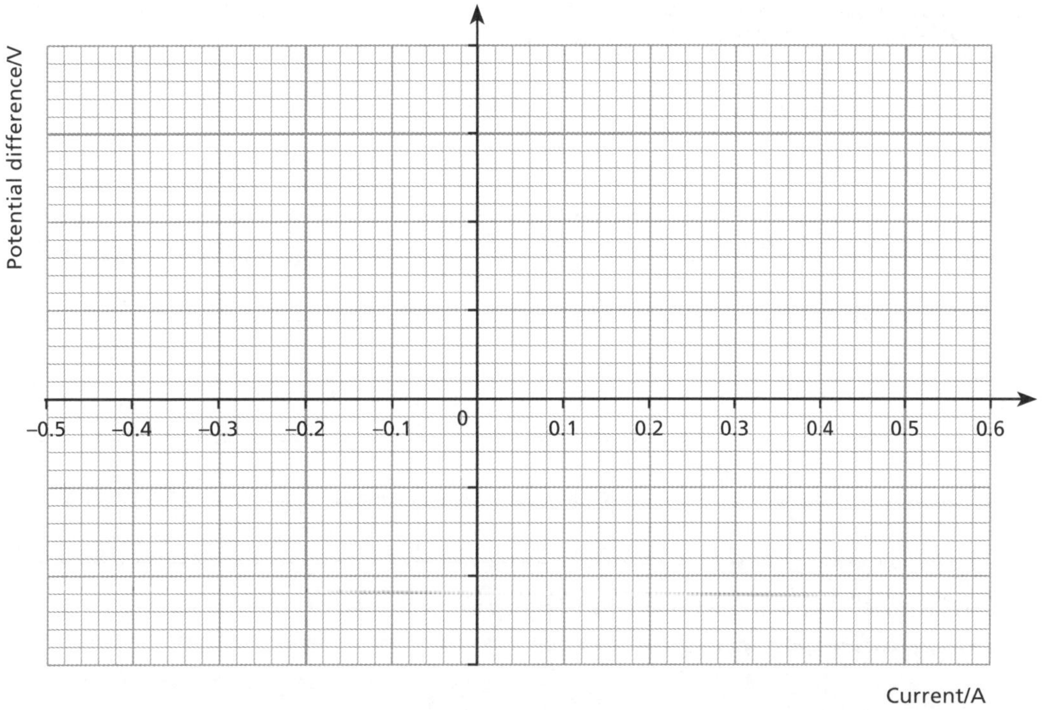

6 Electricity P1 • Grade 6–7

This data shows the potential difference being applied to a diode and the current flowing through it.

Plot a graph showing the relationship between these variables. **[4 marks]**

Potential difference/V	−4	−3.5	−3	−2.5	−2	−1.5	−1	−0.5	0	0.5	1	1.5	2	2.5	3	3.5	4
Current/mA	0	0	0	0	0	0	0	0	0	0	0	2	20	40	60	80	100

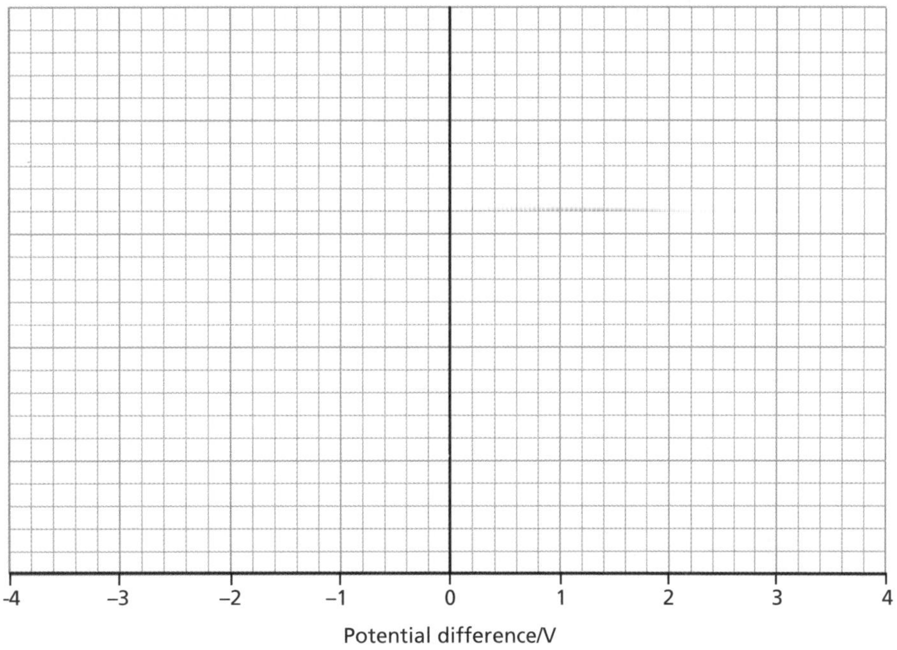

7 Cell Biology P1 • Grade 8–9

The table shows the results of an osmosis experiment.

Potato cylinders were left in sucrose solution and their percentage change in mass calculated.

Concentration of sucrose in mol per dm^3	Percentage change in mass
0.0	12.0
0.2	8.4
0.4	0.8
0.6	–3.8
0.8	–6.4

Plot the results of the experiment on the grid. Include:

- a label and a scale for the *y*-axis
- a line of best fit. **[5 marks]**

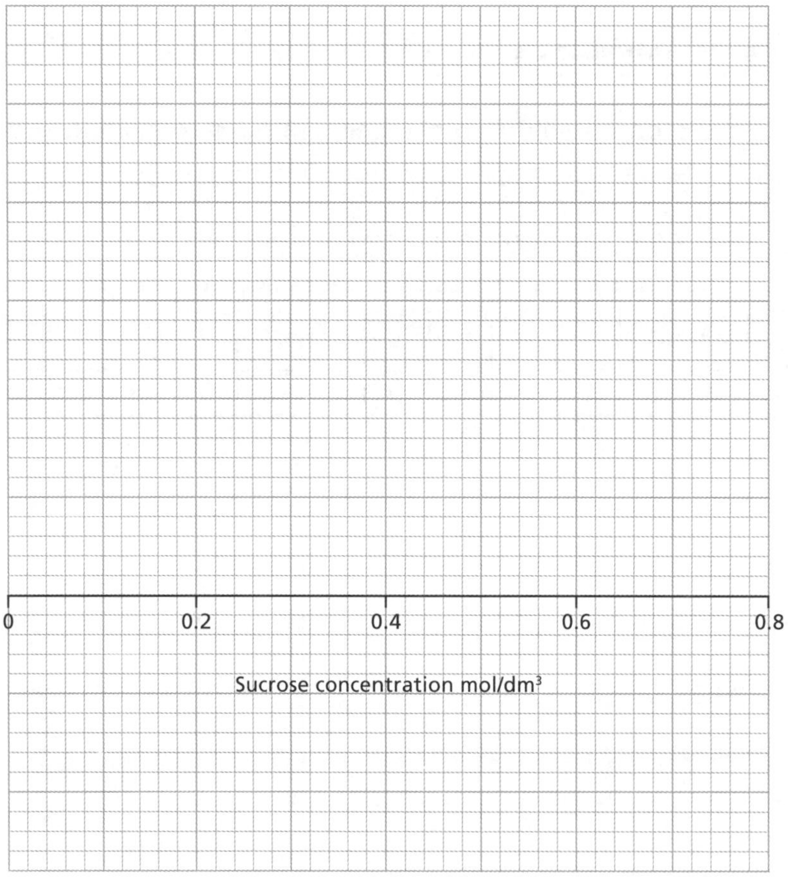

8 The Rate and Extent of Chemical Change P2 • Grade 8–9

A student investigated the rate of reaction between marble chips and hydrochloric acid (HCl).

The table shows the results.

Time (s)	Volume of gas (dm^3)
0	0.000
30	0.030
60	0.046
90	0.052
120	0.065
150	0.070
180	0.076

Plot the data from the table on the graph below. **[3 marks]**

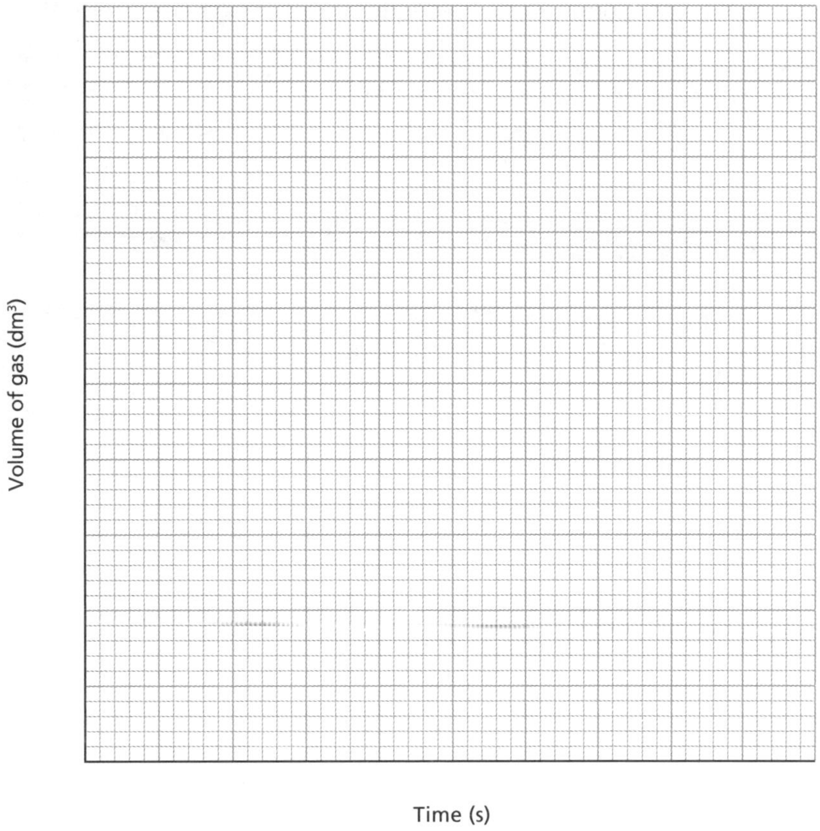

The stopping distance of a car consists of two components: the thinking distance and the braking distance.

a) This data shows the typical thinking distance in metres travelled by a car at various speeds in m/s.

Plot a graph showing this data. **[4 marks]**

Speed / m/s	0	5	10	15	20	25	30
Thinking distance / m	0	3.3	6.7	10.0	13.3	16.7	20.0

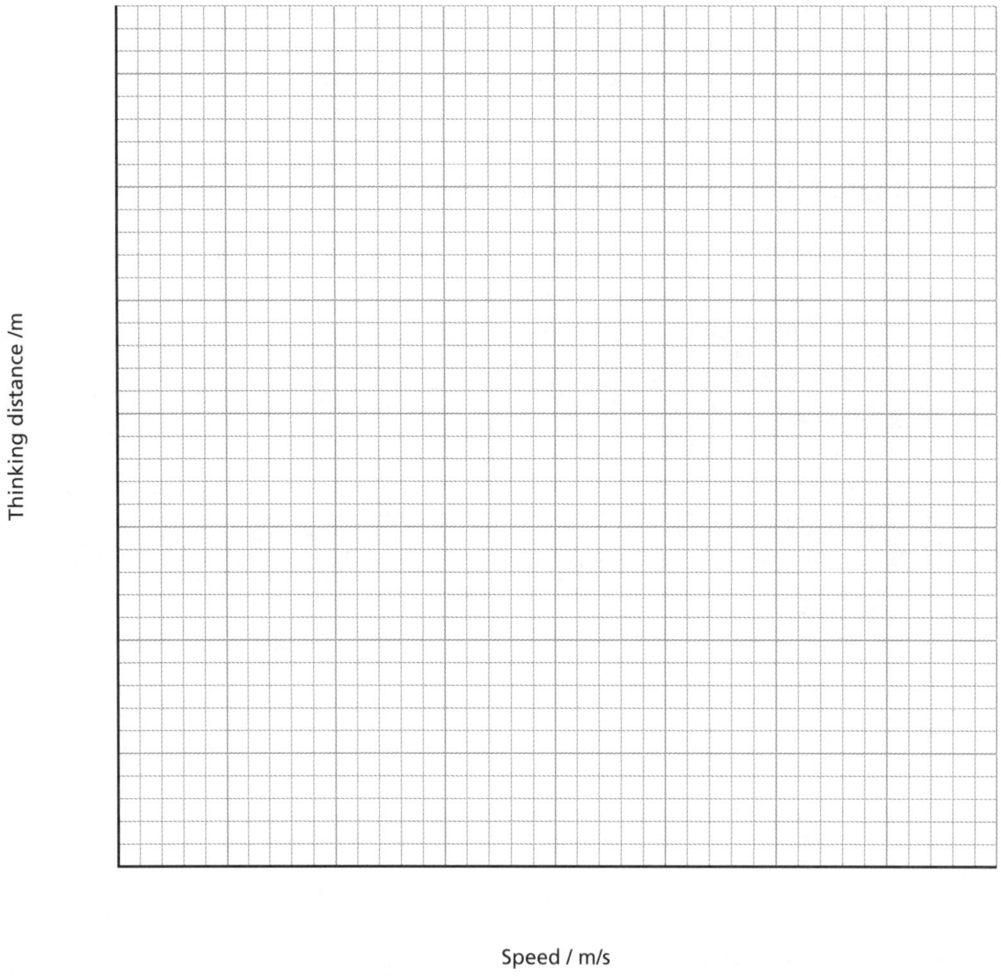

b) This data shows the typical braking distance in metres travelled by a car at various speeds in m/s.

Plot a graph showing this data. **[4 marks]**

Speed / m/s	0	5	10	15	20	25	30
Braking distance / m	0	2	7	16	28	44	63

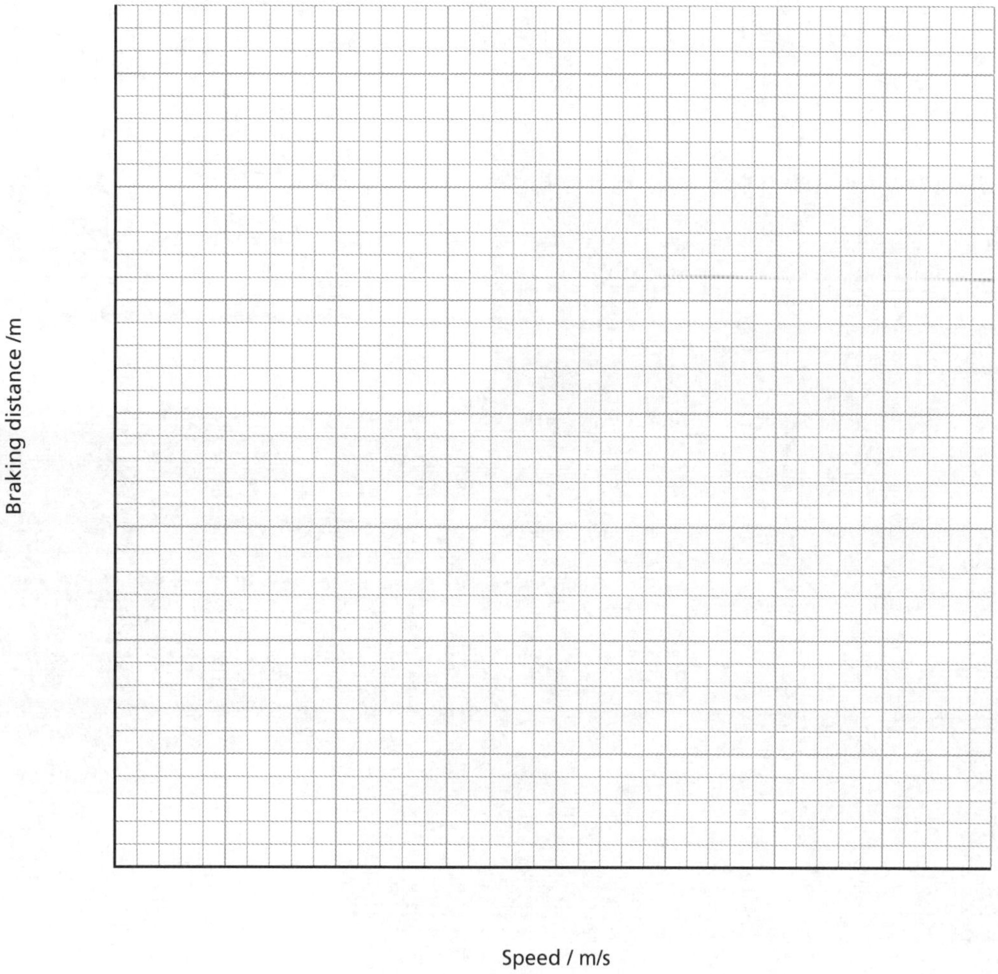

Total score: .... / 35

Compare

Describe the similarities and/or differences between two things, rather than writing about one.

Worked example and more!

TOP TIP
Make sure your answers actually compare the features and do not just write about each one separately.

Example question

1 **Magnetism and Electromagnetism P2 • Grade 4–5**

A student has two rectangular pieces of metal, with similar dimensions. One is a permanent magnet and the other is a piece of magnetic metal.

Compare the two objects in terms of what will happen when another permanent magnet is brought near to first one and then the other. **[4 marks]**

Complete the example

2 Bioenergetics P1 • Grade 4–5

Compare the processes of aerobic respiration and anaerobic respiration in muscle cells. **[5 marks]**

Both of these reactions ....

They are both .... *reactions and use* ....

Aerobic respiration needs .... *but*

....

Anaerobic respiration produces .... *but*

....

Less .... *is released by* .... *respiration.*

3 Bonding, Structure, and the Properties of Matter P1 / Organic Chemistry P2 • Grade 4–5

The diagrams show the structures of two alkane molecules.

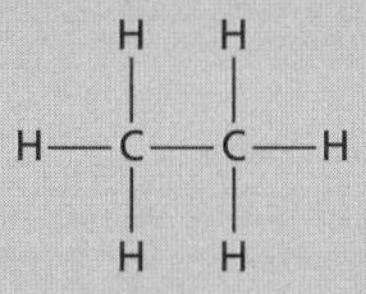

Ethane

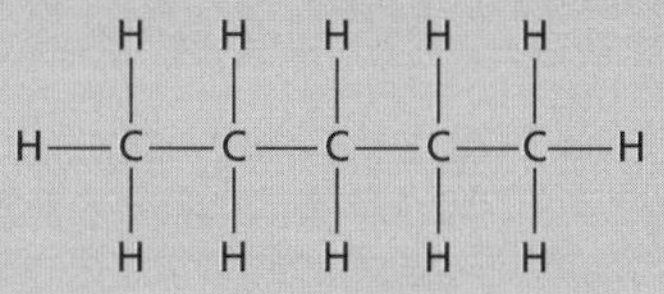

Pentane

The table shows the melting and boiling point values for these two alkanes.

Alkane	Melting point (°C)	Boiling point (°C)
Ethane	–183	–89
Pentane	–130	36

Compare the structure and properties of ethane and pentane. **[6 marks]**

Both ethane and pentane are .... *molecules where the atoms are held together by* .... *bonds, with*

....

between the molecules.

Pentane is a bigger molecule and so has a higher ....

and .... *, meaning that pentane is a liquid at room temperature, whereas ethane is a* ....

Both pentane and ethane are .... *as they contain only hydrogen and carbon. They can be used as fuels and undergo*

.... *to make* ....

Exam practice questions

41

1 Bonding, Structure, and the Properties of Matter P1 • Grade 4–5

The table shows the structure of three different forms of carbon.

Substance	Graphite	Diamond	Buckminsterfullerene
Structure	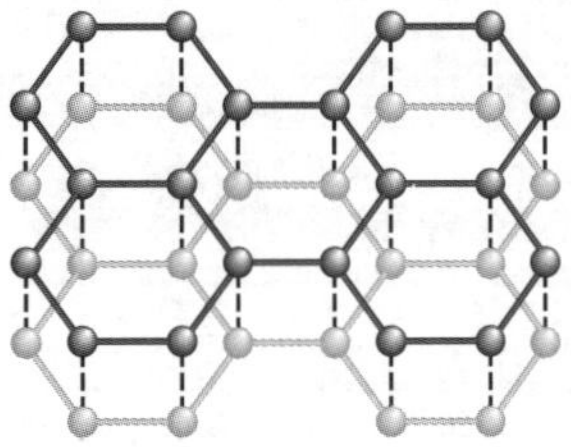	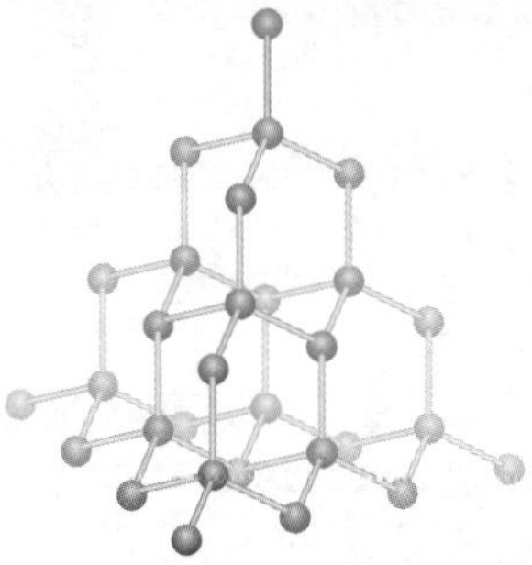	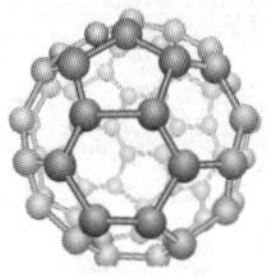

Compare the structure and bonding of the different forms of carbon. **[4 marks]**

2 Using Resources P2 • Grade 4–5

Potable water is water which is safe to drink.

The first stage of making potable water is to select a suitable source.

The second stage is to treat it to ensure it has sufficiently low levels of dissolved salts and microbes.

Compare how easily potable water can be obtained from:

- fresh water (ground water, lake water and river water)
- waste water (sewage). **[6 marks]**

3 Atomic Structure P1 • Grade 4–5

There are different types of ionising radiation. Both alpha and beta radiation contain particles.

Compare the penetrating properties of alpha and beta particles. **[2 marks]**

4 Homeostasis and Response P2 • Grade 6–7

Compare the hormones oestrogen and progesterone.

Include in your answer:

- where the hormones are produced
- the functions of the hormones. **[5 marks]**

5 Organisation P1 • Grade 6–7

The graph shows changes in pressure as blood flows through different parts of the circulatory system.

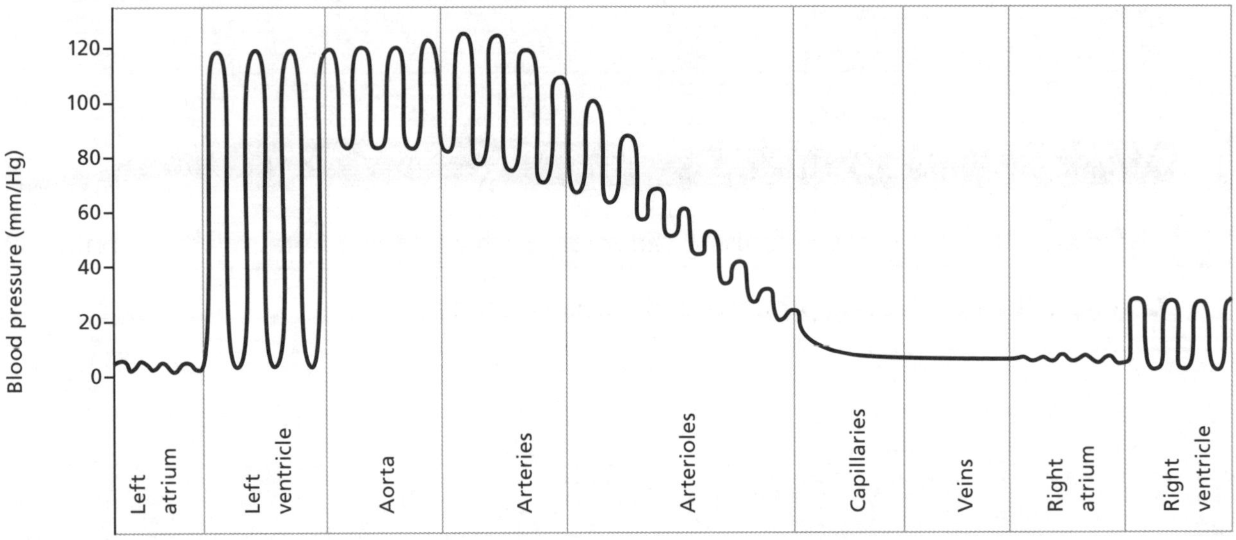

Compare the flow of blood in each of these parts of the circulatory system:

a) left ventricle and right ventricle **[3 marks]**

....

....

....

....

....

....

....

b) aorta and capillaries **[3 marks]**

....

....

....

....

....

....

....

6 Atomic Structure and the Periodic Table P1 • Grade 6–7

Lithium and sodium both react with water.

The picture shows lithium reacting with water.

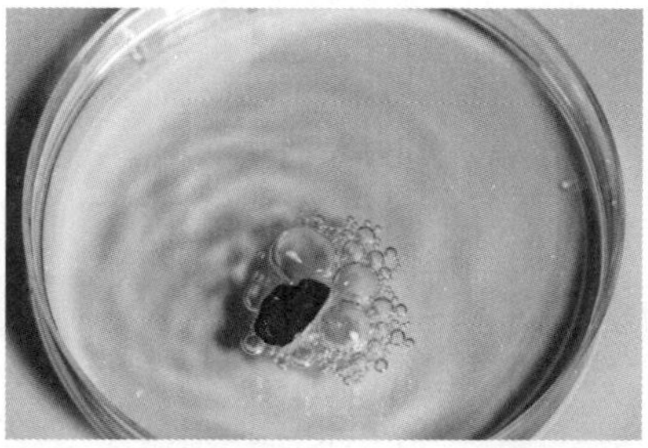

Compare what is seen when lithium reacts with water and when sodium reacts with water.

[4 marks]

7 Waves P2 • Grade 6–7

This diagram shows how light travels from a fish in a pond to the eyes of a person standing on the side. It also shows where the fish appears to be to that person. The solid lines show how the light actually travels and the broken lines show the path it appears to travel.

Compare the actual and apparent paths. **[2 marks]**

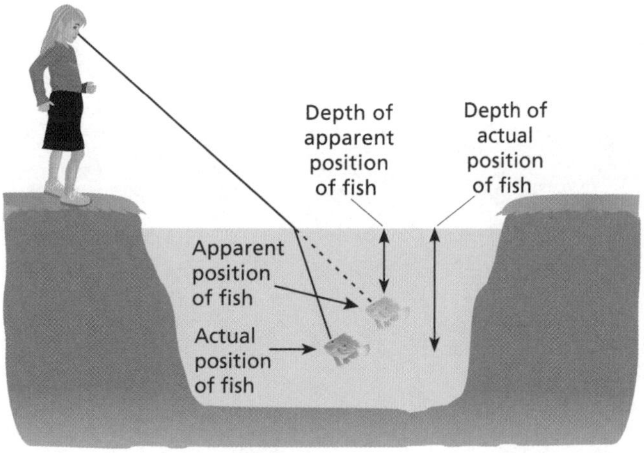

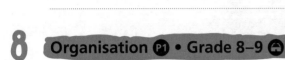

8 Organisation P1 • Grade 8–9

Lipids do not dissolve in water. If they are added to water, they form large droplets which float on the water.

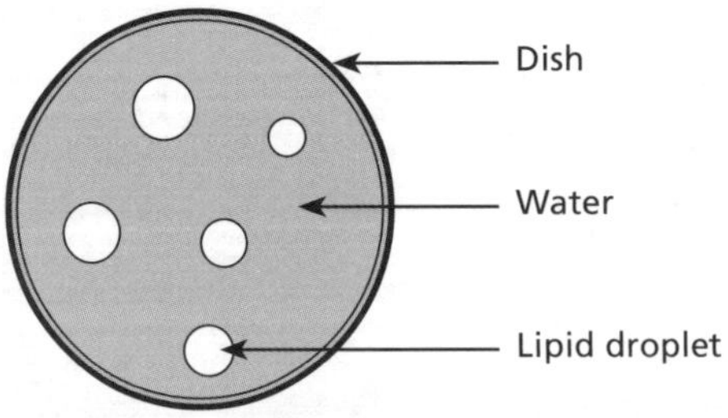

A student sets up an experiment with three dishes containing lipid droplets.

They add different substances to each of the dishes.

The substances added and the results are shown in the diagram.

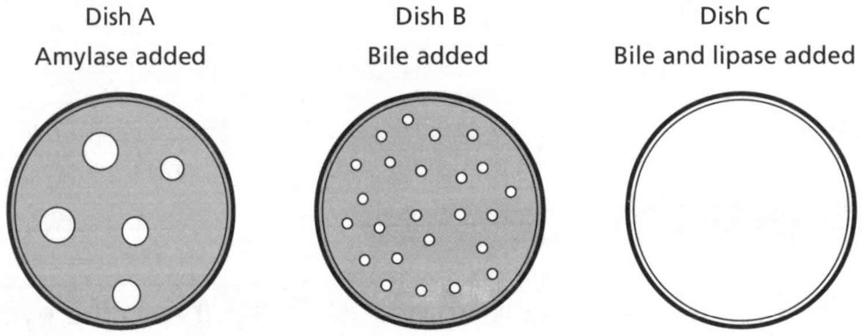

Compare the results produced in each of the dishes with the dish containing just water and lipids. Include explanations for any differences. **[6 marks]**

9 **Forces** P2 • **Grade 8–9**

Diagram A shows the velocity–time graph for an object dropped from a height into water. Diagram B shows the velocity–time graph of a parachutist descending from an aircraft and then opening their parachute.

Compare the graphs, identifying the similarities and differences. **[6 marks]**

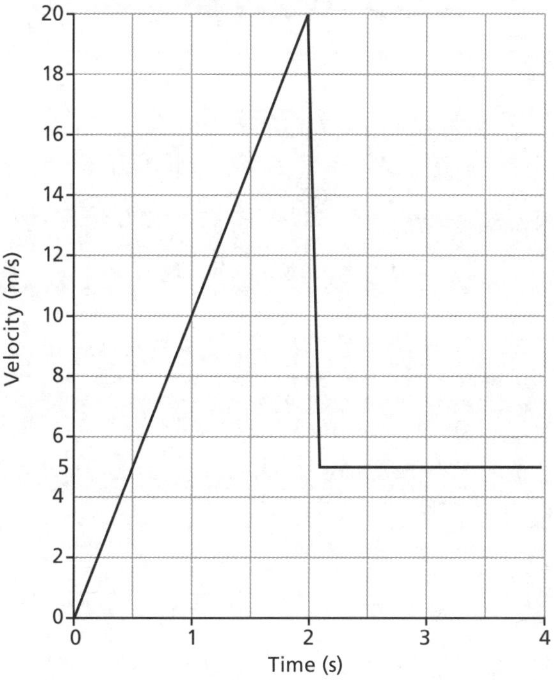

Graph A (object hits water at t = 2 s)

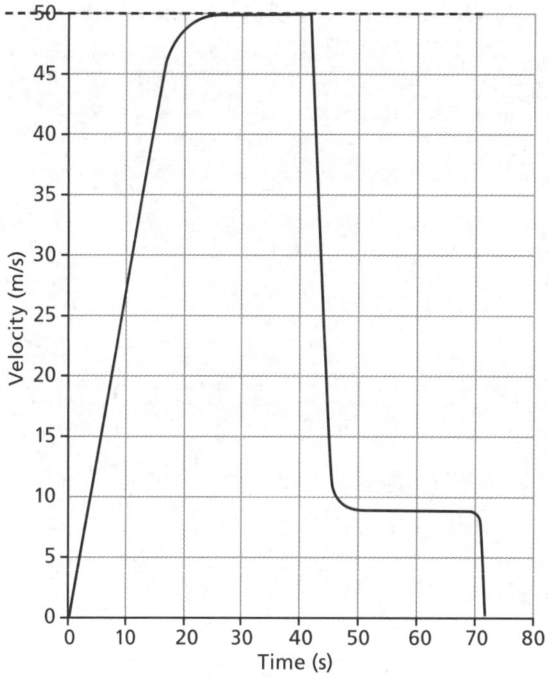

Graph B (parachute opens at t = 42 s)

Total score: .... **/ 41**

Estimate

Find an approximate value.

Worked example and more!

TOP TIP
It may be a calculation, where the result is not exact but based on sampling, or it could involve a graph where you need to extend a line to find an approximate value.

Example question

1 Ecology P2 • Grade 4–5

Some students are investigating how many mosquito larvae live in their school pond.

They put a quadrat on the surface of the pond and count the number of mosquito larvae inside the quadrat. They do this four times in different places on the pond's surface.

The table shows the results.

	Quadrat 1	Quadrat 2	Quadrat 3	Quadrat 4
Number of larvae	12	10	7	11

The area of each quadrat is 0.25 m^2 and the area of the pond is 12 m^2.

Estimate the total number of mosquito larvae in the pond. **[3 marks]**

Complete the example

2 Energy P1 • Grade 4–5

The graph shows the relationship between the load applied to a spring and the extension of the spring.

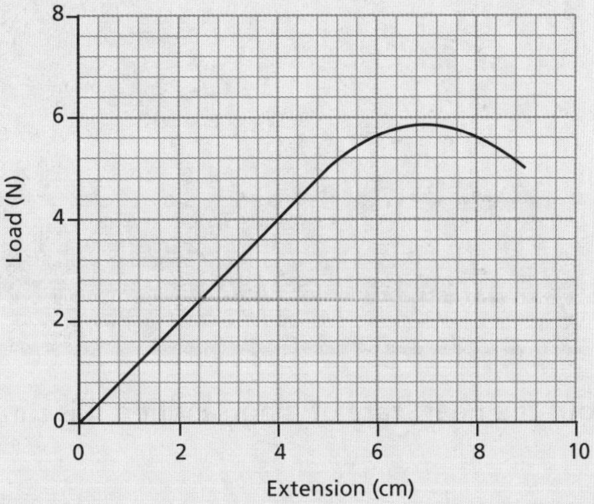

Look on the graph to find the point where the line starts to bend. This is the point where the spring starts to exceed its elastic limit.

Estimate the load at which the spring starts to exceed its elastic limit. **[2 marks]**

3 Atomic Structure and the Periodic Table P1 • Grade 6–7

Element X has two stable isotopes. Their mass numbers are 63 and 65.

The percentage abundance of each isotope is:

- 70% of $^{63}_{29}X$
- 30% of $^{65}_{29}X$

Estimate the relative atomic mass of X.

Tick (✓) **one** box. **[1 mark]**

This question is not asking you to complete a full calculation. You are being asked to look at the numbers and make a judgement call.

The relative atomic mass is a weighted average considering the mass and abundance of the isotopes. There is more of the lighter isotope than the heavier isotope. Therefore, the weighted average will be closer to the lighter isotope than the heavier isotope.

Less than 63 ☐

Between 63 and 64 ☐

Between 64 and 65 ☐

Greater than 65 ☐

Exam practice questions

16

1

Bioenergetics P1 • Grade 4–5

The photograph shows a racehorse. When a racehorse runs, its heart rate increases.

The graph shows data about the heart rate of a horse when it is running at different speeds.

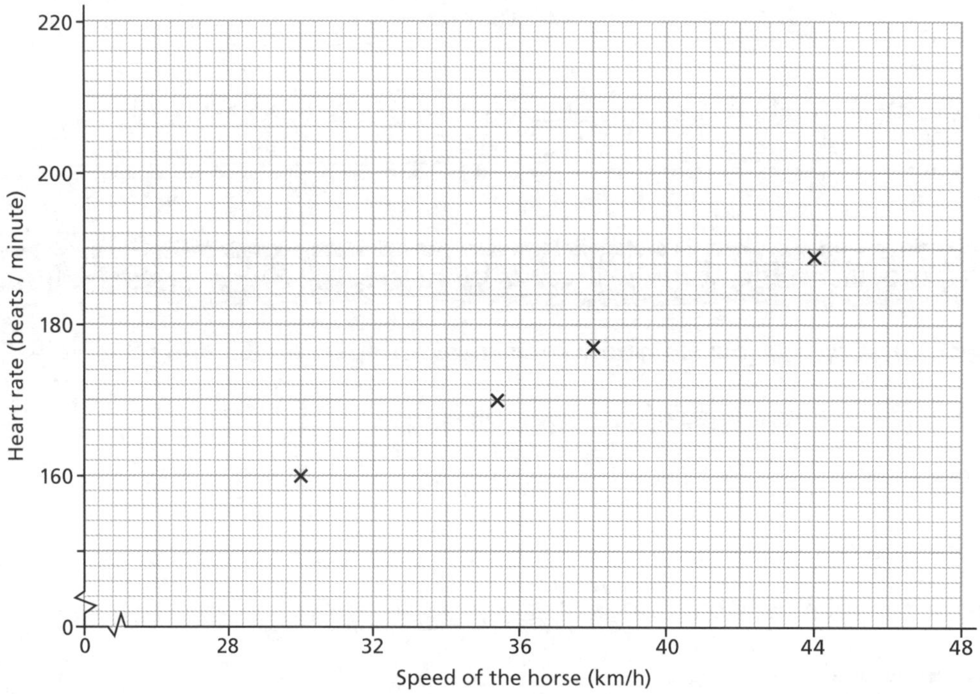

When the heart rate of a horse is above 200 beats per minute, the horse starts to rely on anaerobic respiration.

Estimate the maximum speed the horse can run without relying on anaerobic respiration. Show on the graph how you worked out your answer. **[3 marks]**

Speed = ... km per hour

2 Ecology P2 • Grade 4–5

Students investigate beetles living in an area of the school grounds.

They use a method called capture-recapture to estimate the population size of the beetles. They catch beetles from the area, count them, mark them, and then let them go. This is the first sample.

The next day they catch beetles from the area again. This is the second sample.

The table shows their results.

Number of beetles caught in the first sample	18
Number of beetles caught in the second sample	10
Number of beetles caught in the second sample that were previously marked	4

Estimate the population of beetles in the area.

Use this formula to work out your answer. **[2 marks]**

$$\textbf{Population size} = \frac{\textbf{number in 1st sample} \times \textbf{number in 2nd sample}}{\textbf{number in 2nd sample previously marked}}$$

....

Population size = ...

3 Atomic Structure and the Periodic Table P1 • Grade 4–5

The bar chart shows the densities of some alkali metals.

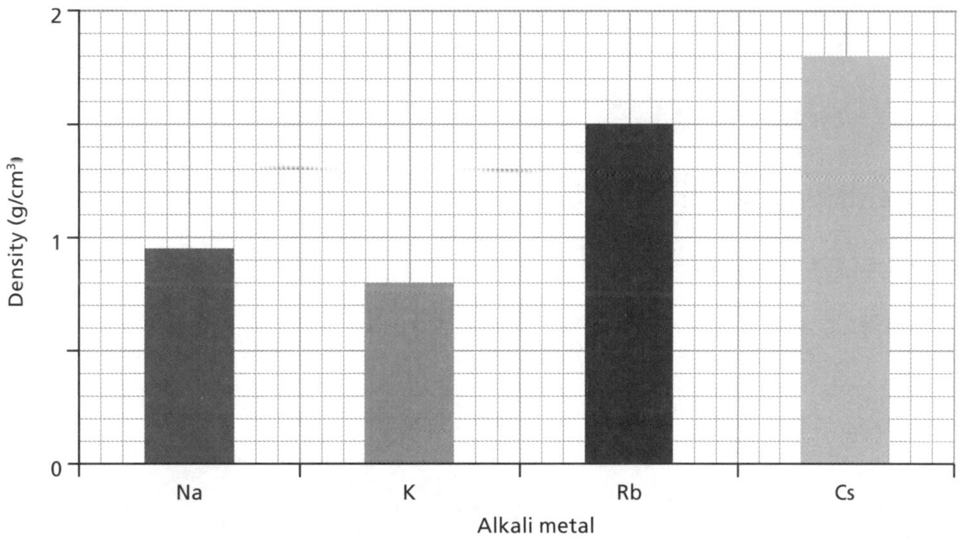

Estimate the density of lithium. **[1 mark]**

....

4 Atomic Structure and the Periodic Table P1 • Grade 4–5

Halogens are non-metal elements. The table shows the boiling point of the Group 7 halogens.

Element	Boiling point (°C)
Fluorine	–188
Bromine	60
Iodine	184
Astatine	337

Estimate the boiling point of chlorine. **[1 mark]**

....

5 Electricity P1 • Grade 4–5

A diode will allow current to flow in one direction but not in the other direction.

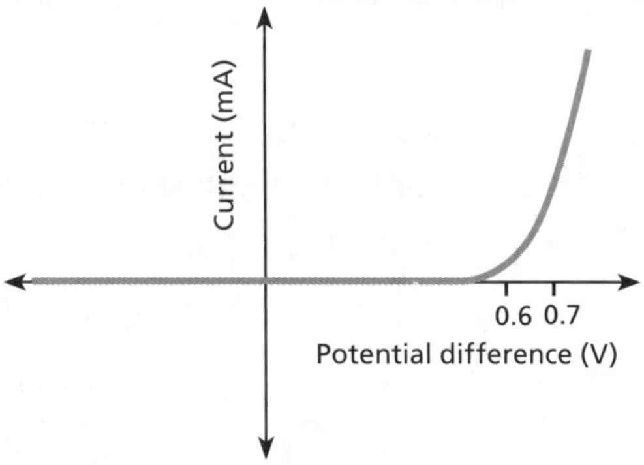

Estimate the voltage at which current starts to flow through the diode when the potential difference is flowing in the correct direction. **[1 mark]**

....

6 Waves P2 • Grade 4–5

This image shows a light ray being refracted as it enters water.

The angle of incidence is 45°.

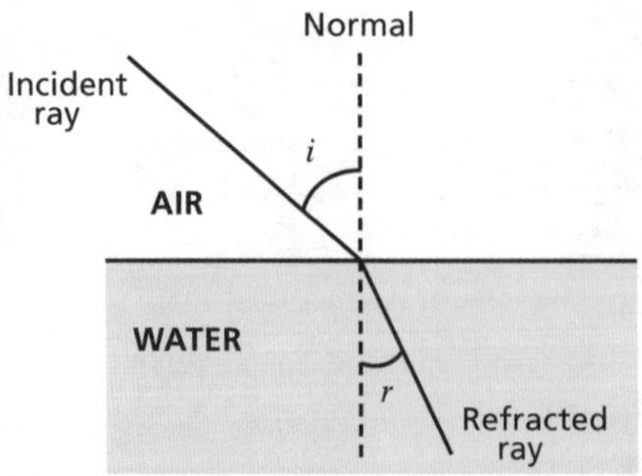

Estimate the angle of refraction. **[1 mark]**

....

7 Atomic Structure P1 • Grade 4–5

A piece of radioactive material is decaying. The number of counts per second is recorded every minute. Some of the results are shown here.

Time from start / min	0	1	2	3	4	5
Count per second	100	82	66	**A**	42	**B**

Estimate the two missing readings. **[2 marks]**

A: .... **B:** ....

8 Bioenergetics P1 • Grade 6–7

Plants produce carbon dioxide by respiration and use it in photosynthesis.

The graph shows how the rates of these processes vary at different times in 24 hours. The crosses (×) show the rate of uptake of carbon dioxide by photosynthesis.

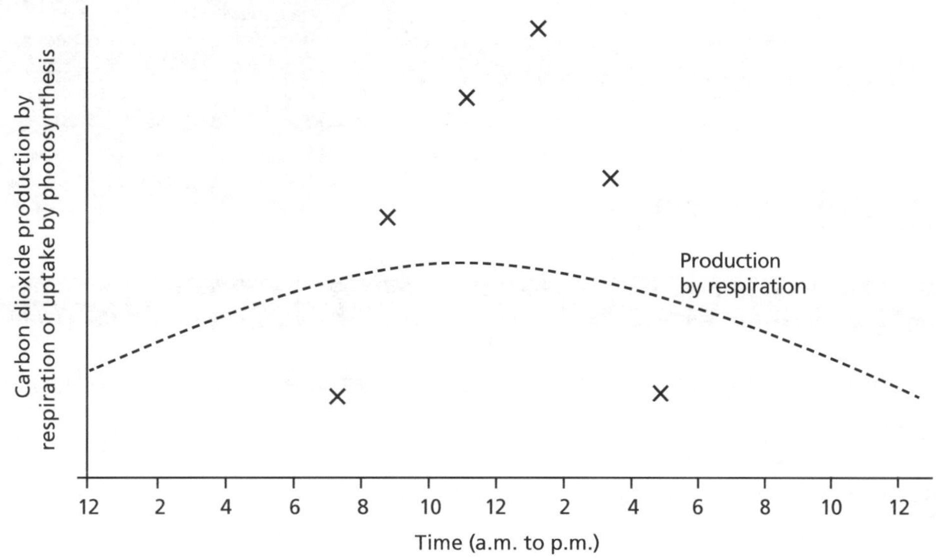

At a plant's compensation point, the rate of photosynthesis equals the rate of respiration.

Estimate the times that this plant reaches its compensation points.
Show on the graph how you worked out your answers. **[3 marks]**

Times = ...

9 Chemistry of the Atmosphere P2 • Grade 6–7

The percentage of water vapour in the atmosphere can vary.

4.2 dm^3 of air contains 0.05 dm^3 of water vapour.

Estimate the percentage of water vapour in the air. Give your answer to 1 significant figure. **[2 marks]**

....

Total score: .... / 16

Worked example and more!

Predict

Give a plausible outcome or result.

TOP TIP
A prediction doesn't have to be what will actually happen but it should show your scientific knowledge and understanding.

Example question

1 The Rate and Extent of Chemical Change P2 • Grade 4–5

A student investigated the rate of reaction between hydrochloric acid and magnesium ribbon.

The graph shows their results.

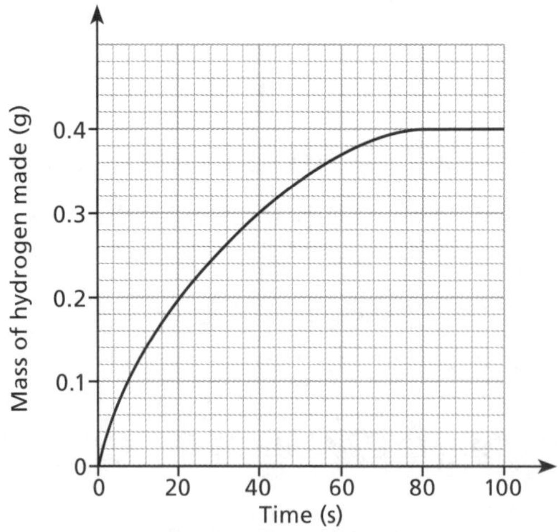

Predict the time taken for the reaction to be complete.

Give your answer in minutes.

Give your answer to three significant figures. **[3 marks]**

Reaction complete at .... minutes

Complete the example

2 Atomic Structure and the Periodic Table P1 • Grade 4–5

Halogens are Group 7 elements. The table gives information about the physical appearance of the halogens at room temperature.

Halogen	Physical appearance at room temperature
Fluorine	Pale yellow gas
Chlorine	Pale green gas
Bromine	Brown liquid
Iodine	Grey solid
Astatine	

Predict the physical appearance of astatine. **[2 marks]**

There is 1 mark for the colour and 1 mark for the correct state at room temperature.

3 Electricity P1 • Grade 6–7

Dorothy has a set of fairy lights that are powered by mains electricity. There are twenty 12 V lamps, connected in series, connected to the 240 V supply.

a) Predict what will happen if one of the lamps has blown. **[1 mark]**

Remember that this is a series circuit with one route for the current to take around the circuit. A lamp has blown, causing a break.

b) Dorothy wants to get the lamps working so she removes the blown lamp and its holder, connecting the wires so that there are now 19 in the circuit. She is relieved to see that they work.

Predict the brightness of the lamps compared to when all 20 were working. **[1 mark]**

Remember that previously in a series circuit the potential difference of the supply is shared between all of the components and now there are fewer components. Think about what will now happen to the potential difference across each of the remaining lamps.

Exam practice questions

1 **The Rate and Extent of Chemical Change P2 • Grade 4–5**

A student investigated the rate of reaction between magnesium ribbon and hydrochloric acid. The equipment used and a graph of the results are shown below.

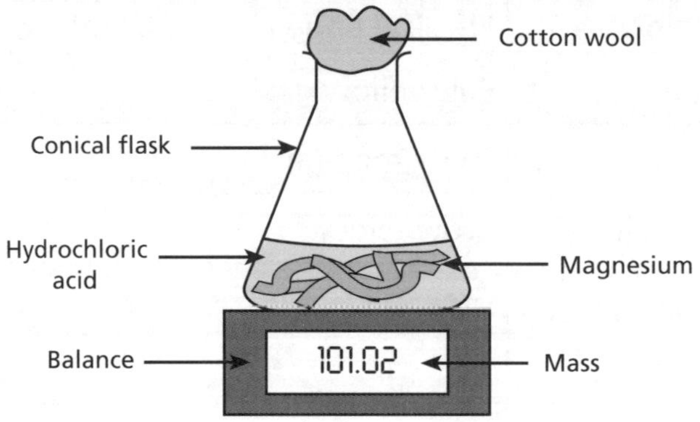

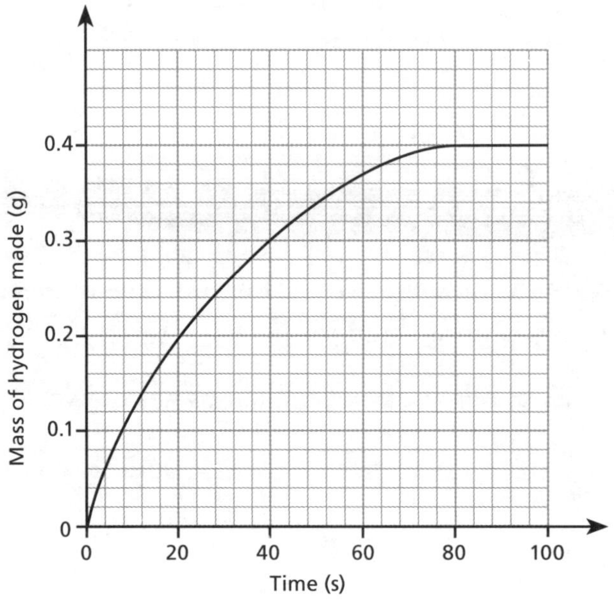

The reaction was monitored for 100 seconds and there was magnesium left behind.

a) Predict the effect on the rate of reaction if a higher concentration of hydrochloric acid was used. **[1 mark]**

....

b) Predict the effect on the maximum mass of hydrogen produced if magnesium powder was used instead of magnesium ribbon. **[1 mark]**

....

c) Predict the effect of increasing the temperature. **[1 mark]**

....

2 Energy P1 • Grade 4–5

Two cups of coffee are poured at the same time into identical cardboard cups and one of them has a plastic lid placed on top.

The volumes and temperature of coffee are the same.

Predict which serving of coffee will cool down quicker and suggest why. **[2 marks]**

3 Particle Model of Matter P1 • Grade 4–5

A beaker has equal volumes of water and oil placed in it.

The water has a density of 1 g/cm^3 and the oil has a density of 0.85 g/cm^3.

The liquids don't mix but settle out as separate layers.

Predict which layer will be on top and suggest why. **[2 marks]**

4 Atomic Structure P1 • Grade 6–7

The graph shows the decay curve of a radioactive isotope.

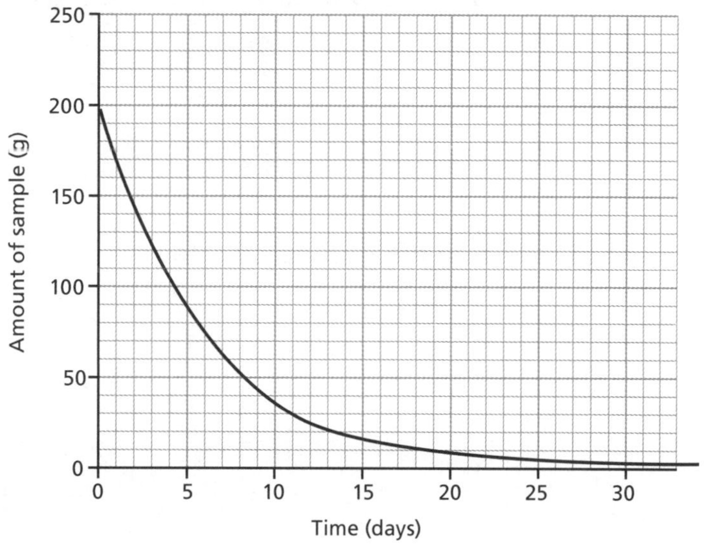

Predict how long it will take for three half lives to elapse, using the graph. **[4 marks]**

5 **The Rate and Extent of Chemical Change P2 / Energy Changes P1 /• Grade 6–7**

The Haber process is used in industry to manufacture ammonia.

The figure shows a diagram of the process.

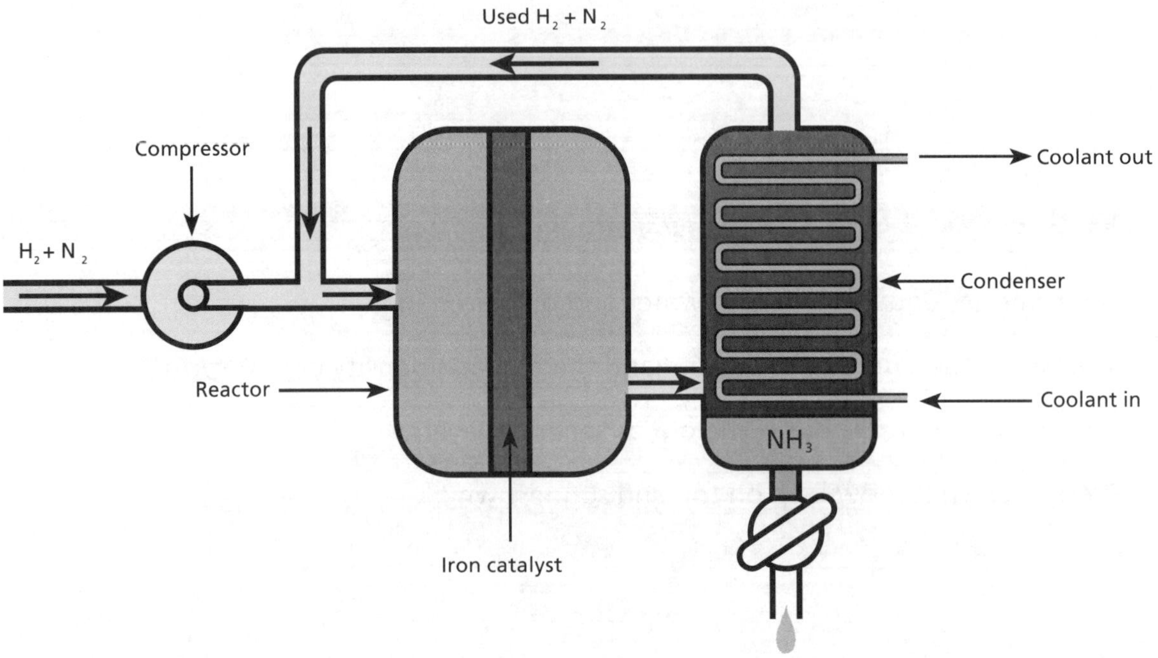

The balanced symbol equation for this reaction is:

$N_2(g) + 3H_2(g) \rightleftharpoons 2NH_3(g)$

a) Predict the effect of increasing the pressure on the position of equilibrium. **[2 marks]**

....

....

....

b) Predict the effect of removing the iron-based catalyst on the Haber process. **[4 marks]**

....

....

....

....

In industry, sulfuric acid is produced using the Contact Process. The diagram shows the Contact Process.

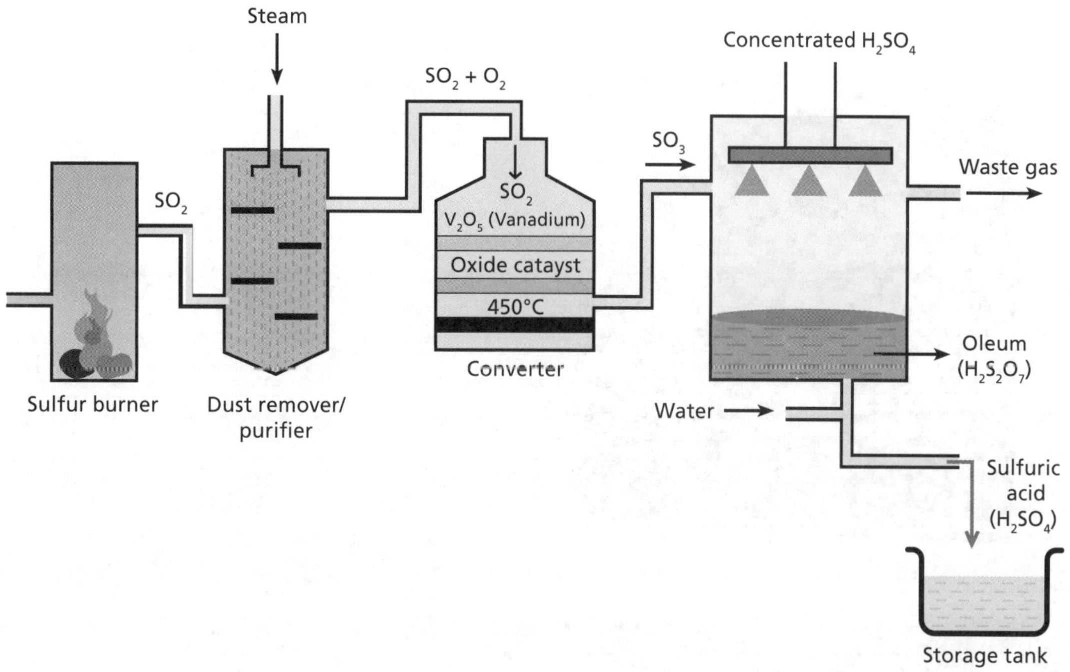

A reversible reaction happens in the converter.

The balanced symbol equation for this reaction is:

$2SO_2(g) + O_2(g) \rightleftharpoons 2SO_3(g)$

The forward reaction is exothermic.

Predict the effect of increasing temperature on the position of equilibrium. **[2 marks]**

....

....

....

Total score: .... / 19

Evaluate

Worked example and more!

Use the information supplied, as well as your knowledge and understanding, to consider evidence for and against when making a judgement / claim.

TOP TIP
Consider questions such as:
What is the judgement?
How is it supported and opposed by evidence?
How well is the evidence connected to the judgement?

Example question

1 **Chemical Changes P1 • Grade 4–5**

Zinc (Zn) is a metal. It is extracted from zinc oxide (ZnO). All other solid products from the extraction method must be separated from the zinc.

The table shows information about three possible methods to extract zinc from zinc oxide.

Method	Reactant	Relative cost	Products
1	Hydrogen gas	High	Zinc solid Water gas
2	Coke	Low	Zinc solid Carbon dioxide gas
3	Aluminium	Low	Zinc solid Aluminium oxide solid

Evaluate the three possible methods for extracting zinc from zinc oxide. **[4 marks]**

Complete the example

2 **Organisation P1 • Grade 4–5**

A student designed an investigation to find the optimum temperature for amylase to work.

This is their method:

1. Add 1 cm^3 of amylase to 5 cm^3 starch solution in a test tube.
2. Place this tube in a water bath at 20°C and start timing.
3. Every 30 seconds take a sample and test for starch.
4. Note the time that the starch test gives a negative result.
5. Repeat with the water bath at 30, 40, 50 and 60°C.

The table shows the student's results.

Temperature of the water bath in °C	20	30	40	50	60
Time taken for a negative starch test in seconds	210	120	90	150	300

The student concluded that the optimum temperature for amylase is 40°C.

Evaluate the student's conclusion.

Refer to the method in your answer. **[4 marks]**

The shortest time is .... so this supports the student's conclusion, as this is the ....

However, the shortest time could be anywhere between ....

This is because the student only tested ....

The student also .... before they were allowed to reach the ....

Only one reading was taken at .... / there were no ....

3 Electricity P1 • Grade 4–5

A teacher presents a class of students with a model showing what happens when current flows around a circuit.

The teacher uses a continuous loop of cord and has a group of students holding the cord loosely so it can pass through their hands.

The teacher is gripping the cord and makes it move around through the students' hands.

The teacher suggests that it is rather like when a power supply makes a current flow.

Evaluate the strengths and weaknesses of this model. **[6 marks]**

The model is an effective one because it shows that charged particles originate in the circuit and don't all start from .... It also shows that these particles all set off in motion ....
The model shows that the current flow is the same .... If one of the pupils starts to grip the cord harder, their hand will get warmer due to friction and this shows how .... However, the model only works for a series .... and it is also inaccurate because .... Overall, the value of the model is ....

Exam practice questions

32

1 Organisation P1 • Grade 4–5

Graph A gives information about the mass of butter and margarine eaten in the USA between 1910 and 2010.

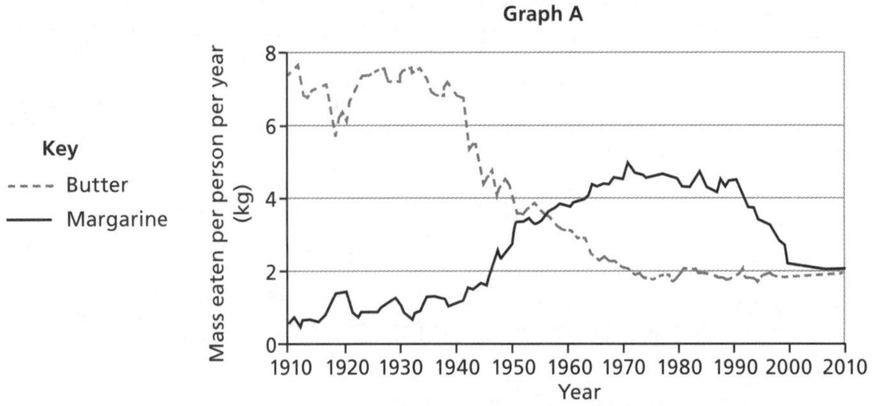

Graph B gives information about the number of people in the USA who died from heart disease between 1910 and 2010.

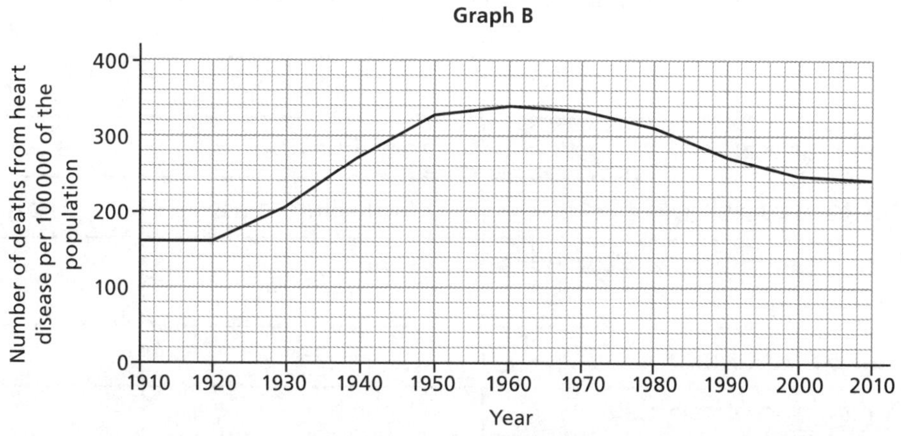

A student says that the graphs show that butter is a healthier food than margarine.

Evaluate this statement using information from **Graph A** and **Graph B**. **[6 marks]**

2 Using Resources P2 • Grade 4–5

The table shows information about two different materials used to make drinks bottles.

	Glass	Plastic
Raw material	Sand, limestone, salt	Crude oil
Bottle material	Soda-lime glass	Polypropene
Maximum temperature used in production	1600°C	850°C
Number of times reused	25	0
Percentage of recycled material used in new bottles	50	10
Fossil fuel use to produce and transport (arbitrary units)	4320	2639

Evaluate the sustainability of the production of drinks bottles made from soda-lime glass and polypropene.

Use the table and your own knowledge. **[6 marks]**

3 Organisation P1 • Grade 6–7

Patients who have operations to treat heart disease can develop dangerous blood clots or bleeding afterwards.

They can be given drugs such as aspirin or warfarin.

The graph gives information about the results of taking these drugs.

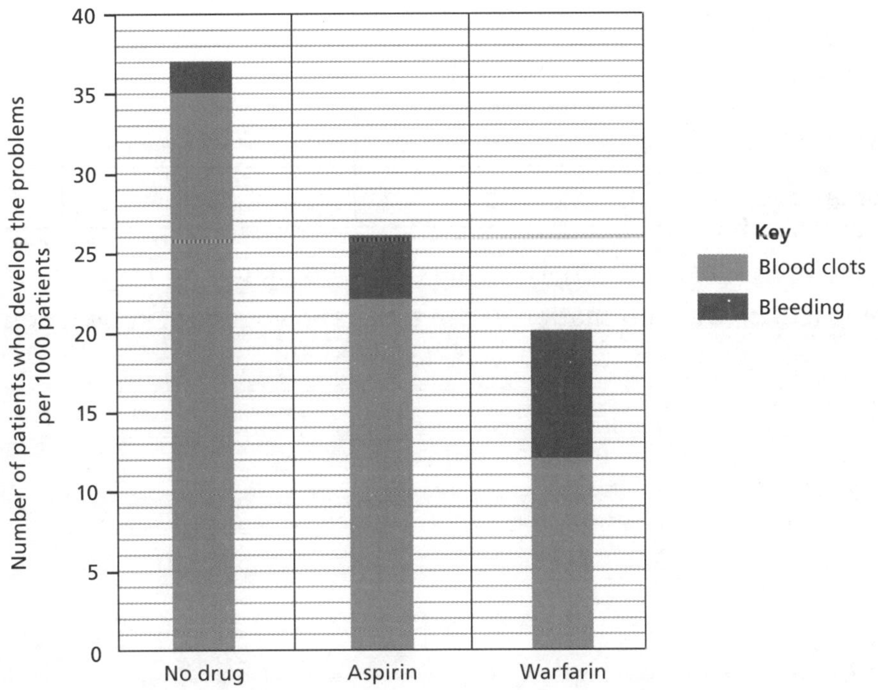

Evaluate the use of warfarin and aspirin in patients who have had these operations. **[4 marks]**

....

....

....

....

....

....

....

....

....

....

4 Using Resources P2 • Grade 6–7

Food plates can be made from ceramics, polymers or paper. The table shows information about plates with the same diameter.

	Ceramic	Polymer	Paper
Raw material	Mined clay	Crude oil	Wood
Maximum packed in delivery box	50	100	500
Average use	1000	400	1
Recycle	No	Yes	Yes
Biodegradable	No	No	Yes

Evaluate the use of these materials for making food plates. You should use features of life cycle assessments (LCAs), the information in the table and your own knowledge. **[4 marks]**

5 Atomic Structure P1 • Grade 6–7

A flour manufacturer wants to set up a system to check that their packets of flour have the required amount in them, without having people looking into every packet.

After flour has been put in the packets they will pass between a radioactive source and a detector. If the detector shows a higher reading, the level of flour is too low. They use a beta source with a half-life of around 30 years.

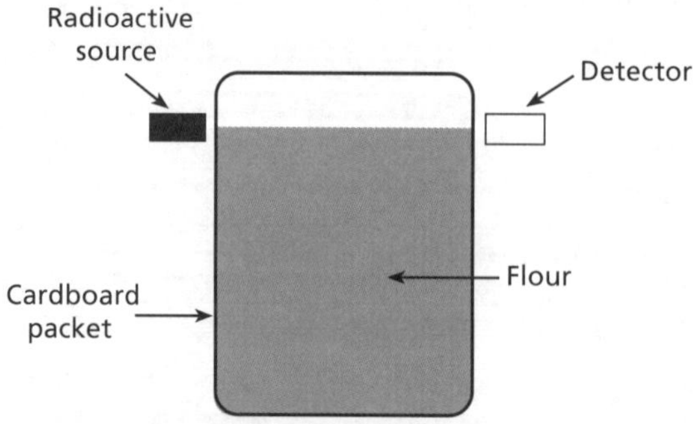

Evaluate this as a way of checking the level of flour. **[6 marks]**

6 Magnetism and Electromagnetism P2 • Grade 6–7

A teacher sets up a demonstration to show how a generator produces a potential difference. They set up a coil of wire connected at both ends to a voltmeter and get a bar magnet. They push the magnet in and out of the coil and show that when the magnet is moving it produces a potential difference across the ends of the coil.

Evaluate this as a model to show how a generator produces a potential difference. **[6 marks]**

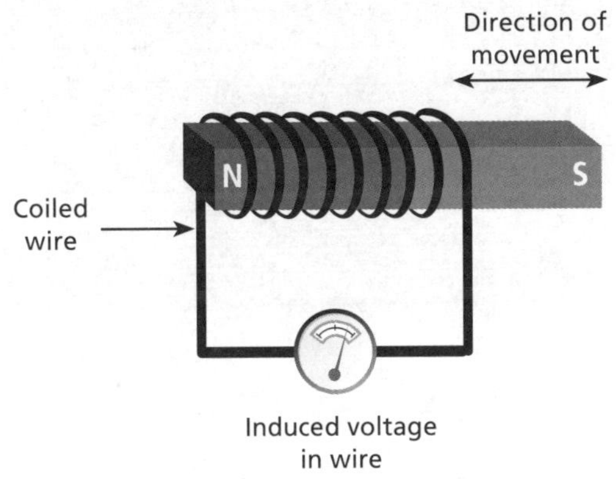

Teacher demonstration

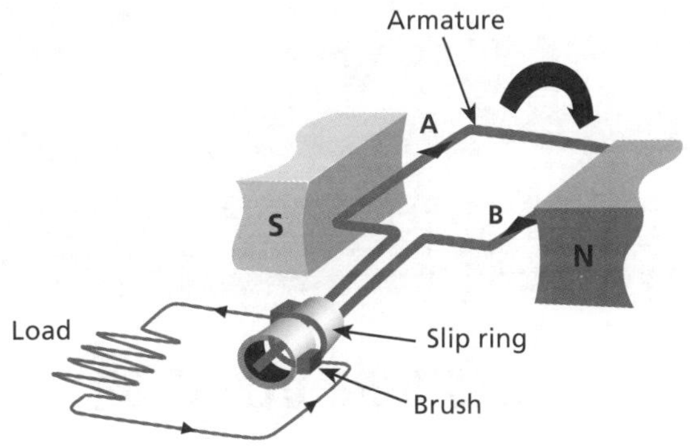

Simple generator

Total score: .... / 32

Justify

Support a case or argument with evidence. This evidence is usually from data provided in the question.

TOP TIP
Unlike 'Evaluate' questions, you do not need to give arguments for and against.

Worked example and more!

Example question

1 **Atomic Structure and the Periodic Table P1 • Grade 4–5**

The model of the structure of the atom has changed over time.

In one experiment, positively charged alpha radiation was fired at a sheet of very thin gold foil. The diagram shows the experiment.

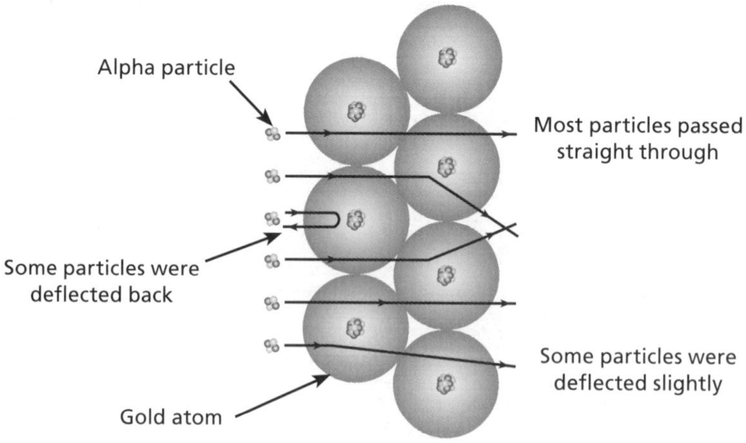

The data from the experiment was used to conclude that:

- atoms were mainly empty space
- atoms had a small positive centre, where most of the mass is found.

Justify the conclusions. **[6 marks]**

Complete the example

2 Organisation P1 • Grade 4–5

A patient goes to see their doctor.
The doctor measures the patient's mass and height as:

- mass = 100 kg
- height = 1.8 m

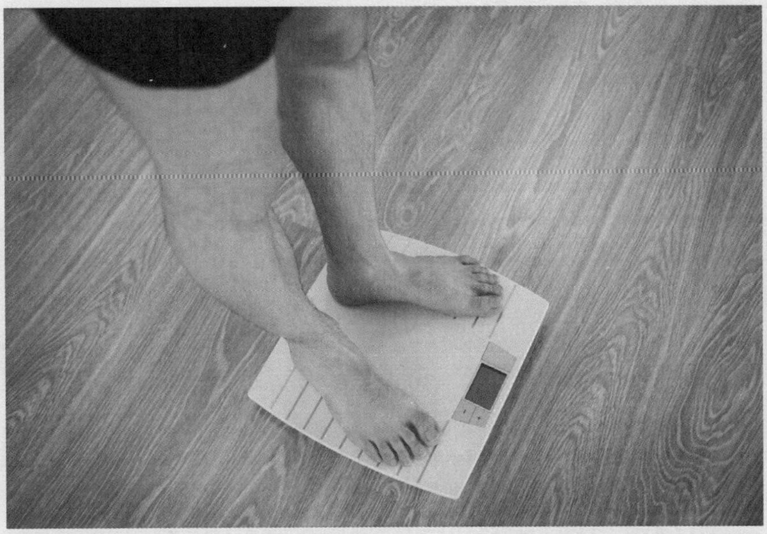

The doctor then looks at this BMI information.

BMI is a way of finding out if a person's body mass is healthy for their height.

$$\text{BMI} = \frac{\text{mass in kg}}{(\text{height in m})^2}$$

Category	BMI
underweight	<18.5
normal	18.5–24.9
overweight	25.0–30.0
obese	>30.0

The doctor says that the patient should lose 20 kg.

Justify the doctor's advice. **[4 marks]**

The patient's BMI can be worked out as: $100 \div 1.8^2 =$ ....

That means that they are .... *so need to lose weight.*

If the patient loses 20 kg, their BMI becomes .... ,

which is in the .... *range.*

3 Forces P2 • Grade 4–5

Some students are investigating how the gradient of a ramp affects the motion of a trolley rolling down it.

At each gradient they time the interval between the trolley being released from the top of the ramp and reaching the bottom of the ramp.

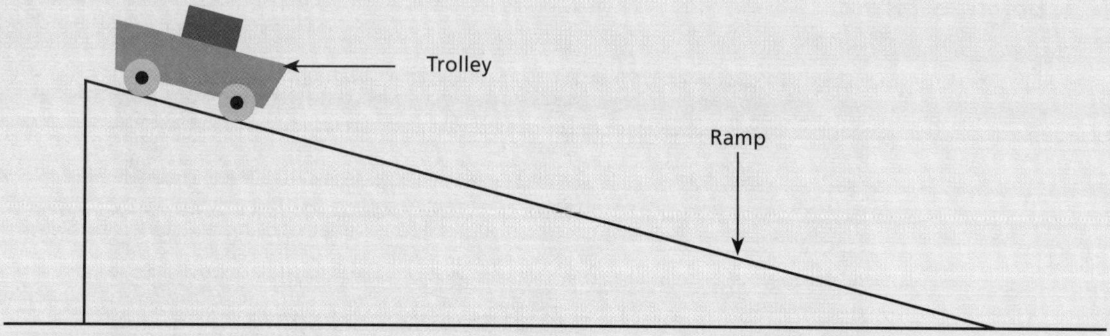

At one gradient they record the time intervals as being:

8.2 s 7.9 s 8.1 s 10.9 s

a) Justify their decision to make repeat readings. **[2 marks]**

Repeat readings are important because there are reasons why the value obtained could vary. There might be a slight pause in ...., an error in .... or the vehicle might ....

b) Justify their decision to eliminate the final reading and calculate the mean of the other three. **[2 marks]**

The first three readings are .... with small gaps between, but the .... is significantly different with a ....
Taking the mean of .... will give an answer nearer to the true value.

Exam practice questions

26

1

Chemical Changes P1 • Grade 4–5

A student investigated the reaction of magnesium with different types of acid.

This was the method used:

1. $10\ cm^3$ of the same concentration of each acid or pure water was measured and put into separate, labelled test tubes.
2. 0.1 g of magnesium metal was added to each test tube.
3. The reaction was observed.

Here is a diagram of the results.

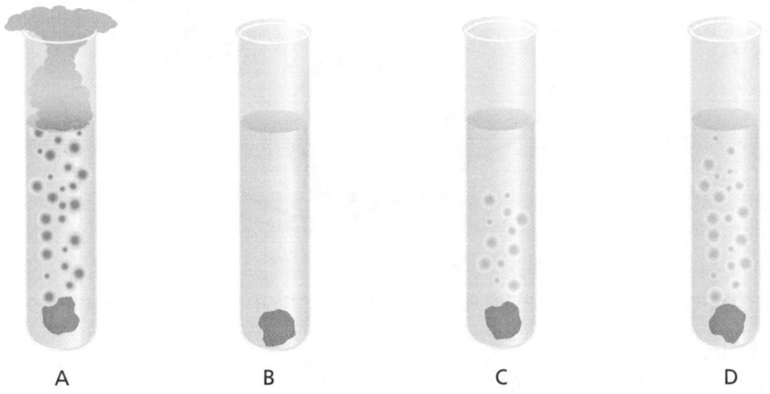

a) Justify that test tube B was the control and contained pure water. **[4 marks]**

....

....

....

....

....

b) Write the four liquids in order of reactivity with the most reactive first.

Justify your order of reactivity. **[3 marks]**

....

....

....

....

....

2 Electricity P1 • Grade 4–5

Some students need to measure the resistance of a component as part of their practical investigation.

They could do so by using a power supply to make a current flow through it, measuring the potential difference across the component and the current flow and then dividing the p.d. by the current.

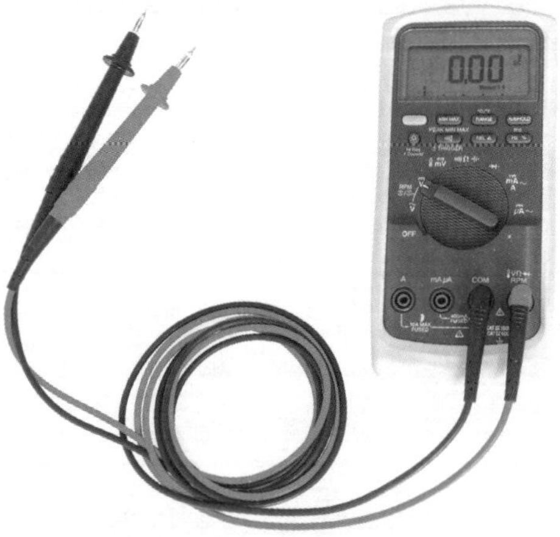

Instead, they decide to use a resistance meter (or ohmmeter) such as this one and measure the resistance directly.

Justify their decision. **[3 marks]**

Long distance runners can assess their fitness by knowing the maximum rate that they can use oxygen. This is called their **VO_2 Max**.

Successful long distance runners normally have a VO_2 Max in the range 60–85.

VO_2 Max can be estimated using this formula:

$$VO_2 \text{ Max} = \frac{15 \times \text{maximum heart rate}}{\text{resting heart rate}}$$

The graph shows an athlete's heart rate as they exercise.

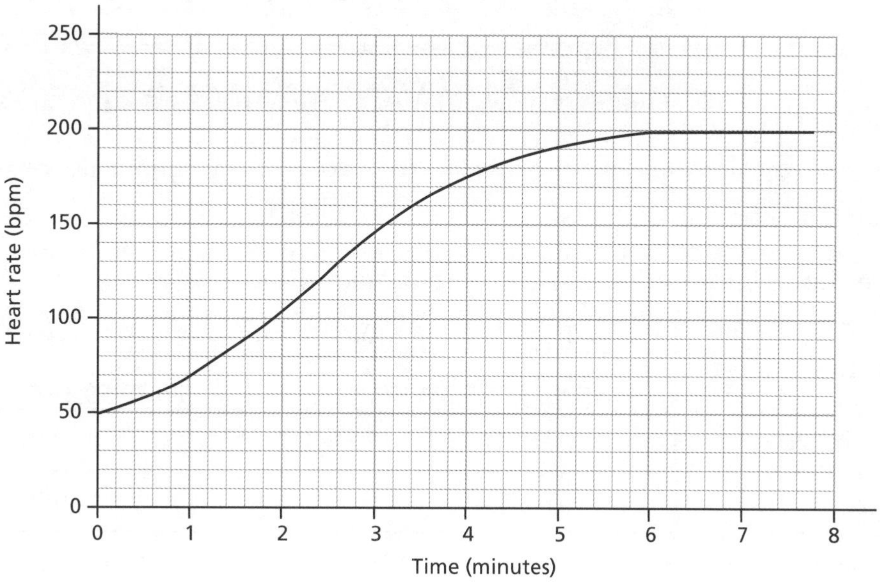

The athlete thinks that they are fit enough to be a long distance runner but need to further improve their fitness.

Justify the athlete's view. **[4 marks]**

The picture shows Lake Michigan, a large lake in North America.

Scientists are concerned about the level in the lake of toxic chemicals called PCBs.
Four main rivers flow into the lake.

The table shows information about the four main rivers.

Name of river	Volume of water flowing in m^3 per second	Concentration of PCBs in the water in micrograms per m^3
Calumet	10	55
Fox	90	50
Grand	190	2
St Joseph	200	1

The scientists claim that the Fox river is causing about four times as much pollution as the other three rivers put together.

Justify the scientists' statement using information from the table. **[4 marks]**

5 Organic Chemistry P2 • Grade 8–9

Crude oil is a mixture of hydrocarbons.

Justify the need for cracking of hydrocarbons. **[4 marks]**

6 Forces P2 • Grade 8–9

An engineer comes up with two designs for a funicular railway, which will carry passengers up and down a steep cliff.

One idea (A) is to have a single car pulled up and lowered down by a motor. The car has a counterweight to balance the weight. As the car comes up, the counterweight goes down and vice versa.

A

B

The other idea (B) is to have a pair of cars attached to each other by a long rope which goes over a pulley at the top, so that as one goes up the other comes down. Both cars have water tanks. The one at the top has the tank filled so it is the heavier one; the water is drained away when that car reaches the bottom.

Both systems have braking systems so that the motion is smooth and safe.

Select the best design idea for the engineer to use.

Justify your selection. **[4 marks]**

Total score: .... / 26

Mixed Questions

1 Infection and Response P1 • Grade 4–5

2 hours 5 mins

a) Measles is a disease caused by a virus.

Children are usually given a vaccination to protect them against measles.

Describe how the body responds when a vaccinated person encounters the measles virus.

[4 marks]

....

....

....

....

b) In 2016, there were 531 cases of measles in the UK. 420 of these cases were in people who had not been vaccinated. A number of these cases were linked to music festivals and other large public events.

Calculate the percentage of people who caught measles in 2016 who had not been vaccinated. Give your answer to 2 significant figures. **[2 marks]**

....

....

Percentage = ...

c) How is measles spread? **[1 mark]**

Tick (✔) **one** box.

By air ☐

By direct contact ☐

By water ☐

By insect vector ☐

d) AIDS is a disease that is also caused by a virus.

Describe **one** way that the virus causing AIDS is spread. **[1 mark]**

....

e) Explain why it is difficult to treat diseases such as measles and AIDS with drugs. **[3 marks]**

2 Inheritance, Variation and Evolution P2 • Grade 4–5

a) Mendel used the term 'breeding true' in his experiments.

What term is used to describe the genotype of an organism that 'breeds true'? **[1 mark]**

b) The figure shows how the sperm and egg cells are formed in humans by meiosis.

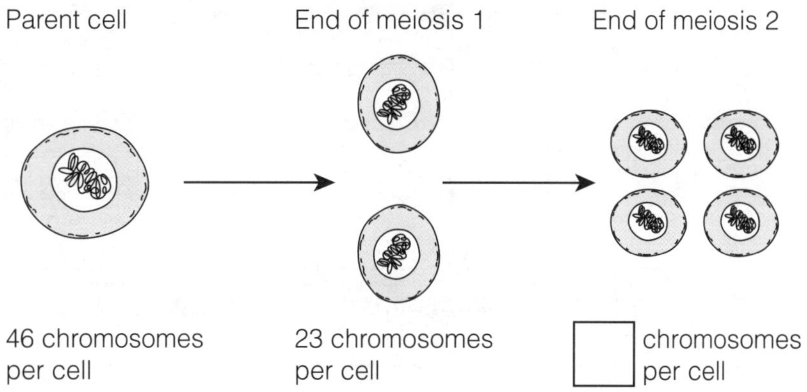

Complete the figure by writing how many chromosomes will be present in each cell at the end of meiosis 2. **[1 mark]**

c) Name the organ where meiosis occurs to produce the male gametes. **[1 mark]**

d) If a male gamete carrying an X chromosome fuses with an egg cell, what will be the sex of the offspring? Explain your answer. **[2 marks]**

e) In asexual reproduction, a different type of cell division is involved.

Name the type of cell division involved in asexual reproduction. **[1 mark]**

f) Sexual reproduction in animals requires the fusion of an egg and sperm cell.

Name the two gametes involved in sexual reproduction in plants. **[1 mark]**

3 Homeostasis and Response P2 • Grade 6–7

This question is about hormones.

a) Thyroxine is a hormone.

Cerys does not produce enough thyroxine. She gains weight easily.

Explain why. **[2 marks]**

....

....

....

b) The figure shows how production of thyroxine is controlled.

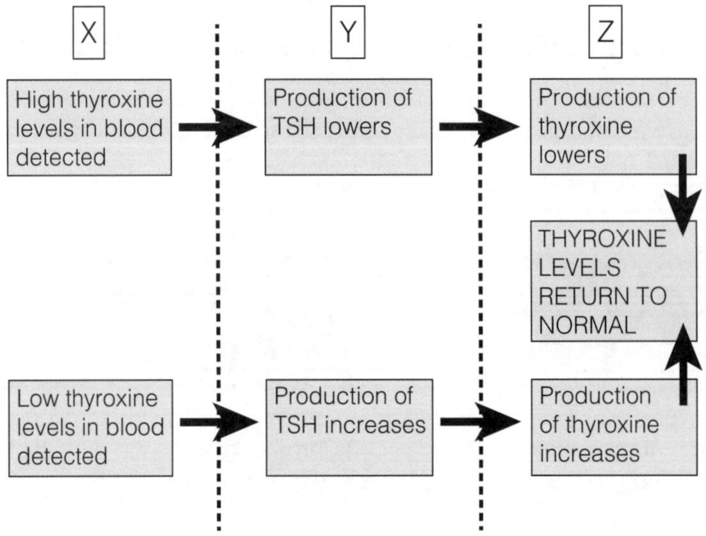

Which letter represents the process that the pituitary gland is responsible for? **[1 mark]**

....

c) Where in the body is thyroxine produced? **[1 mark]**

....

d) Cerys goes to the GP to get some test results. She feels anxious. Her heartbeat increases. Cerys is producing the 'flight or fight' hormone.

What is the name of this hormone? **[1 mark]**

....

e) Hormones produced by the pancreas are responsible for controlling blood glucose levels.

Explain how blood glucose levels are controlled with reference to these hormones and the mechanism of negative feedback. **[6 marks]**

....

....

f) The graph shows how the blood glucose levels of a person without diabetes change shortly after eating a meal.

Draw on the graph the results you would expect for a person with Type 1 diabetes. **[2 marks]**

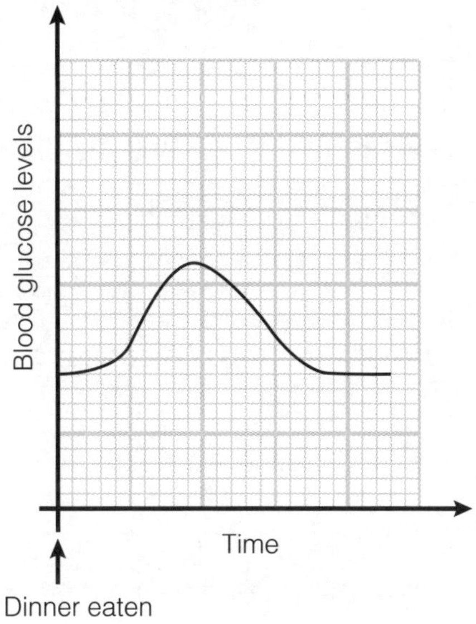

g) What is the normal treatment for someone who has Type 1 diabetes? **[1 mark]**

4 Organisation P1 • Grade 6–7

Substances can move in and out of cells by diffusion.

a) What is diffusion? **[2 marks]**

b) The structure shown in the figure is found in the lungs.

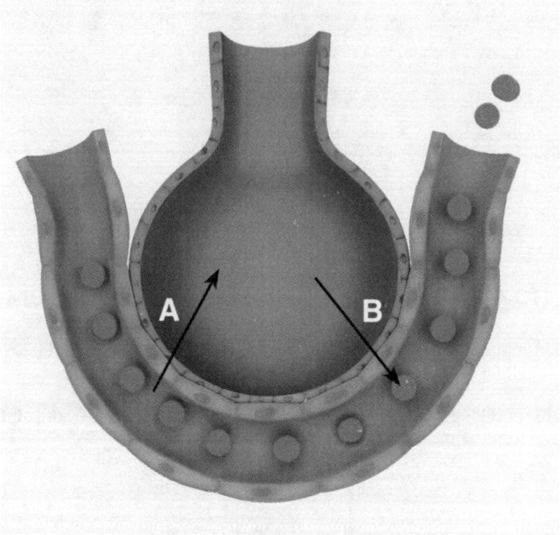

Name the substances represented by arrows A and B. **[1 mark]**

A ....

B ....

c) Explain how the structure of the lungs / alveoli are adapted to maximise the rate of diffusion. **[4 marks]**

....

....

....

....

d) Some students wanted to investigate how temperature affected diffusion.

They set up the following apparatus and placed it in a water bath at 10°C.

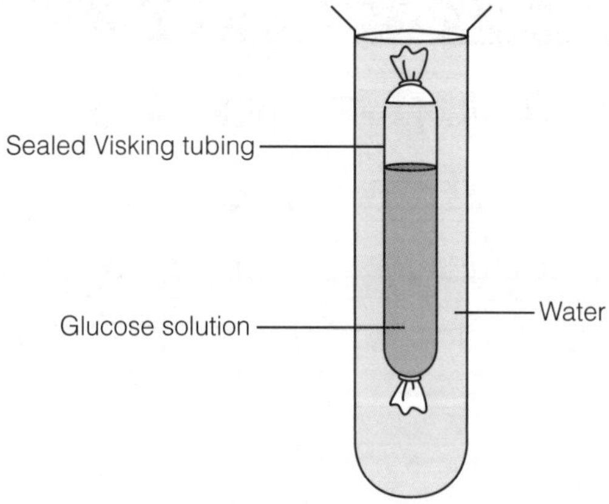

After every minute, for eight minutes, they dipped a glucose testing stick into the water.

The glucose testing stick changes from blue to brown when a certain concentration of glucose is reached.

The students repeated the test at 15°C, 20°C and 25°C.

Suggest **two** factors the students needed to control to make the test fair. **[2 marks]**

e) The table shows the students' results.

Time (minutes)	Colour of glucose testing stick at different temperatures			
	10°C	**15°C**	**20°C**	**25°C**
0	Blue	Blue	Blue	Blue
1	Blue	Blue	Blue	Blue
2	Blue	Blue	Blue	Brown
3	Blue	Blue	Brown	Brown
4	Blue	Blue	Brown	Brown
5	Blue	Brown	Brown	Brown
6	Brown	Brown	Brown	Brown
7	Brown	Brown	Brown	Brown
8	Brown	Brown	Brown	Brown

One student concluded that doubling the temperature doubles the rate of diffusion.

What data from the table supports this conclusion? **[1 mark]**

f) Explain why the rate of diffusion increases as the temperature increases. **[1 mark]**

5 Ecology P2 • Grade 6–7

A community of organisms inhabit a rock pool on a beach.

a) Name two biotic factors and two abiotic factors that will affect the numbers and types of organisms in the rock pool. **[2 marks]**

Biotic:

Abiotic:

b) In the rock pool there are plant plankton and shrimp.

The graph shows the changing numbers of both throughout a year.

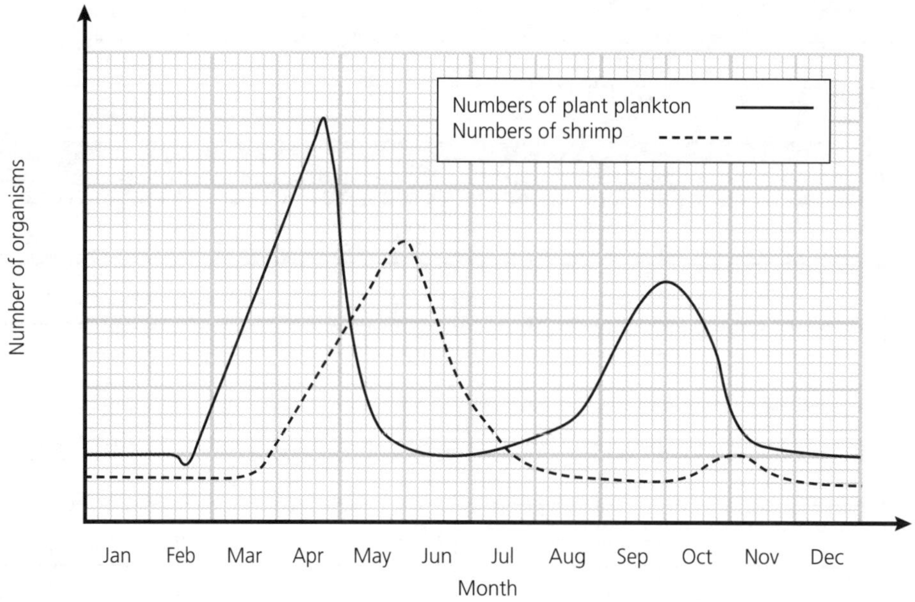

Explain why the numbers of each organism change throughout the year. **[4 marks]**

....

....

....

....

....

....

....

....

....

c) Scientists studying the diversity of organisms in rock pools recorded the information shown in the table.

Maximum depth of rock pool at low tide in cm	Average number of different organisms found
20	3
40	3
60	7
80	11
100	14

Describe the pattern in the results. **[1 mark]**

d) Suggest one reason for this pattern. **[1 mark]**

6 Atomic Structure and the Periodic Table P1 • Grade 4–5

An atom of phosphorus has the symbol $^{31}_{15}P$.

a) Give the number of protons, neutrons and electrons in this atom of phosphorus. **[3 marks]**

Number of protons = ...

Number of neutrons = ...

Number of electrons = ...

b) Why is phosphorus in Group 5 of the periodic table? **[1 mark]**

7 Using Resources P2 • Grade 4–5

This question is about the manufacture of cars.

A manufacturing company produces a LCA for the cars it produces.

a) What does LCA stand for? **[1 mark]**

b) Why is a LCA useful to customers? **[1 mark]**

c) Give **one** factor, other than the LCA, that customers might consider when buying a car. **[1 mark]**

d) Which **one** of the steps below is **not** part of the LCA of a car? **[1 mark]**

Tick (✔) **one** box.

The top speed of the car ☐

How much of the car can be recycled ☐

The effect on the environment of extracting the raw materials to produce the car ☐

The amount of carbon dioxide produced in the manufacture of the car ☐

8 Using Resources P2 • Grade 4–5

Shopping bags can be made from plastic or paper.

Explain the environmental impact of making bags from paper and from plastic. **[4 marks]**

9 Quantitative Chemistry P1 • Grade 6–7

Here are the relative atomic masses (A_r) of the elements in ammonium sulfate:

nitrogen = 14

hydrogen = 1

sulfur = 32

oxygen = 16

a) Calculate the relative formula mass (M_r) of ammonium sulfate, $(NH_4)_2SO_4$. **[2 marks]**

Relative formula mass = ...

b) What is the mass of two moles of ammonium sulfate? **[1 mark]**

a) Rutherford's assistants, Geiger and Marsden, carried out an experiment to give evidence for the plum pudding model of the atom.

They set up the apparatus shown in the figure and fired alpha particles at a strip of gold foil.

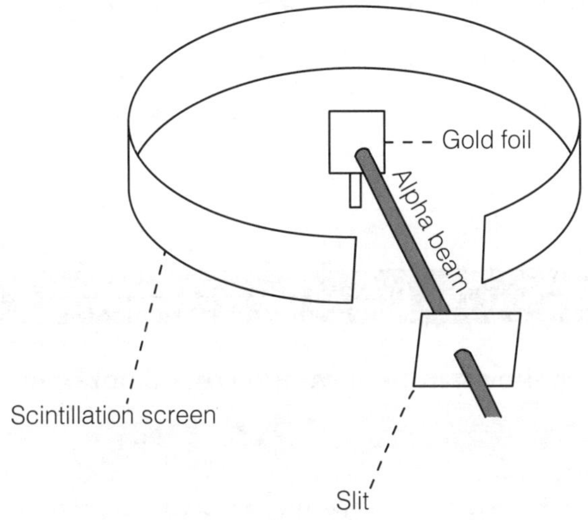

Suggest why the experiment was carried out in a vacuum. **[2 marks]**

b) Geiger and Marsden predicted that the plum pudding model was correct.

Show on the figure what would have happened if Geiger and Marsden's prediction was correct. **[2 marks]**

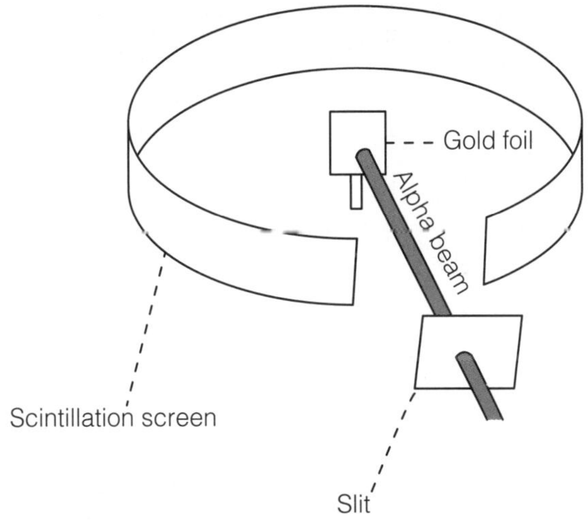

c) Rutherford analysed the results of the experiment.

He said: "It was almost as incredible as if you fired a 15-inch shell (a large bullet) at a piece of tissue paper and it came back and hit you."

Explain the connection between firing alpha particles at a gold foil strip and Rutherford's statement. **[4 marks]**

d) Give **two** conclusions that can be made from Geiger and Marsden's experiment. **[2 marks]**

11 Bonding, Structure, and the Properties of Matter P1 • Grade 8–9

A molecule of water is shown in the dot and cross diagram in the figure.

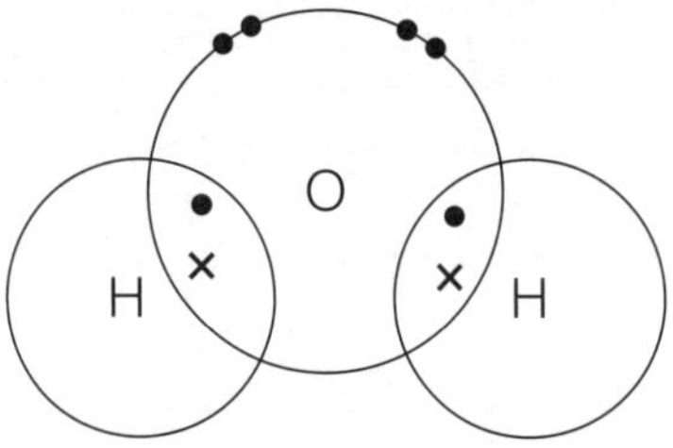

a) Suggest **one** advantage and **one** disadvantage of using the dot and cross diagram to show the structure of water. **[2 marks]**

Advantage:

Disadvantage:

b) Magnesium is a Group 2 metal. The structure of magnesium can be shown using the metallic model in the figure.

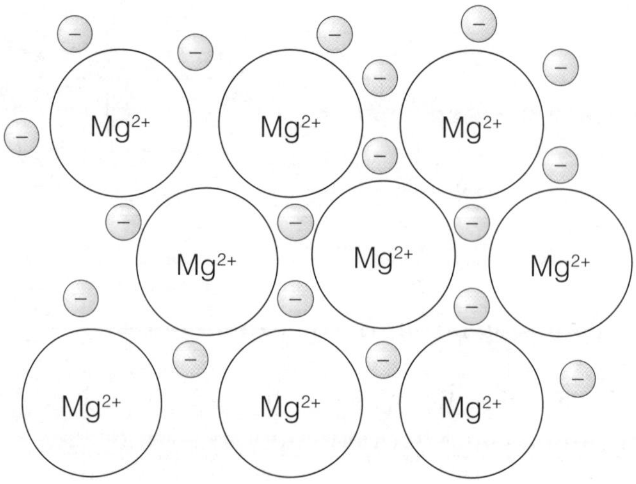

Suggest **one** advantage and **one** disadvantage of using the metallic model to show the structure of magnesium. **[2 marks]**

Advantage:

....

....

Disadvantage:

....

....

c) The structure of diamond can be shown using the ball and stick model in the diagram.

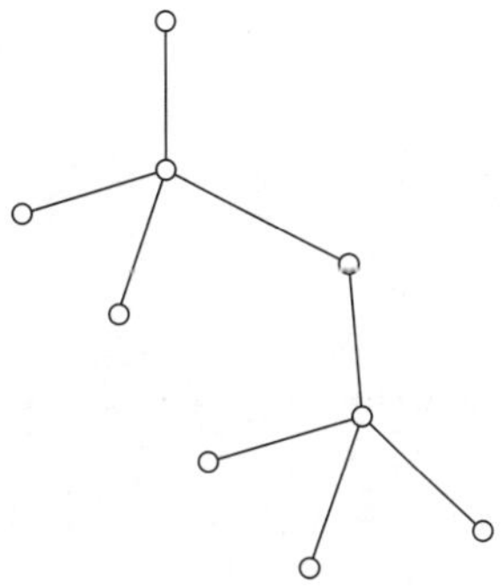

Suggest **one** advantage and **one** disadvantage of using the ball and stick model to show the structure of diamond. **[2 marks]**

Advantage:

....

....

Disadvantage:

....

....

12 Organic Chemistry / Chemistry of the Atmosphere P2 • Grade 8–9

The products released into the atmosphere when fossil fuels are burnt can cause problems.

a) Draw one line from each pollutant to the environmental problem it causes. **[2 marks]**

Pollutant	**Environmental problem**
	Global dimming
Carbon particles	Global warming
Nitrogen oxides	Acid rain
	Thinning of the ozone layer

Petrol contains octane: C_8H_{18}. Octane is a hydrocarbon.

b) Explain why octane is described as a hydrocarbon. **[2 marks]**

....

c) Complete the equation below to show the complete combustion of octane. **[2 marks]**

C_8H_{18} + ... O_2 → .... $CO_2 + 9H_2O$

d) If there is a limited supply of oxygen then incomplete combustion can occur.

Incomplete combustion of fuels can produce carbon monoxide.

Name **one** other product. **[1 mark]**

....

e) Why is carbon monoxide **not** easy to detect? **[1 mark]**

....

f) Why is the production of carbon monoxide a problem? **[1 mark]**

....

13 Electricity P1 • Grade 4–5

The graph shows how the resistance of a component X varies with light intensity.

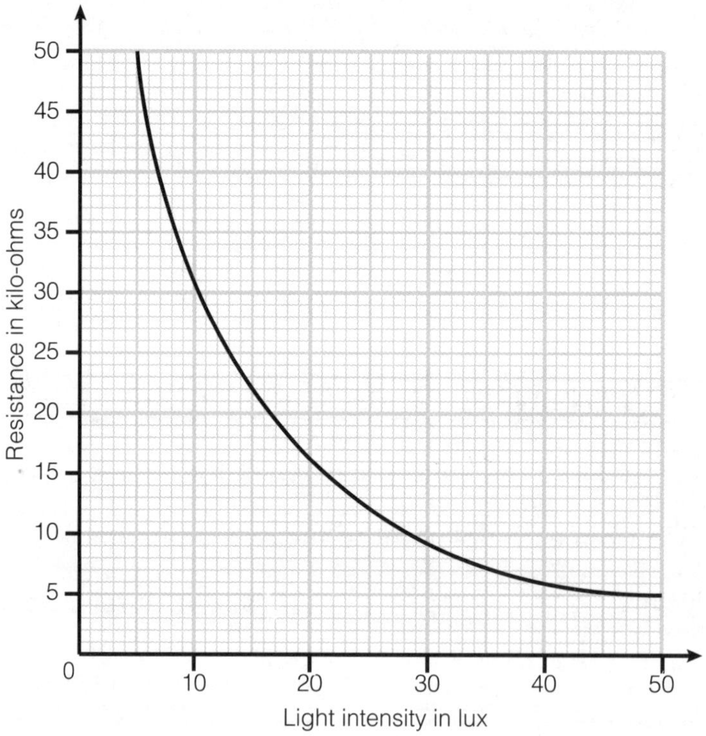

a) Name component X. **[1 mark]**

....

b) What is the resistance of component X when the light intensity is 35 lux? **[1 mark]**

....

c) When the light intensity is 35 lux, the current through the circuit is 0.0003 A.

Calculate the reading on the voltmeter when the light intensity is 35 lux. **[2 marks]**

....

....

....

14 Energy P1 • Grade 4–5

A heater is used to heat a 1.5 kg metal block.

The table shows how the temperature of the block increased over time.

Time in s	Temperature in °C
0	20.3
60	22.8
120	24.9
180	28.0
240	31.2
300	35.1

The graph shows how temperature changes over time.

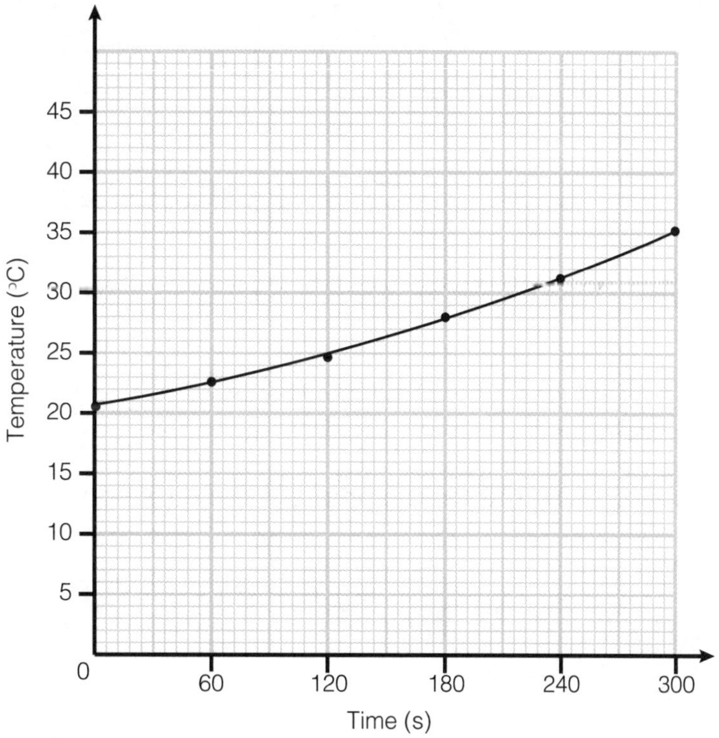

a) Calculate the gradient of the graph. **[2 marks]**

....

b) The heater provides thermal energy at a rate of 54 W.

Use the value for the gradient of the graph to calculate the specific heat capacity of the metal block.

Explain how specific heat capacity is related to the change in thermal energy. **[3 marks]**

15 Magnetism and Electromagnetism P2 • Grade 4–5

The figure shows a constant current passing through a straight wire in the downward direction indicated by the arrow.

A magnetic plotting compass is positioned near the wire as shown.

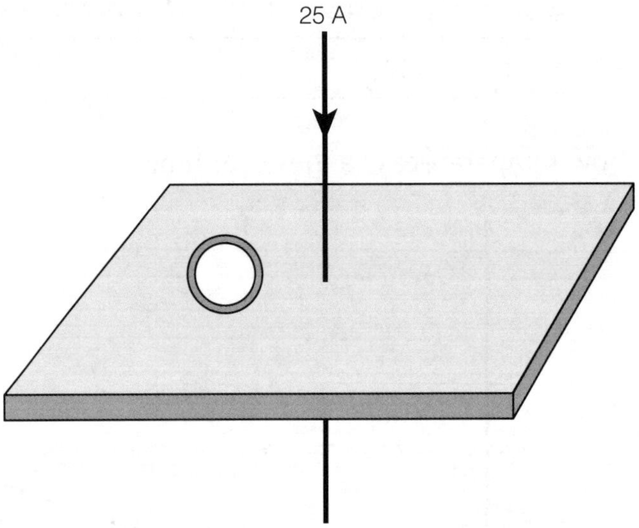

a) On the figure, draw an arrow to show the direction the magnetic needle inside the compass is pointing. **[1 mark]**

b) Explain the reason why the needle points in the direction you have shown. **[2 marks]**

c) The figure shows the Earth, with magnetic South (geographic North) at the top and magnetic North (geographic South) at the bottom.

Draw magnetic field lines to show the Earth's magnetic field. **[2 marks]**

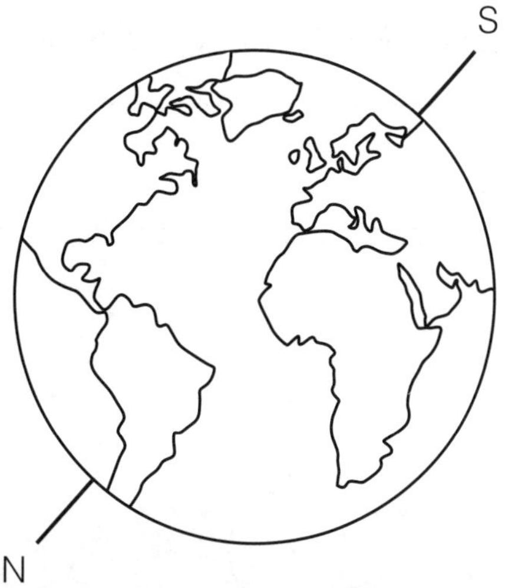

16 Forces P2 • Grade 6–7

A type of toy called a Newton's Cradle can be explained using physics.

The figure shows a Newton's Cradle with two spheres. Each sphere has a mass of 10 g. They are at rest.

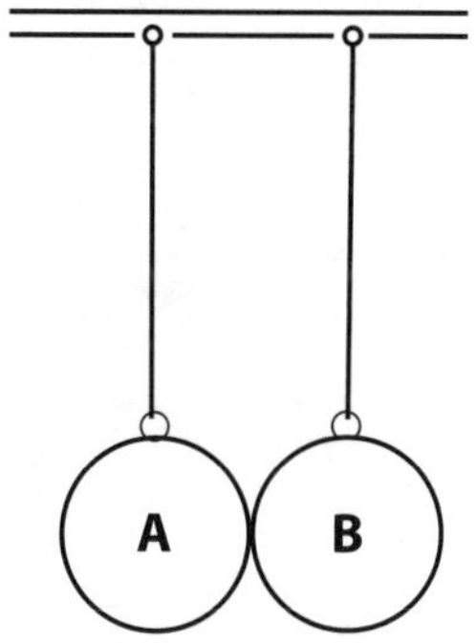

a) Explain, using ideas about forces, why the spheres are stationary. **[3 marks]**

....

....

....

....

Sphere A is raised to the left and released. It takes one second to hit sphere B. See the figure.

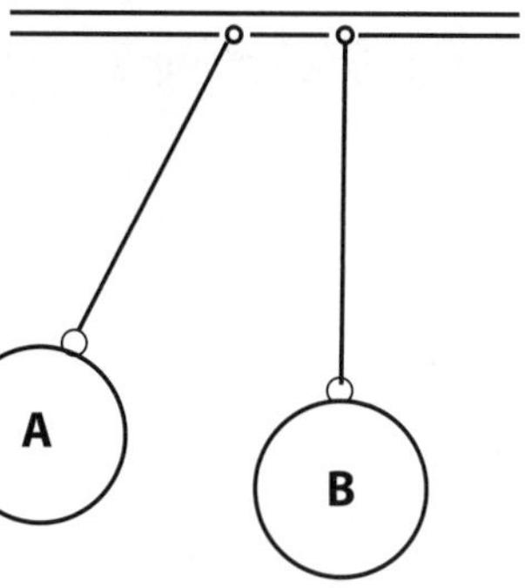

b) Draw the position of sphere B and its wire two seconds after the release of sphere A. **[1 mark]**

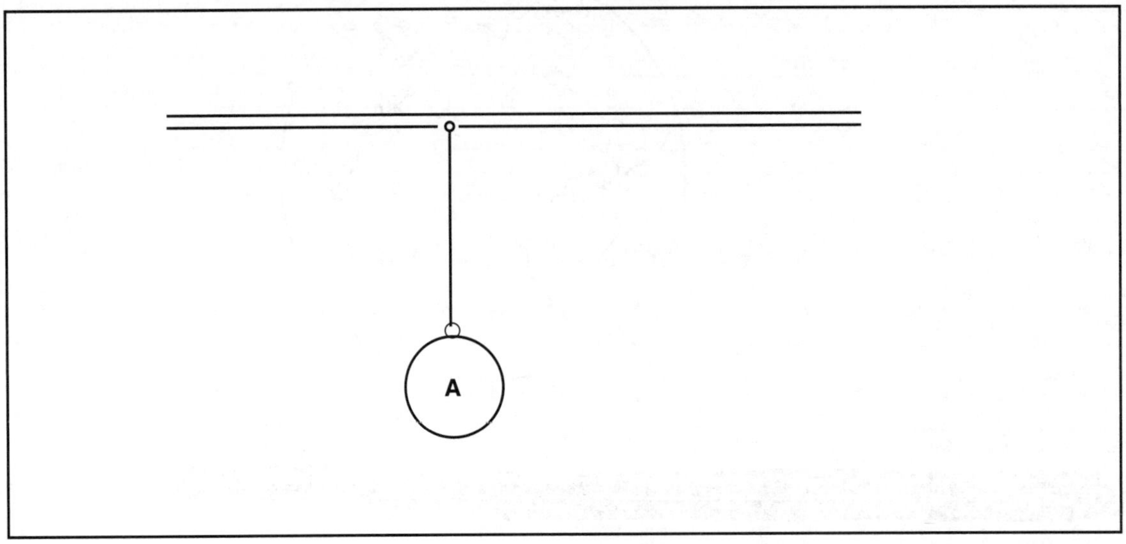

c) Explain what happens to the spheres from the moment sphere A is released up to two seconds later.

Use ideas of momentum, energy and Newton's Laws in your answer. Assume conservation of energy. **[6 marks]**

....

....

....

....

....

....

....

....

....

....

....

d) In reality, the spheres are not operating in a vacuum.

Suggest what would happen to the spheres over time. **[1 mark]**

....

17 Forces (P2) • Grade 6–7

A car travelling at 31.1 m/s skids to a stop in 5.17 s.

a) Determine the distance the car skids (assume uniform acceleration). **[5 marks]**

b) Explain what the difference would be to the stopping distance if the driver had been over the legal alcohol limit. **[2 marks]**

c) Describe what would happen if, rather than a car, the driver had been driving a lorry with a mass 5 times that of the car. **[1 mark]**

Total score: / 124

Index of Topics

This grid tells you which questions in this book offer practice for each of the specification topics across the three subjects in Combined Science.

Topic	Page	Question	Example question	Complete the example	Exam practice question
BIOLOGY					
Cell Biology, Paper 1	4	1	✓		
	6	1			✓
	15	4			✓
	39	6			✓
	44	3			✓
	61	8			✓
	62	10			✓
	66	1	✓		
	77	3		✓	
	82	9			✓
	85	2		✓	
	87	4			✓
	100	2			✓
	110	1	✓		
	112	2			✓
	135	2		✓	
	136	1			✓
	137	4			✓
	144	1	✓		
	146	2			✓
	146	3			✓
	147	4			✓
	148	5			✓
	161	3			✓
	163	6			✓
	168	2			✓
	172	7			✓
Organisation, Paper 1	7	4			✓
	13	2		✓	
	15	5			✓
	21	2		✓	
	22	1			✓
	25	6			✓
	31	3			✓
	44	2			✓
	50	1	✓		
	57	2		✓	
	64	15			✓
	68	2			✓
	72	9			✓
	89	8			✓
	100	1			✓
	112	1			✓
	122	2			✓
	145	2		✓	
Organisation, Paper 1 (cont.)	146	1			✓
	150	1	✓		
	160	2			✓
	180	5			✓
	182	8			✓
	197	2		✓	
	198	1			✓
	201	3			✓
	205	2		✓	
	216	4			✓
Infection and Response, Paper 1	28	1	✓		
	30	1			✓
	54	10			✓
	78	1			✓
	78	2			✓
	121	2		✓	
	138	5			✓
	212	1			✓
Bioenergetics, Paper 1	16	6			✓
	27	10			✓
	37	2		✓	
	58	2			✓
	68	1			✓
	152	1			✓
	177	2		✓	
	186	1			✓
	189	8			✓
	209	3			✓
Homeostasis and Response, Paper 2	6	3			✓
	30	2			✓
	43	3		✓	
	44	1			✓
	55	14			✓
	86	1			✓
	99	3		✓	
	102	5			✓
	106	1			✓
	118	11			✓
	122	1			✓
	132	10			✓
	133	11			✓
	140	11			✓
	154	5			✓
	165	2		✓	
	179	4			✓
	215	3			✓

Topic	Page	Question	Example question	Complete the example	Exam practice question
Inheritance, Variation and Evolution, Paper 2	38	2			✓
	39	5			✓
	48	11			✓
	49	14			✓
	58	1			✓
	62	9			✓
	75	15			✓
	105	2		✓	
	108	6			✓
	125	10			✓
	131	6			✓
	169	3			✓
	213	2			✓
Ecology, Paper 2	6	2			✓
	37	1			✓
	52	1			✓
	80	6			✓
	114	5			✓
	127	2		✓	
	128	1			✓
	155	6			✓
	158	1	✓		
	167	1			✓
	184	1	✓		
	187	2			✓
	210	4			✓
	217	5			✓
CHEMISTRY					
Atomic Structure and the Periodic Table, Paper 1	9	8			✓
	14	1			✓
	14	2			✓
	32	5			✓
	40	7			✓
	48	13			✓
	56	1	✓		
	59	3			✓
	77	2		✓	
	85	3		✓	
	86	2			✓
	113	3			✓
	135	3		✓	
	146	1	✓		
	181	6			✓
	185	3		✓	
	187	3			✓
	188	4			✓
	191	2		✓	
	204	1	✓		
	219	6			✓
	222	10			✓
Bonding, Structure, and the Properties of Matter, Paper 1	12	1	✓		
	33	8			✓
	40	8			✓
	45	5			✓
	49	15			✓
	63	12			✓
	67	2		✓	

Topic	Page	Question	Example question	Complete the example	Exam practice question
Bonding, Structure, and the Properties of Matter, Paper 1 (cont.)	86	2			✓
	88	5			✓
	90	9			✓
	94	3			✓
	94	4			✓
	107	4			✓
	111	2		✓	
	116	7			✓
	177	3		✓	
	178	1			✓
	222	11			✓
Quantitative Chemistry, Paper 1	18	8			✓
	54	11			✓
	70	4			✓
	74	12			✓
	83	10			✓
	118	12			✓
	120	1	✓		
	123	3			✓
	123	4			✓
	124	6			✓
	131	7			✓
	139	7			✓
	139	8			✓
	141	12			✓
	156	8			✓
	221	9			✓
Chemical Changes, Paper 1	8	6			✓
	25	7			✓
	26	8			✓
	26	9			✓
	29	2	✓		
	32	6			✓
	41	10			✓
	51	3		✓	
	54	11			✓
	59	4			✓
	74	12			✓
	103	7			✓
	105	3		✓	
	115	6			✓
	118	12			✓
	120	1	✓		
	123	4			✓
	124	6			✓
	130	4			✓
	143	2			✓
	143	3			✓
	143	4			✓
	151	2		✓	
	156	7			✓
	166	3		✓	
	196	1	✓		
	207	1			✓

Topic	Page	Question	Example question	Complete the example	Exam practice question
Energy Changes, Paper 1	5	2		✓	
	45	4			✓
	52	3			✓
	91	10			✓
	93	1			✓
	97	9			✓
	98	1	✓		
	109	7			✓
	129	3			✓
The Rate and Extent of Chemical Change, Paper 2	21	3		✓	
	22	2			✓
	48	6			✓
	72	10			✓
	73	11			✓
	92	1	✓		
	93	1			✓
	94	2			✓
	106	2			✓
	113	4			✓
	128	2			✓
	136	2			✓
	169	4			✓
	173	8			✓
	190	1	✓		
	192	1			✓
	194	5			✓
	195	6			✓
Organic Chemistry, Paper 2	31	4			✓
	35	11			✓
	36	1	✓		
	43	2		✓	
	49	15			✓
	52	2			✓
	69	3			✓
	74	12			✓
	143	1			✓
	177	3			✓
	211	5			✓
	223	12			✓
Chemical Analysis, Paper 2	10	9			✓
	17	7			✓
	59	4			✓
	127	3		✓	
Chemistry of the Atmosphere, Paper 2	9	7			
	31	4			
	53	4			
	103	8			
	131	7			
	189	9			
	223	12			
Using Resources, Paper 2	62	11			✓
	67	2		✓	
	69	3			✓
	79	3			✓
	139	8			✓
	141	2		✓	
	156	8			
Using Resources, Paper 2 (cont.)	178	2			
	200	2			
	202	4			
	219	7			
	220	8			
PHYSICS					
Energy, Paper 1	19	10			✓
	20	1	✓		
	34	9			✓
	35	10			✓
	38	3			✓
	46	7			✓
	47	8			✓
	47	9			✓
	53	6			✓
	53	7			✓
	79	4			✓
	95	5			✓
	104	1	✓		
	106	3			✓
	117	9			✓
	119	13			✓
	123	5			✓
	126	1	✓		
	131	5			✓
	141	13			✓
	145	3		✓	
	148	6			✓
	151	3		✓	
	162	5			✓
	185	2		✓	
	193	2			✓
	225	14			✓
Electricity, Paper 1	33	7			✓
	39	4			✓
	42	1	✓		
	55	13			✓
	63	13			✓
	70	5			✓
	80	5			✓
	87	3			✓
	95	6			✓
	96	7			✓
	102	6			✓
	111	3		✓	
	117	10			✓
	121	3		✓	
	125	8			
	132	8			✓
	132	9			✓
	154	4			✓
	161	4			✓
	170	5			✓
	171	6			✓
	188	5			✓
	191	3		✓	

Topic	Page	Question	Example question	Complete the example	Exam practice question
Electricity, Paper 1 (cont.)	198	3		✓	
	208	2			✓
	224	13			✓
Particle Model of Matter, Paper 1	13	3		✓	
	34	9			✓
	61	6			✓
	84	1	✓		
	108	5			✓
	116	8			✓
	124	7			✓
	125	9			✓
	138	6			✓
	139	9			✓
	152	3			✓
	160	1			✓
	193	3			✓
Atomic Structure, Paper 1	10	10			✓
	23	3			✓
	53	8			✓
	54	9			✓
	71	7			✓
	81	7			✓
	179	3			✓
	189	7			✓
	193	4			✓
	202	5			✓
Forces, Paper 2	5	3		✓	
	14	3			✓
	24	4			✓
	40	9			✓
	51	2		✓	
	54	12			✓
	57	3		✓	
	61	7			✓
	64	14			✓
	67	3		✓	
	71	8			✓
	75	14			✓
	76	1	✓		
	82	8			✓
	89	7			✓
	93	2		✓	
	101	3			✓
	101	4			✓
	109	8			✓
	134	1	✓		
	137	3			✓
	157	9			✓
	159	2		✓	
	164	1	✓		
	174	9			✓
	183	9			✓
	206	3		✓	
	211	6			✓
	227	16			✓
	229	17			✓

Topic	Page	Question	Example question	Complete the example	Exam practice question
Waves, Paper 2	11	11			✓
	11	12			✓
	18	9			✓
	47	10			✓
	53	5			✓
	60	5			✓
	71	6			✓
	74	13			✓
	88	6			✓
	97	8			✓
	99	2		✓	
	149	7			✓
	181	7			✓
	188	6			✓
Magnetism and Electro-magnetism, Paper 2	29	3		✓	
	37	3		✓	
	39	4			✓
	176	1	✓		
	203	6			✓
	226	15			✓

Answers

Extended answer questions in this workbook contain a model full-mark answer. In the exam, extended response questions are marked according to your level of response and there are 2 marks for each level. Examiners will look at the overall quality of your answer.

Pages 4–11: Choose

Complete the example

2. A = reactant
B = activation energy
C = overall energy change
D = product

3. 7750 N

Exam practice questions

1. a) plasmid **[1]**
b) nucleus **[1]**

2. Feeding – D **[1]**
Photosynthesis – B **[1]**
Respiration – C **[1]**

3. A = Receptor **[1]**
B = Sensory neurone **[1]**
C = Synapse of a relay neurone **[1]**
D = Motor neurone **[1]**
E = Effector **[1]**

4.  **[1]**

5. fusion **[1]**
DNA **[1]**
variation **[1]**

6. increase **[1]**
limiting **[1]**
excess **[1]**
evaporating **[1]**

7. A = carbon dioxide **[1]**
B = oxygen **[1]**
C = nitrogen **[1]**

8. metallic **[1]**

9. a) carbon dioxide **[1]**
b) oxygen **[1]**
c) hydrogen **[1]**
d) chlorine **[1]**

10. a) ${}^{4}_{2}He$ **[1]**
alpha decay **[1]**
b) ${}^{0}_{-1}e$ **[1]**
beta decay **[1]**

11. wavelength; closer together **[2]**

12. a) D **[1]**
b) straight barrier **[1]**

Pages 12–19: Give

Complete the example

2. b) Genes/genetic factors / Age

3. In any order: Breadth/width; height

Exam practice questions

1. a) Halogens **[1]**
b) Cl_2 **[1]**
c) Br^- (*Accept* Br^{1-} *and* Br^{-1}) **[1]**
K^+ (*Accept* K^{1+} *and* K^{+1}) **[1]**

2. Protons 11; Electrons 11 **[1]**
Neutrons 13 **[1]**

3. The change in speed **[1]**
The change in direction **[1]**
The weight of the vehicle **[1]**

4. a) Osmosis involves movement of water molecules whereas diffusion is movement of particles. **[1]**
Osmosis always involves a semi-permeable membrane whereas diffusion may not. **[1]**
b) Active transport is movement of particles against a concentration gradient / from low to high concentration, rather than from high to low concentration as with diffusion. **[1]**
Active transport requires energy from respiration whereas diffusion does not. **[1]**

5. a) Use random numbers to produce coordinates. **[1]**
b) Measure the length and width / area of the field. **[1]**

6. a) Concentration of nitrate ions **[1]**
b) g or kg **[1]**
c) *Any two from:* light (intensity); water; temperature; mass / volume of soil; soil type or (soil) pH; other mineral content of the soil; number of plants; starting mass of barley; height / age of barley; type / variety of barley; harvested at the same time **[2]**

7. Step 1: Pencil is insoluble in water / It prevents the start line from running into the results. **[1]**
Step 3: To ensure the solvent wicks through the paper / To prevent samples from dissolving into the solvent / To ensure that separation happens. **[1]**

8. a) 6.02×10^{23} **[1]**
b) $0.00024 = 0.24$ g **[1]**
Moles = $\frac{0.24}{63.5} = 0.00378$ **[1]**
Number of atoms = $0.00378 \times 6.02 \times 10^{23}$ **[1]**
Number of atoms = 2.27556×10^{21} **[1]**
$= 2.28 \times 10^{21}$ **[1]**

9. *In any order:* tension in the string; rate of oscillation; distance between oscillator and pulley. **[3]**

10. *In any order:* length of tube; number of turns; temperature increase. (*Allow* starting temperature and final temperature *and allow* mass, *though it is not needed.*) **[3]**

Pages 20–27: Identify

Complete the example

2. a) C
   b) B
3. a) Concentration of hydrochloric acid
   b) Time (taken for cross to disappear)

Exam practice questions

1. a) A **[1]**
   b) A and D **[2]**
   c) B **[1]**
2. a) Volume of gas **[1]**
   b) *Accept one from:* concentration of hydrogen peroxide; volume of hydrogen peroxide; temperature of reaction mixture **[1]**
3. a) Alpha **[1]**
   b) Aluminium **[1]**
   c) Gamma **[1]**
   d) Lead **[1]**
4. Mass **[1]**
   Velocity **[1]**
5. a) – d)

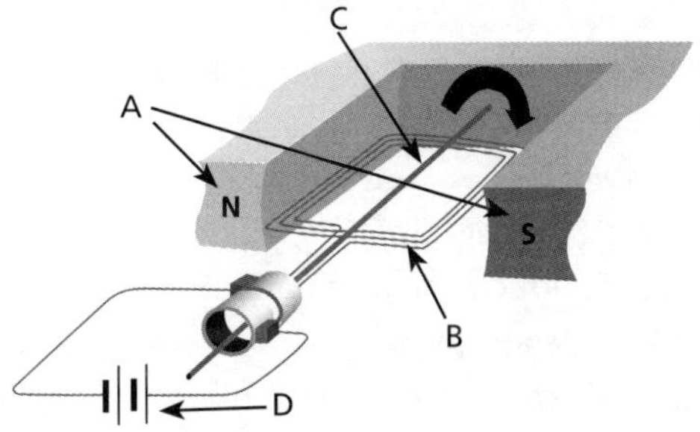

[5]

6. P **[1]**
   The mean and the median are both 4. **[1]**
7. a) Stage 1: (thermal) decomposition **[1]**
   Stage 2: REDOX
   (*Accept* displacement) **[1]**
   b) Carbon (*Accept* graphite) **[1]**
8. a) Fe_2O_3 (*Accept* iron oxide *or* iron ore) **[1]**
   b) CO_2 / carbon dioxide **[1]**
9. a) Na^+ **[1]**
   H^+ **[1]**
10. B **[1]**

Pages 28–35: Name

Complete the example

2. b) Copper sulfate (*Accept* copper(II) sulfate)
3. a) *Two from:* Iron / Fe; Cobalt / Co; Nickel / Ni
   b) Steel

Exam practice questions

1. Rose black spot – fungus **[1]**
   Malaria – protist **[1]**
   Measles – virus **[1]**
2. a) Pituitary gland **[1]**
   b) Progesterone, luteinising hormone (LH) and oestrogen **[3]**
3. a) X = Enzyme **[1]**
   Y = Substrate **[1]**
   Z = Product **[1]**
   b) Lock and key **[1]**
4. a) Methane / CH_4 **[1]**
   b) Combustion (*Accept* oxidation) **[1]**
   c) Carbon dioxide / CO_2 **[1]**
5. Electron **[1]**
6. a) Bromine **[1]**
   b) Lead **[1]**
7. a) Variable resistor **[1]**
   b) Directly proportional **[1]**
8. a) Metallic bonding **[1]**
   b) Electrons **[1]**
   c) Ionic bonding **[1]**
   d) Ions **[1]**
9. a) Condensing **[1]**
   b) Latent heat of vaporisation (*Allow* specific heat of vaporisation) **[1]**
10. *Any two from:* Solar; Wind; Biofuel / Biodiesel **[2]**
11. a) Fractional distillation and cracking **[1]**
    b) Carbon dioxide and water **[1]**
    c) Ethanol **[1]**

Pages 36–41: Write

Complete the example

2. a) Glucose → **Ethanol** + **Carbon dioxide**
   b) Bread, *plus any one from* beer, wine, cider
3. force on a conductor at right angles to a magnetic field carrying a current = magnetic flux density × current × length (*Accept* F = B I l)

Exam practice questions

1. a) Primary consumers **[1]**
   b) Apex consumers/predators **[1]**
   c) Secondary consumers **[1]**
2.

Controlled by their genes	Caused by the environment	Controlled by their genes and caused by the environment
Tom and Jake have brown eyes **[1]**	Jake has a scar **[1]**	Tom is 160 cm tall **[1]** Jake's body mass is 60 kg **[1]**

3. *In any order:* mass of the solid; specific latent heat of the solid. **[2]**
4. *In any order:* number of turns on the coil; current flowing through the coil; use of an iron core in the coil. **[3]**
5. a) Genus; species **[2]**
   b) Binomial (system) **[1]**

c) Domain [1]

6. a) Plasmids [1]
b) Mitochondria [1]
c) Chloroplasts [1]

7. $2K + 2H_2O \rightarrow 2KOH + H_2$
(1 mark for correct reactants in either order; 1 mark for correct products in either order; 1 mark for correct balancing) [3]

8. The caesium (atom) loses [1]
one (outer shell) electron. [1]
The bromine (atom) gains [1]
one electron. [1]

9. Momentum = mass × velocity (Momentum = m × v) [1]

10. a) $2Cl^- \rightarrow Cl_2 + 2e^-$
(1 mark for correct reactant formula; 1 mark for correct product formulae in either order; 1 mark for correct balancing) [3]
b) $Cu^{2+} + 2e^- \rightarrow Cu$
(1 mark for correct reactant formulae in either order; 1 mark for correct product formula; 1 mark for correct balancing) [3]

Pages 42–49: Complete

Complete the example

2. C_5H_{12}

3. **FSH**
Oestrogen
Progesterone
LH

Exam practice questions

1.

Hormone	Site of production	Function
insulin	pancreas	**controls blood glucose levels [1]**
testosterone	**testes [1]**	controls production of secondary sexual characteristics
thyroxine	**thyroid gland [1]**	**controls the metabolic rate [1]**

2. *Labels completed clockwise from top left:*
Vena cava [1]
Aorta [1]
Left atrium [1]
Right ventricle [1]

3. increases [1]
water; partially [2]
0.5 [1]

4. surroundings [1]
decrease / get lower / fall [1]
exothermic reactions / exothermic changes / exothermic chemical reactions / exothermic chemical changes. [1]

5. 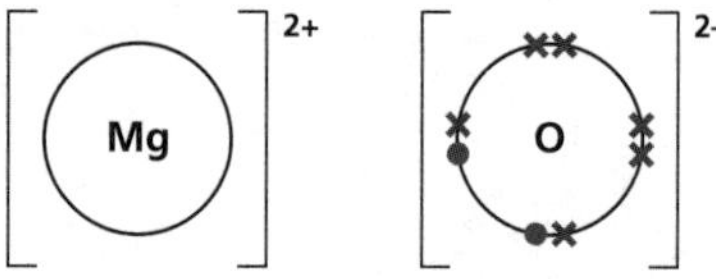

(1 mark for correct charge on magnesium ion; 1 mark for no electrons in the outer shell of magnesium ion; 1 mark for correct charge on oxide ion; 1 mark for eight electrons in the outer shell of oxide ion) [4]

6. a) magnesium + hydrochloric acid → magnesium chloride + hydrogen
(1 mark for each in either order) [2]
b) The independent variable is concentration (of hydrochloric acid). [1]
The dependent variable is mass. [1]

7. a) Gravitational potential [1]
b) Gravitational potential [1]
c) Elastic potential [1]

8. A liquid [1]
B mixture of solid and liquid [1]
C solid [1]

9. kinetic [1]

10. A Lamp/light source [1]
B Motor [1]
C Water/water tray [1]
D Viewing screen/wave pattern [1]
E Wooden bar/rod [1]

11. red-green colour blindness / polydactyly / cystic fibrosis [1]
(*Accept other correct characteristics.*)
genotype [1]
phenotype [1]
dominant [1]
homozygous [1]
multiple / many [1]

12. a) moles (*Accept* mol) [1]
b) Avogadro constant (*Accept* 6.02×10^{23}) [1]

13. a) salt (*Accept* ionic compound) [1]
b) Cl_2 **[1]** and Br_2 **[1]** *(Must be in this order.)*

14. A = Insulin gene is cut out of human DNA [1]
B = Plasmid is cut open [1]
C = Insulin gene is inserted into plasmid [1]
D = Plasmid is inserted into a bacterium [1]

15. 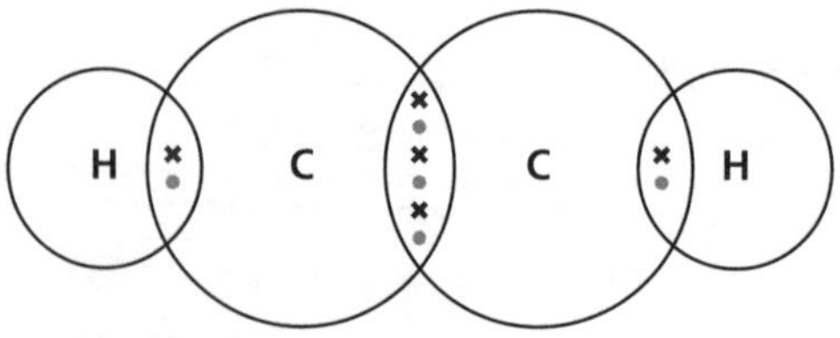

(1 mark for 6 shared electrons in the overlap between the two carbon atoms; 1 mark for 2 shared electrons in the overlap between each carbon and hydrogen atom.) [2]

Pages 50–55: Define

Complete the example

2. The rate at which **velocity** changes. (*Accept* change in speed and/or direction.)
3. **a)** Gain of **oxygen** and loss of **electrons**.
   b) Loss of **oxygen** and gain of **electrons**.

Exam practice questions

1. **a)** All the living organisms / biotic factors and all the non-living / abiotic factors in an area / habitat. **[1]**
   b) All the organisms / populations living in a habitat. **[1]**
2. A molecule that contains only carbon **[1]**
   and hydrogen atoms. **[1]**
3. **a)** Transfers energy to the surroundings **[1]**
   so the temperature of the surroundings increases. **[1]**
   b) The minimum amount of energy that particles must have to react. **[1]**
4. Water that is safe to drink. **[1]**
5. The rate at which a wave passes a fixed point. **[1]**
6. Energy which is stored in an object due to it being in motion. **[1]**
7. The amount of energy needed to increase the temperature of one kilogram of a material by one degree C. **[1]**
8. The amount of time for the level of activity of a particular sample to drop to half its level. **[1]**
9. The process by which an object is exposed to ionising radiation. **[1]**
10. **a)** The state of physical and mental well-being. **[1]**
    b) Something that leads to an increased rate of disease. **[1]**
11. The reactant that is completely used up. **[1]**
12. The product of the mass of an object and its velocity. **[1]**
13. A measure of the energy per unit of charge transferred between two points. **[1]**
14. **a)** The regulation of the internal conditions of a cell or organism **[1]**
    to maintain optimum conditions for function. **[1]**
    b) A change in a variable causes a response that corrects the variable **[1]**
    back to the normal level. **[1]**

Pages 56–65: Describe

Complete the example

2. Bile is **alkaline** and so neutralises **acid** released in the **stomach**.
   Bile also **emulsifies fats**.
   This means that bile **increases** the rate of **fat digestion** by lipase.
3. The graph shows the relationship between distance and **time**. On a graph like this if the line is horizontal it means that the object is **stationary**. If the line has a positive gradient it means that the object is **moving away from the starting point**.
   In this graph the object starts off by travelling at a **steady speed** and then **stops**. It then moves at a greater **steady speed**, then **stops** and finally **returns to the starting point**.

Exam practice questions

1. From parts of organisms that have not decayed. **[1]**
   Because the conditions needed for decay are absent. **[1]**
   Parts of the organism are replaced by minerals. **[1]**
   As preserved footprints / burrows / rootlet traces / bones / teeth. **[1]**
2. As the percentage of oxygen increases, the breathing rate decreases. **[1]**
   At higher levels, the breathing rate levels off. **[1]**
   Minimum breathing rate is about 14 breaths per minute. **[1]**
3. **a)** In order of their increasing atomic masses. **[1]**
   b) Mendeleev left gaps for elements that he thought had not been discovered. **[1]**
   Mendeleev changed the order based on atomic masses / ordered the elements by their chemical reactions. **[1]**
   c) No gaps **[1]**
   Group 0 / Noble gases discovered. **[1]**
   Elements listed by increasing atomic number. **[1]**
4. Chlorine: damp litmus paper **[1]**
   bleached / turns white **[1]**
   Hydrogen: a burning splint **[1]**
   pop sound **[1]**
   Oxygen: glowing splint **[1]**
   relights **[1]**
5. **Transverse:** Shake the slinky from side to side or up and down to make transverse waves. **[1]**

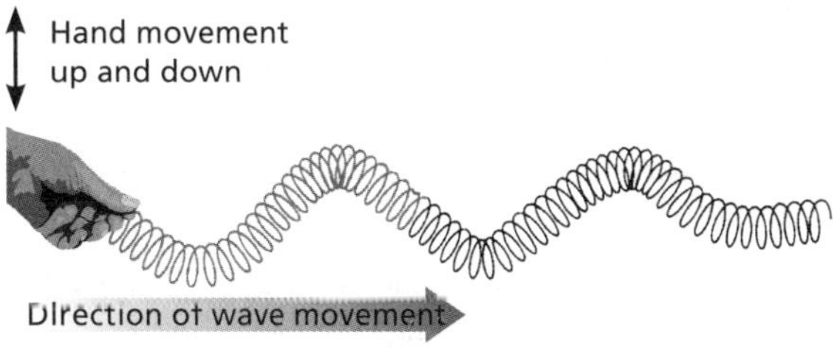

[1]

Longitudinal: Push the slinky backwards and forwards to make longitudinal waves. **[1]**

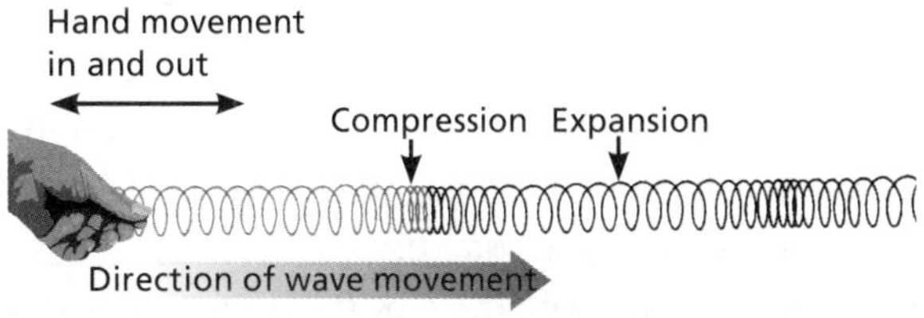

[1]

6. Use a balance to determine the mass of the object. **[1]**
   Use a container large enough to fit the object in but do not insert it yet. *(Ideally the container should be a Eureka can but a beaker with a spout can be used.)* **[1]**
   Fill the container completely with water and use a measuring cylinder to catch any water overflowing. **[1]**

Suspend the object using a thread and lower it into the container so that all the displaced water is captured. **[1]**
Record the volume of the displaced water. **[1]**
Divide the mass of the object by the volume to determine the density. **[1]**

7. Decelerating / negative accelerating **[1]**
8. Gain different sub-cellular structures. **[1]**
Become specialised for a particular role. **[1]**
9. *Description should include any five points from:* DNA contains two strands wound in a double helix; DNA is a polymer made from nucleotides; Each nucleotide consists of a sugar, phosphate and base; There are four bases, A, C, G and T; The strands consist of alternating sugar and phosphate groups; The strands are held together by attractions of the bases; In the complementary strand, a C is always linked to a G on the opposite strand, and a T is linked to an A. **[5]**
10. *Description should include any five points from:* Before a cell can divide, it needs to grow; The cell increases the number of sub-cellular structures or ribosomes or mitochondria; The DNA replicates to form two copies of each chromosome; Mitosis occurs; One set of chromosomes is pulled to each end of the cell and the nucleus divides; The cytoplasm and cell membranes divide to form two identical cells. **[5]**
11. Use bacteria **[1]**
to produce leachate solutions / solution which contain copper compounds. **[1]**
Electrolysis of solution (containing a copper compound) **[1]**
or displacement (of copper) from solution (containing a copper compound). **[1]**
12. Silica forms a giant covalent structure **[1]**
where the atoms are held together by shared **[1]**
pairs of electrons **[1]**
in strong covalent bonds. **[1]**
13. Set the resistor up with a power supply, voltmeter and ammeter. **[1]**
The voltmeter should be in parallel with the resistor to measure the potential difference across it and the ammeter should be in series with it to measure the current flowing through it. **[1]**
Connect the circuit and record readings on both meters. **[1]**
If the reading on the ammeter exceeds the maximum value on the scale add a fixed resistor in series with the resistance being measured but ensure the voltmeter is only connected across the resistor being measured. **[1]**
Divide the potential difference by the current to determine the resistance of the resistor. **[1]**
If the supply voltage is altered calculate the resistance from the readings at each setting. This should have the same value so is a good way of checking the result. **[1]**

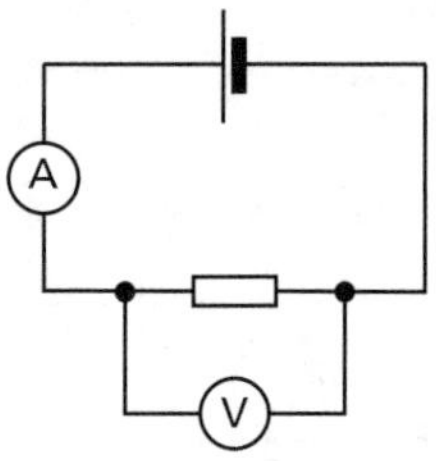

14. They will need a selection of weights which are of known values. **[1]**
With no weight on the spring they should mark the position of the pointer as zero. **[1]**
Add various weights until they find a weight (or combination of weights) that stretches the spring to near the end of the scale. **[1]**
Remove the weights and make sure the pointer goes back to the zero mark. **[1]**
Adding those weights back on they should mark the position of the pointer. **[1]**
Divide the scale between that mark and zero into equal steps, e.g. if the load is 7 N then the distance on the scale should be divided into seven equal intervals, each of which will represent 1 N. **[1]**
15. *Description should include any five points from:* Measure the position of the water meniscus on the scale; Measure a certain length of time; Measure the meniscus again and calculate the difference in the two readings; Multiply up the value to give the water uptake per hour; Convert the distance the meniscus moved to volume; Using the cross-sectional area of the tube multiplied by the distance moved. **[5]**

Pages 66–75: Why / What / Which…

Complete the example

2. **a)** Mixture
Formulation
b) In pure metals, the layers of **atoms / ions** easily **slide** over each other, but in alloys, the different sizes of **atoms / ions** distort the layers so they can't **slide** as easily.
3. Speed is a **scalar** quantity and only has **magnitude**. Velocity is a **vector** quantity and has **direction** as well as **magnitude**.

Exam practice questions

1. **a)** Act as a heat shield / Stop the water in the beaker heating up. **[1]**
b) Rate of photosynthesis / Number of bubbles given off in a certain time. **[1]**
2. **a)** Red blood cell **[1]**
b) So that it can fit in more haemoglobin / adapted to carry more oxygen. **[1]**

3. a) Propene [1]
   b) Collect the used plastic bottles. [1]
   Wash them. [1]
   Melt them. [1]
   Re-shape them into new bottles. [1]
4. a) Mass is conserved / no atoms are gained or lost [1]
   b) Carbon dioxide / a gas is made [1]
   and escapes. [1]
5. a) It is reduced. [1]
   b) To reduce energy loss on transmission. [1]
   c) Step-down transformer [1]
6. Radiators transfer energy to the surroundings to heat the room. [1]
   The effectiveness of the transfer depends upon the colour of the radiator. Matt black is the colour that is most effective at radiating energy. [1]
7. Alpha [1]
8. a) The object is stationary. [1]
   b) The object is travelling at a constant velocity. [1]
9. a) A [1]
   b) C, D and E [1]
   c) D [1]
10. a) Copper(II) oxide and copper(II) carbonate only [1]
    b) By using an electric heater/Bunsen burner [1]
11. a) Top pan balance [1]
    b) No further mass change [1]
12. a) CH_3COOH [1]
    b) Is an aqueous solution [1]
    c) 0.02 mol [1]
13. a) At right angles to the mirror. [1]
    b) With a broken line. [1]
    c) It is used to measure the angles of the light rays. [1]
14. a) To record the position of the car at that instant. [1]
    b) To determine the distance the car has travelled in the time [1]
    between the two photographs being taken. [1]
    c) Speed = Distance between the two positions ÷ Time taken to travel between the two positions [1]
15. Some sperm have an X chromosome and some have a Y. [1]
    X and Y chromosomes are different sizes. [1]

Pages 76–83: Use

Complete the example

2. Nucleus
3. The students are correct because at 0.55 mol/dm^3 the line crosses the **x-axis** and so there is no **(percentage) loss** in mass.
   This means that there is no net movement of **water**.
   Therefore the inside and outside of the potato cells must have the **same concentration**.

Exam practice questions

1. This method does not use expensive / complicated equipment. [1]
   It is also very easy, so that people do not need a lot of training / experience / knowledge to be able to administer the vaccine. [1]
2. D [1]
   Release of toxins in the body cause fever. [1]
3. 20 : 2 [1]
   = 10 : 1 [1]
4. a) The purpose is to produce light so any other outputs are not useful. [1]
   The thermal output is not useful and is 3.2 J. [1]
   b) Efficiency = Useful energy transferred out ÷ Total energy supplied × 100
   = 0.8 ÷ 4 × 100 [1]
   = 20% [1]
5.

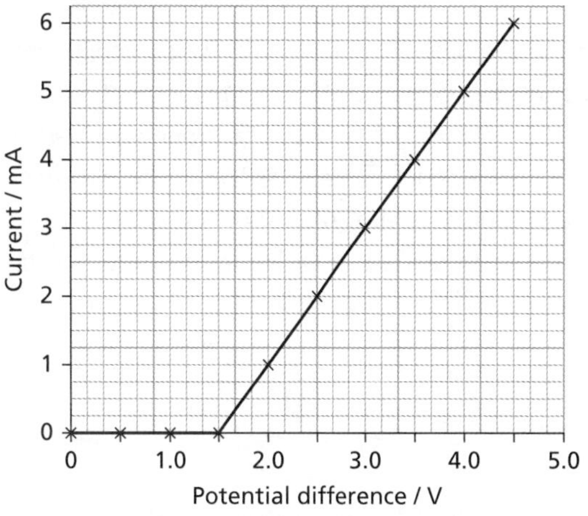

(2 marks for plotting data +/– 2 squares correct, 1 mark for line of best fit, 1 mark for each correct scale (x-axis and y-axis).) [4]

6. The number of lynx peak after the number of hares. [1]
   As there is more food for the lynx, their numbers increase. [1]
   This causes the hare numbers to then drop as more are eaten. [1]
7. a)

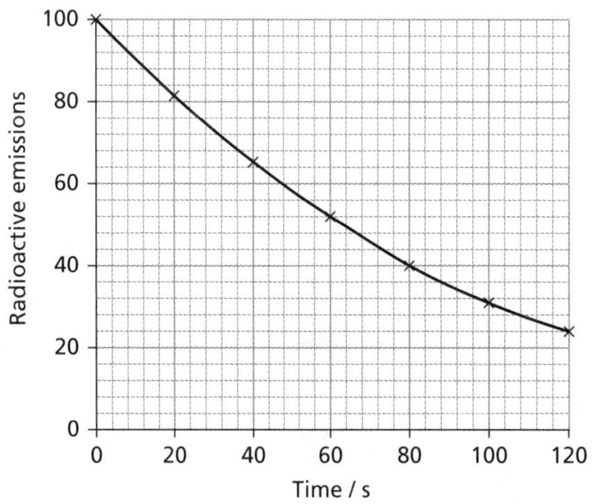

(1 mark for correct y-axis label, 1 mark for correct y-axis scale, 2 marks for plotting data +/– 2 squares.) [4]

b)

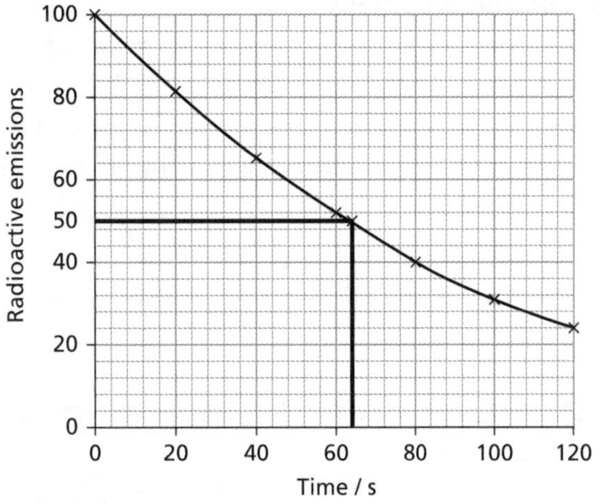

(1 mark for selecting two values of activity, the second half of the first; 1 mark for reading time values and calculating time interval, 1 mark for getting answer of 64 s) **[3]**

Note that the half life is the time taken for the activity to drop to half its original level. The example here shows the working if going from a level of 100 to (half of 100) 50 but it is correct to go from any given value of activity to half that level as long as both values appear on the graph. The value of the half life will be the same (within a margin of error) and get the available marks.

8. v = 6 m/s, u = 0 m/s and s = 2 m. Therefore 36 – 0 = 2 × a × 2 **[1]**

so 36 = 4a **[1]**

therefore a = 9 m/s^2 **[2]**

9. Calculations of surface area to volume ratio for red blood cells: shrew 2.42 v mouse 1.75. **[1]**

Therefore, shrew's red blood cells have a larger surface area to volume ratio. **[1]**

They can take up and release oxygen quicker to supply the shrew's greater demand for oxygen. **[1]**

10. a) Only one spot on the chromatogram. **[1]**

b) $\frac{6}{12}$ **[1]**

= 0.5 **[1]**

Pages 84–91: Draw

Complete the example

2. *Diagram drawn the same shape with clear lines and no shading. Any two from:* the cell membrane; cytoplasm; nucleus *should be labelled.*

3.

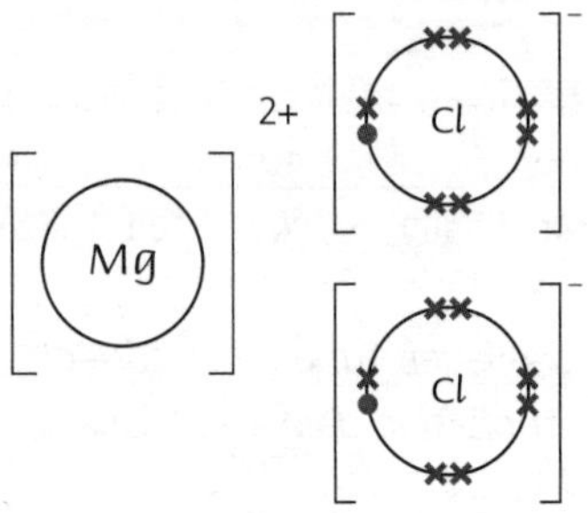

Exam practice questions

1. *Diagram should be completed as follows:*

Sensory neurone drawn entering dorsal root and labelled. **[1]**

Motor neurone drawn leaving ventral root and labelled. **[1]**

Relay neurone drawn connecting sensory and motor neurones and labelled. **[1]**

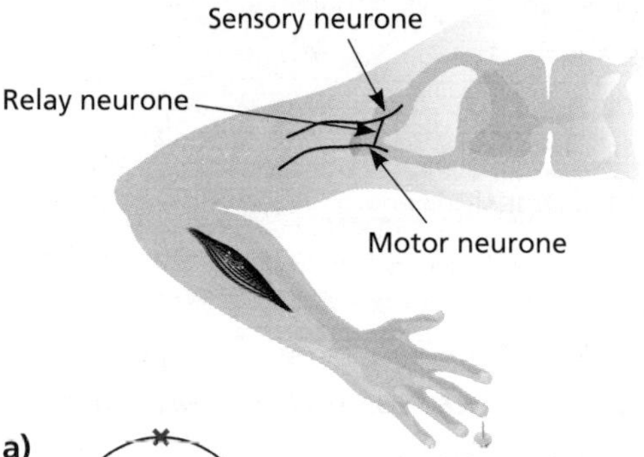

2. a)

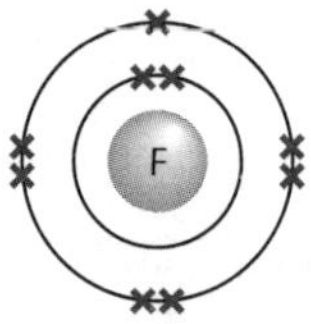

(1 mark for 9 electrons in total; 1 mark for two electrons in the first shell and seven electrons in the outer shell) **[2]**

b)

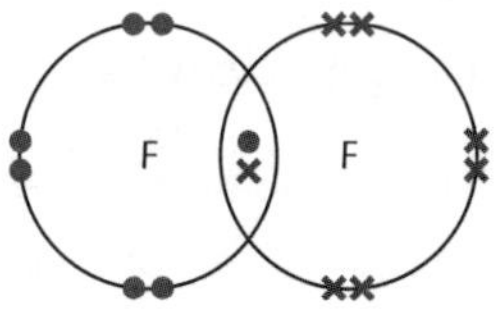

(1 mark for a shared pair of electrons between the atoms; 1 mark for each atom having 7 electrons in their outer shell) **[2]**

3.

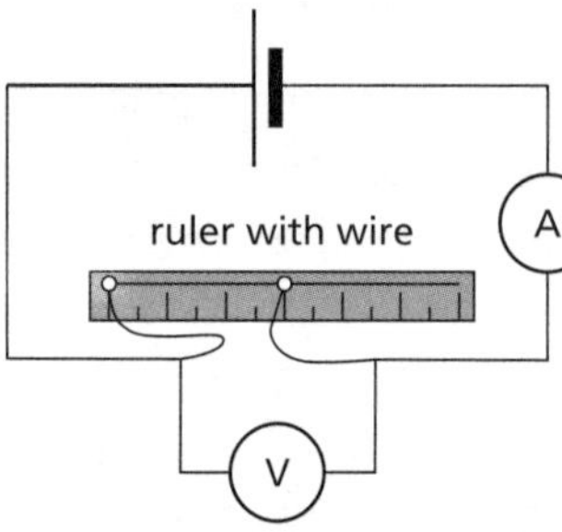

(1 mark for ammeter; 1 mark for voltmeter; 1 mark for ruler; 1 mark for wire.) **[4]**

4. 2 micrometres – 2 × 10^{-6} m **[1]**

2 centimetres – 2 × 10^{-2} m **[1]**

5. a)

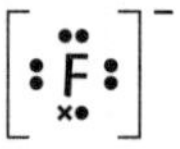

(1 mark for eight electrons in the outer shell; 1 mark for charge) **[2]**

b)

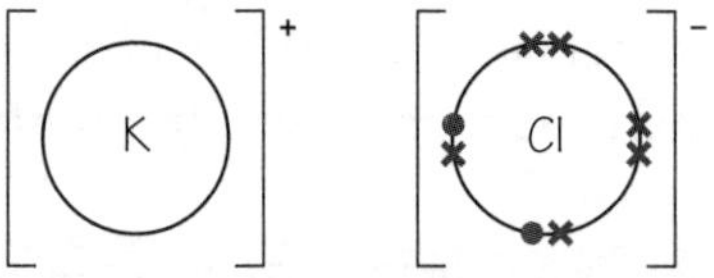

(1 mark for no electrons in potassium outer shell; 1 mark for charge on potassium ion; 1 mark for 8 electrons in the chloride outer shell; 1 mark for charge on chloride ion) **[4]**

6.

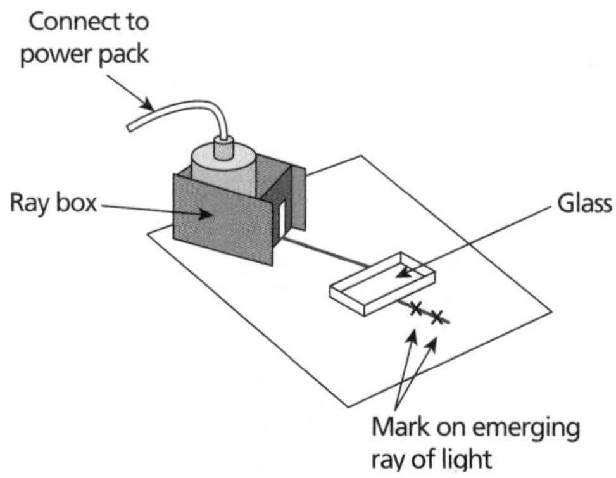

(1 mark for ray box lamp; 1 mark for incident ray; 1 mark for block; 1 mark for showing emerging ray of light.) **[4]**

7.

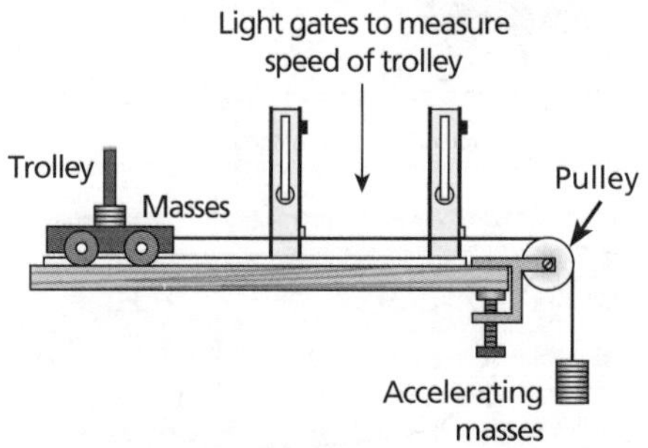

(1 mark for trolley on ramp; 1 mark for pulley; 1 mark for masses on trolley; 1 mark for accelerating masses.) **[4]**

8. *Tangent drawn correctly at 40 seconds.* **[1]**

Correct expression of slope, e.g. (100 – 40) ÷ 76 **[1]**

Correct rate of reaction = 0.79 **[1]**

9.

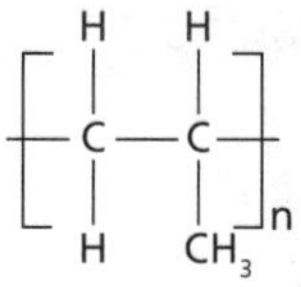

(1 mark for correct structure; 1 mark for square brackets; 1 mark for no double bond and bond stretching through the square brackets; 1 mark for subscript $_n$) **[4]**

10.

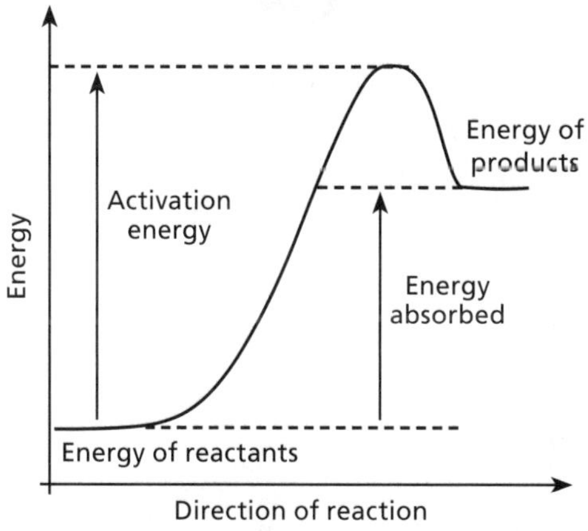

(1 mark for energy of reactants lower than energy of products; 1 mark for activation energy labelled; 1 mark for energy absorbed labelled.) **[3]**

Pages 92–97: Sketch

Complete the example

2.

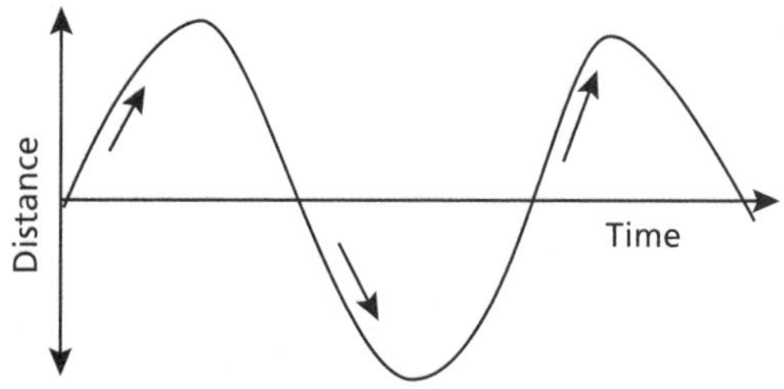

Exam practice questions

1.

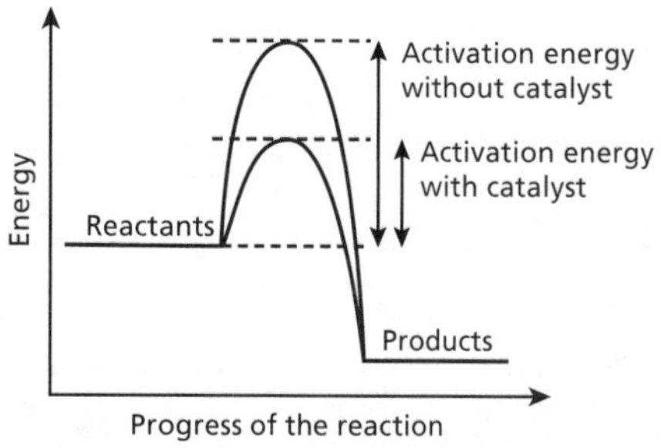

[2]

2.

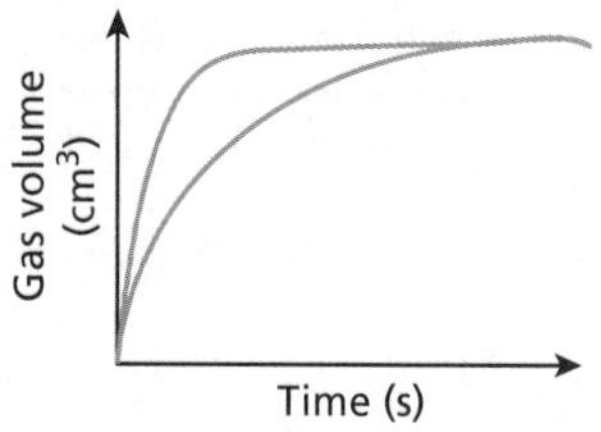

(1 mark for line starting at origin; 1 mark for steeper curve; 1 mark for lines finishing at the same height) **[3]**

3.

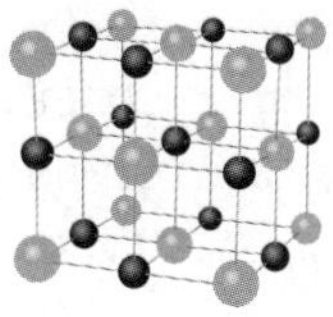

or

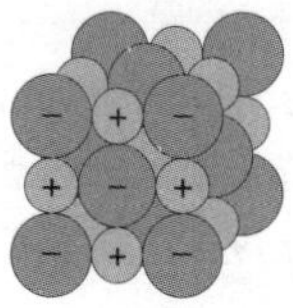

(1 mark for attempt to show 3D; 1 mark for at least 5 sodium ions and 5 chloride ions; 1 mark for a repeating pattern where the chloride is surrounded / connected by 4 sodium ions and each sodium is surrounded / connected to chloride ions.) **[3]**

4.

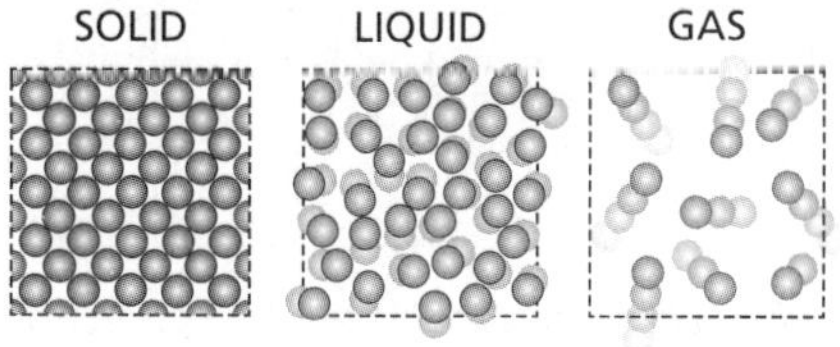

(1 mark for diagrams showing particles in a rigid pattern with no spaces for a solid; 1 mark for particles in a random pattern with small spaces, but with particles touching other particles, for a liquid; 1 mark for particles in a random pattern with big spaces between them for a gas) **[3]**

5.

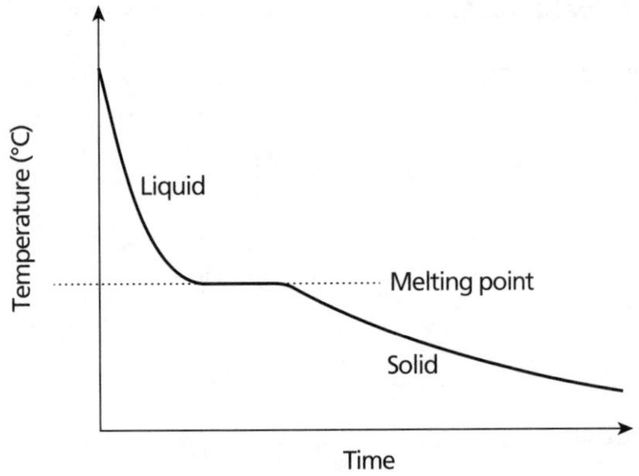

(1 mark for curved line labelled liquid; 1 mark for horizontal line labelled melting point; 1 mark for curved line labelled solid.) **[3]**

6.

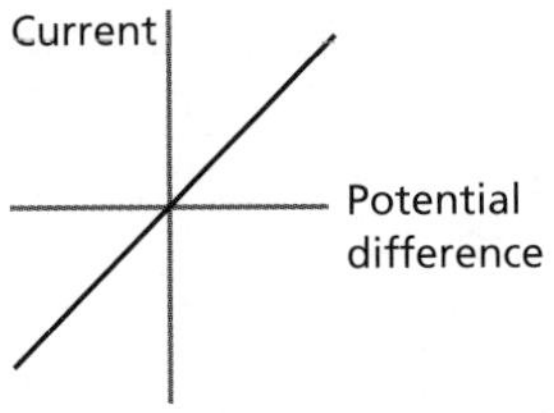

(1 mark for line going through the origin; 1 mark for positive gradient and straight line) **[2]**

7.

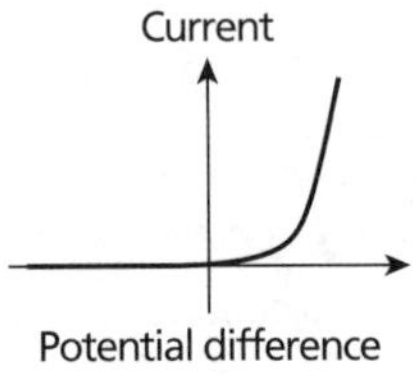

(1 mark for line to left of vertical axis being horizontal and on axis; 1 mark for line to right of vertical axis curving upwards; 1 mark for line then becoming straight with a positive gradient.) **[3]**

8.

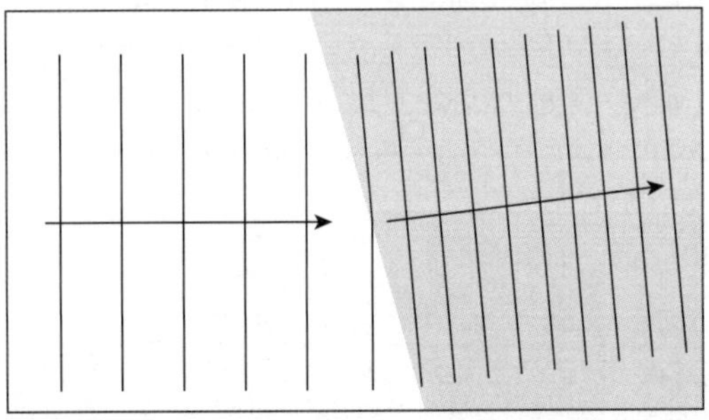

(1 mark for parallel straights lines in deeper area to left; 1 mark for parallel rays in shallow area with changed direction; 1 mark for rays in shallower area being closer together.) **[3]**

9.

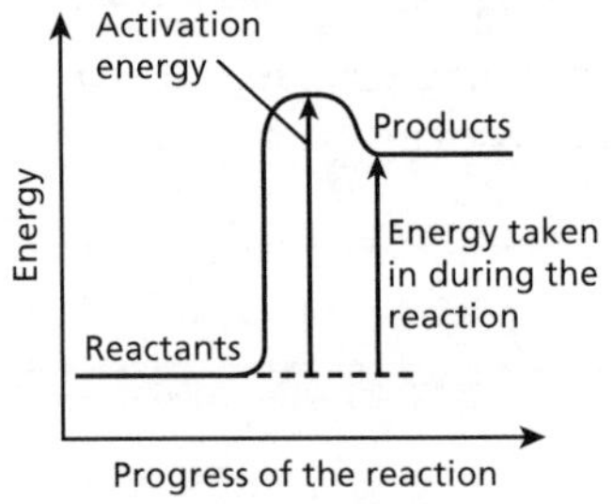

(1 mark for products higher than reactants; 1 mark for activation energy shown) **[2]**

Pages 98–103: Label

Complete the example

2.

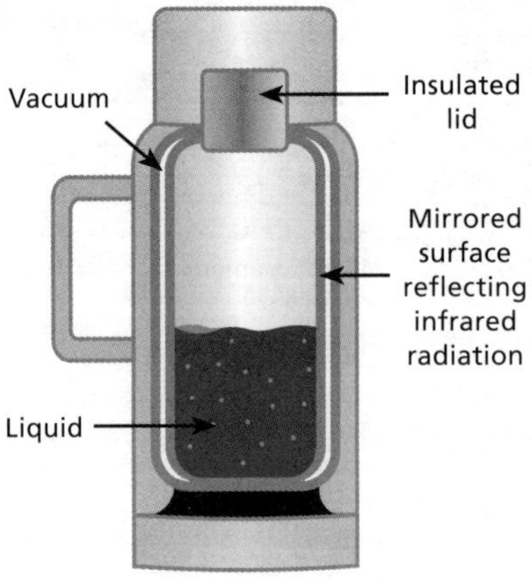

3.

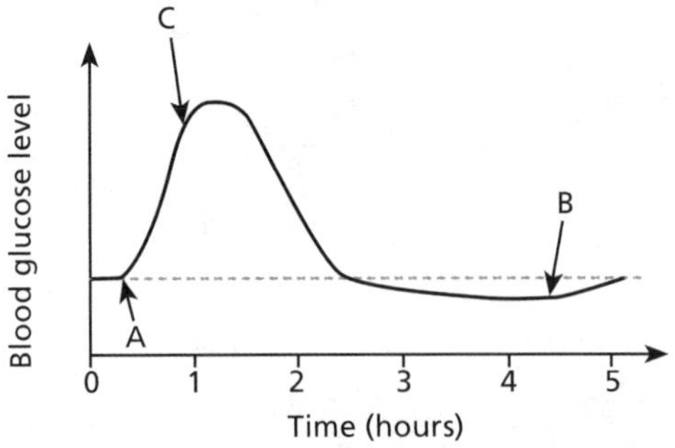

Exam practice questions

1.

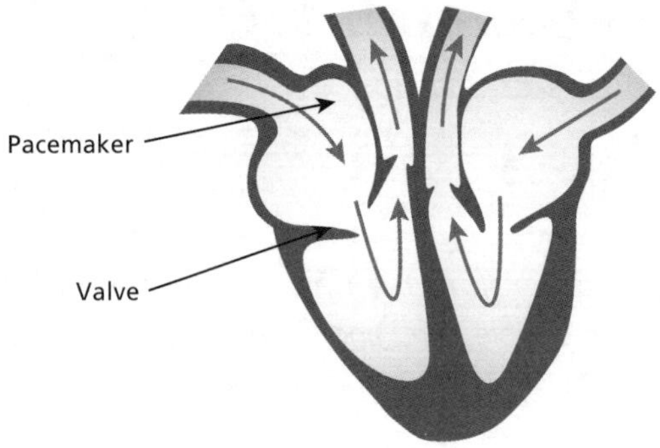

[2]

2. R = first, second or third cell from the left **[1]**
   S = fourth cell from the left **[1]**
   T = third cell from the left **[1]**

3.

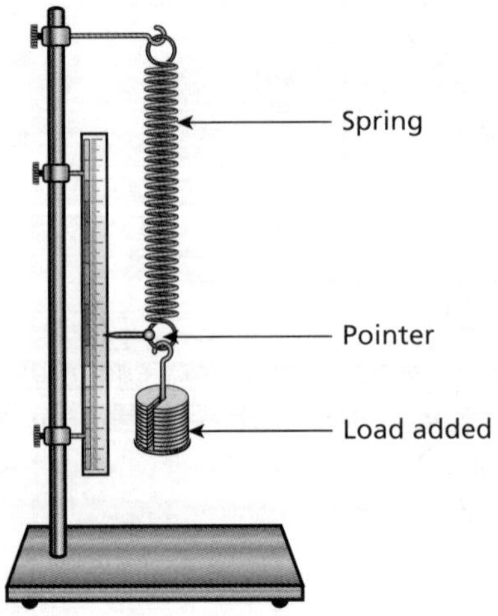

[3]

4.

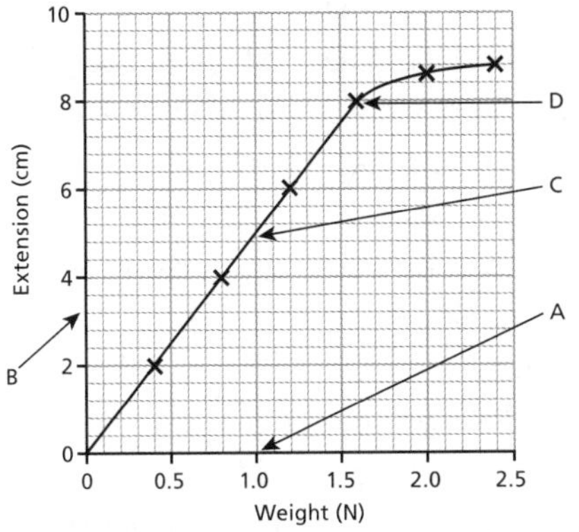

[4]

5.

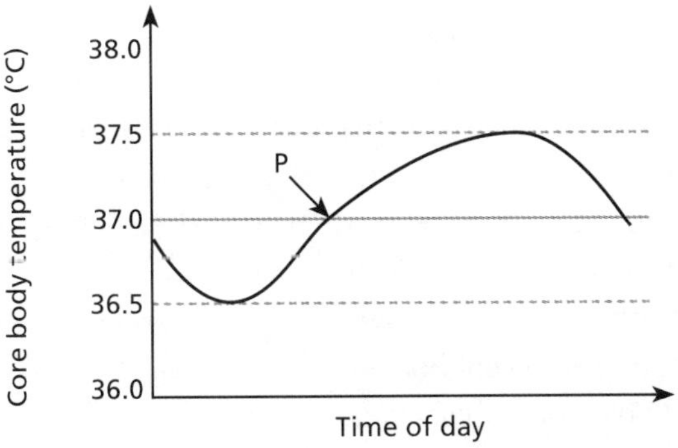

[1]

6.

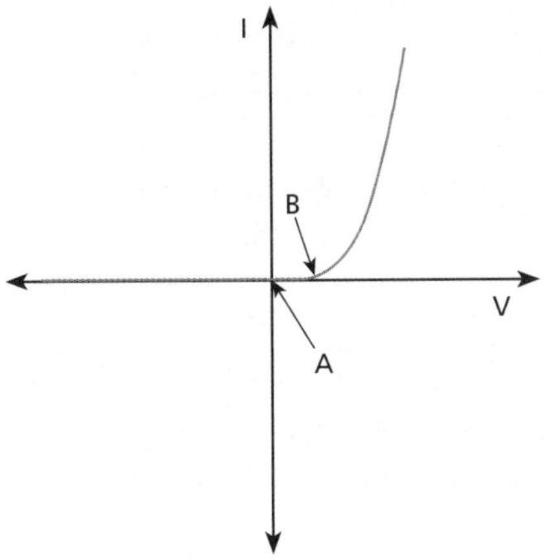

[2]

7.

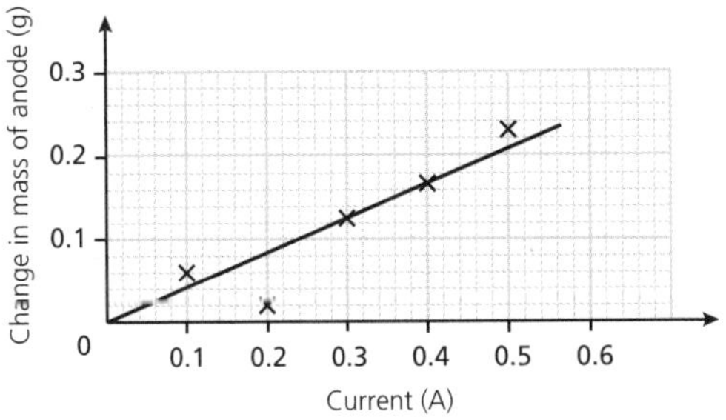

[2]

8. *1 mark for the 78.08% section labelled as* nitrogen *or* N_2; *1 mark for the 20.95% section labelled as* oxygen *or* O_2; *1 mark for the 0.93% section labelled as* argon *or* Ar [3]

Pages 104–109: Suggest

Complete the example

2. A plant may have sexually reproduced and released **seeds**. These were carried to the area and germinated to produce a plant.

This plant must then have used **asexual** reproduction many times as all the plants in the area are **genetically** identical.

3. Filter/filtration

Exam practice questions

1. **a)** The pancreas extract contained insulin. [1]
The insulin controlled the blood glucose level. [1]
However, the injected insulin only lasted for a certain time in the body. [1]
b) For: allowed the discovery of insulin / led to treatment for diabetes / saved lives. [1]
Against: ethically wrong to harm animals / dogs may respond differently to humans. [1]

2. Measuring the mass loss as the reaction happens. [1]
Measuring the volume of gas produced during the reaction. [1]

3. **a)** The energy supplied will vary according to the amount of sunlight that day. [1]
b) At some times of year the days are shorter, so less sunlight will be received. [1]
c) It means energy not being used at that time can be stored [1]
and used later on when it is needed. [1]

4. **a)** Covalent [1]
b) Giant (covalent) / giant covalent structure / macromolecule [1]

5. **a)** As the car is approaching a bend the driver will be applying the brakes. [1]
Friction in the brakes causes a transfer of energy from the kinetic store of the car to the thermal store of the brake discs [1]
causing them to radiate energy as light. [1]
b) The car is no longer braking and energy is no longer being radiated. [1]
The energy which was there has been transferred to the surroundings. [1]

6. **a)** Hooke's microscope only magnified 50 times. [1]
Sperm cells are smaller than plant cells. [1]
b) Van Beneden did not make the link between chromosomes and factors controlling characteristics. [1]
Mendel's work remained undiscovered for some time. [1]

7. **a)** *Any one from:* less blue; becomes colourless [1]
b) *Any one from:* didn't stir the solution correctly; the bulb of the thermometer was not in the solution [1]

8. *Any two from:* Some of the people tested could be affected by tiredness or physical exhaustion; Could be under the effect of drink or drugs; Could be of a different age; Could be inattentive / distracted or tense. [2]

Pages 110–119: Explain

Complete the example

2. Carbon nanotubes contain **delocalised electrons**, which are free to **move through the structure** and carry **the charge**.
3. If lamps are connected in series, the potential difference supplied by the **battery / power pack** will be divided between the lamps so if there are more lamps then each of the lamps receives **less** and therefore **becomes dimmer**.
   However, if the lamps are connected in parallel, each of the lamps receives **the whole potential difference**. This means that if more lamps are connected then all of them will receive **the full potential difference** and therefore **be bright**.

Exam practice questions

1. **a)** Acts as a control. [1]
   To show that the water is lost from the plants. [1]
   b) B loses much less water than C. [1]
   The stomata are mainly on the under surface of the leaf [1]
   so in B they are blocked. [1]
2. *Explanation should include four of these points:* Many subcellular structures are too small to be seen with a light microscope; Compared to light microscopes, electron microscopes can see smaller specimens because they have: a greater magnification; a higher resolution; greater resolving power; Transmission electron microscopes (TEM) show structures in cells. [4]
3. **a)** *Explanation should include four points from***:** The atoms get larger / atomic radii increase; Less attraction between the (positive) nucleus and (outer shell) electrons; Outer shell electrons are more easily lost; To become a positive / 1+ ion; More reactive as you go down the group. [4]
   b) The atoms get larger / Atomic radii increase. [1]
   Less reactive as you go down the group [1]
   to become a negative/1– ion. [1]
   Less attraction from the (positive) nucleus to form chemical bonds [1]
   c) Atoms have a stable arrangement of electrons. (*Accept* full outer shell (of electrons)) [1]
4. **a)** Particles have more kinetic energy. [1]
   More collisions in the same time. [1]
   More collisions have higher energy / More collisions occur or exceed the activation energy. [1]
   More successful collisions in the same time. [1]
   b) Powder has more surface area than ribbon. [1]
   More particles exposed for collision at the same time. [1]
   More successful collisions in the same amount of time. [1]
5. **a)** *Any three from:* The crab may not have any natural predators; May be eating many different types of organisms; May be outcompeting other organisms; This could disturb food chains / webs. [3]
   b) Biodiversity makes ecosystems more stable. [1]
   This is because organisms are not just dependant on one other type of organism. [1]
6. **a)** Ions free to move. [1]
   To carry charge / allow current to flow. [1]
   b) Cryolite lowers the melting point. [1]
   Reduces energy use / operating temperature / cost. [1]
   c) Oxygen is formed (at the anode). [1]
   Reacts (immediately) with the carbon of the anode. [1]
   Makes carbon dioxide that is released into the atmosphere. [1]
   Carbon anode burns away / gets smaller. [1]
7. *Explanation should include these points:*
   In diamond:
   Many strong covalent bonds [1]
   need to be broken / overcome [1]
   this takes a lot of energy [1]
   In methane:
   Weak forces of attraction / intermolecular forces between the molecules [1]
   need to be overcome / no covalent bonds are broken and this requires a lower amount of energy [1]
   So, the melting point of methane is lower than diamond. [1]
8. The ice is less dense than the water, which is why it floats and some is above the water surface. [1]
   As the surroundings are warmer, heat is transferred into the ice and water. [1]
   This melts the ice, turning it into water, which occupies a smaller volume. [1]
   It only needs the space that the submerged part of the ice occupied. So the water level does not change. [1]
9. The specific heat capacity of a material indicates the amount of energy needed to raise its temperature by one degree C. [1]
   A high specific heat capacity means that it will take a lot of energy to cause a significant change in temperature. [1]
   This means that the water circulating through the engine can absorb a lot of heat [1]
   without getting near to boiling point. [1]
10. **a)** The resistance is calculated by dividing each of the potential difference readings by the corresponding current flow. [1]
   This gives values for the resistance of (to 2dp): 76.92Ω, 74.07Ω, 78.95Ω, 76.92Ω, 75.76Ω, 76.92Ω, 77.78Ω and 77.67Ω [2]
   These values are relatively constant and there are no outliers. [1]

b) *Any two from (2 marks each):* There may be an error in the meter readings; The temperature of the resistor may have changed a little, causing the resistance to change; The resistances have been rounded off and in some cases this may have increased the interval between them. **[4]**

11. a) Impulse causes neurotransmitter molecules to be released. **[1]**
These molecules diffuse across the gap between the neurones. **[1]**
They join with receptor sites on the relay neurone and stimulate an impulse. **[1]**
b) Neurotransmitter can only be released from sensory neurone; Receptor sites are only on the relay neurone; So the neurotransmitter can only produce a nerve impulse in the relay neurone. **[3]**

12. a) Fully ionises **[1]**
in solution / water. **[1]**
b) Solution A has a concentration of
36.5 ÷ 1000 = 0.0365 g/cm³ **[1]**
Solution B has a concentration of
18.25 ÷ 250 = 0.073 g/cm³ **[1]**
Solution B is more concentrated than solution A. / Solution A is more dilute than solution B. **[1]**

13. They are assuming all the energy stored in the wood is transferred into the water. **[1]**
They can determine how much additional energy the water has and are taking this to be the value of the energy transferred out of the wood. **[1]**
But some energy will be transferred to the air, some absorbed by the equipment and some transferred into the water but then transferred out of it to the surroundings. **[1]**
The energy in the water is therefore a smaller quantity than what was in the wood so the calculated value will be too low. **[1]**

Pages 120–125: Show

Complete the example

2. The therapeutic ratio for drug **A** is **10**, for drug **B** it is **5** and for drug **C** it is **8**.
Therefore, taking drug **A** would be safest, as it has the **highest** ratio so people would be less likely to take a dangerous dose.

3. V = I x R, so I = V ÷ R
12 V ÷ 300 Ω
= 0.04 A

Exam practice questions

1. 6 become pregnant out of a total of 25 **[1]**
So percentage is $\frac{6}{25} \times 100 = 24\%$ **[1]**

2. Minimum percentage with high blood pressure is 33% + 3% **[1]**
So $\frac{36}{100} \times 1\,000\,000 = 360\,000$ **[1]**

3. Percentage yield =
$\frac{\text{mass of actual product made}}{\text{maximum theoretical yield of product}} \times 100$ **[1]**
$= (\frac{\mathbf{15.8}}{\mathbf{63.5}}) \times 100$ **[1]**
= 24.881189 which rounds to 25% **[1]**

4. 125 – 81 = mass of carbon dioxide **[1]**
= 44 g **[1]**

5. Useful output = 125 J and energy supplied = 500 J, so efficiency = 125 ÷ 500 **[1]**
= 25 % **[2]**

6. M_r of Fe_2O_3 = 160 **[1]**
Moles Fe_2O_3 = 1500 ÷ 160 = 9.375 mol **[1]**
Mole ratio is 2 : 1 so need at least 9.375 × 2 = 18.75 mol **[1]**
Mass of Al needed = 18.75 × 27 = 506.25 g **[1]**
which is more than 0.5 kg, so Al is the limiting reagent. **[1]**

7. a) Density = mass ÷ volume **[1]**
Volume = l × b × h = 0.1 × 0.2 × 0.3 = 0.006 m³ **[1]**
Density = 13.5 ÷ 0.006 = 2250 kg/m³ **[2]**
b) Pressure = force ÷ area. When on the largest face this means the area is 0.2 m × 0.3 m, or 0.06 m² and the force is 13.5 kg × 10 N/kg, or 135 N **[1]**
so the pressure is 135 ÷ 0.06, or 2250 N/m² **[1]**
When on the smallest face the force is still 135 N but the area is 0.1 m × 0.2 m, or 0.02 m² so the pressure is 135 ÷ 0.02, or 6750 N/m². **[1]**
2250 × 3 = 6750 so the pressure is three times greater. **[1]**

8. Energy transferred = power × time **[1]**
Time = 60 × 60 × 24 = 86400 s **[1]**
E = 10 W × 86400s = 864000 J **[1]**
or 864 kJ **[1]**

9. Density = mass ÷ volume **[1]**
Volume = 2 × 2 × 2 = 8 cm³ **[1]**
Density = 7.36 g ÷ 8 cm³ = 0.92 g/cm³ **[1]**
Solids will float in liquids which have a greater density and sink in ones which have a lower density. 0.92 is less than 1 so it will float in water but greater than 0.79 so it will sink in methanol. **[1]**

10. Jane must be homozygous recessive and Kevin heterozygous. **[1]**
The probability of a child being affected is 0.25 ($\frac{1}{4}$). **[1]**
Probability it is also a boy is 0.25 × 0.5 ($\frac{1}{4} \times \frac{1}{2}$). **[1]**

Pages 126–133: Determine

Complete the example

2. The percentage of gravestones with lichens in town P is **17**%, in town Q it is **20**% and in town R it is **25**%. Therefore, town **P** contains the most pollution as lichens are more likely to **die**.
3. The colour common in both drinks moved **6.0 cm**.
$R_f = \frac{\textbf{distance moved by substance}}{\textbf{distance moved by solvent}} = \frac{\textbf{6.0}}{\textbf{12.0}}$
= **0.5**

Exam practice questions

1. Caravan site [1]
The beach will have to be closed from June. [1]
2. a) Mean rate of reaction = change in mass ÷ time [1]
= 0.2 ÷ 20 = 0.01 g/s [2]
b) 80 seconds [2]
3. a) Metal [1]
b) °C [1]
c) Calcium, cobalt, copper (*Accept* Ca, Co *and* Cu) [1]
4. a) *Accept any number in the range of 22–26°C* [1]
b) At 80°C 170 g of potassium nitrate [1]
At 50°C 80g of potassium nitrate [1]
170 - 80 = 90 g [1]
5. Efficiency = useful output ÷ input [1]
= 250 ÷ 1000 [1]
= 25 % [2]
6. a) 5 [1]
b) 4 [1]
7. Mass of iron used = 106.00 – 50.00 = 56 g [1]
Moles of iron used = $\frac{56}{56}$ = 1 mole [1]
Mass of oxygen used = 130 – 106 = 24 g [1]
Moles of oxygen molecules = $\frac{24}{32}$ = 0.75 moles [1]
So, there is a mole ratio of 4 : 3 of iron : oxygen molecules [1]
The product has the empirical formula Fe_2O_3 and so the balanced equation is: $4Fe + 3O_2 \rightarrow 2Fe_2O_3$ [1]
8. a) V = I × R [1]
= 0.016 × 10 [1]
= 0.16 V [2]
b) Power loss = $I^2 \times R$ [1]
= $0.016^2 \times 10$ [1]
= 0.00256 W, or 2.56 mW [2]
9. P = I × V, so I = P ÷ V = 960 ÷ 240 [1]
= 4 A [1]
The fuse should be the next size up from 4 A [1]
so it will allow this current to flow but not much more. [1]
The fuse should therefore be 5 A. [1]
10. a) $\pi \times 1^2 \times 500$ [1]
= 1570 cm^3 [1]
b) 1570 × 10 × 20 × 6 [1]
= 1 884 000 cm^3 [1]
11. a) 4 minutes [1]
b) Increases from 80 to 280. [1]
$\frac{200}{80} \times 100$ [1]
= 250% [1]

Pages 134–141: Calculate

Complete the example

2. a) Surface area = 24
Volume = 8
Ratio = 3 : 1
b) **1 ÷ 36 = 0.028**
3. $\frac{\mathbf{(35 \times 75) + (37 \times 25)}}{\mathbf{100}}$ **= 35.5**

Exam practice questions

1. a) 1 μm = 1000 nm [1]
$\frac{1000}{100}$ = 10 times [1]
b) One order of magnitude [1]
2. Quantity of product formed = 404.80 – 403.65 = 1.15 g [1]
Mean rate of reaction = $\frac{\text{quantity of product formed}}{\text{time}}$ **or**
Mean rate of reaction = $\frac{1.15}{90}$ = 0.012 777 78 [1]
= 0.0128 g/s [2]
3. Kinetic energy = $\frac{1}{2}mv^2$ [1]
= $\frac{1}{2} \times \frac{15000}{10}$ [1]
= $\frac{1}{2} \times 1500$ [1]
= 750 000 J / 750 kJ [1]
4. 5 μm = 5 × 10^{-6} m [1]
So it is likely to be a bacterium. [1]
5. Area = π × 152 [1]
= 706.5 mm^2 [1]
So antibiotic A is the best to use as it has the largest clear zone. [1]
6. 334 000 × 0.5 [1]
= 167 000J [1]
7. a) 17 g [1]
b) 0.5 × 17 = 8.5 g [1]
8. a) 14 + (3 × 1) = 17 [1]
b) (mass of nitrogen ÷ relative formula mass of ammonia) × 100 or $\frac{14}{17}$ × 100 [1]
= 82% (*Accept* 82.4%) [1]
9. a) Density = mass ÷ volume, so mass = density × volume.
Volume = 5 × 5 × 5 = 125 cm^3 [1]
Mass = 7.85 × 125 = 981.25 g = 0.98125 kg [2]
b) $\Delta E = m \times c \times (T_2 - T_1)$
= 0.98125 × 502 × (35 – 15) [1]
= 9851.75 J [2]
10. Power output = I × V = 0.48 × 10 000 = 4800 W [1]
Power input = I × V = 5 × 1000 = 5000 W [1]
Efficiency = useful output ÷ input = 4800 ÷ 5000 [1]
= 96% [1]

11. 30 nm = 3×10^{-8} m [1]

Speed = $\frac{3\times10^{-8}}{1.8\times10^{-7}}$ [1]

= 0.17 m/s [1]

12. a) M_r = 25.5 + 1 = 36.5 [1]

Number of moles = $\frac{\text{mass}}{M_r}$ [1]

= $\frac{1.825}{36.5}$ = 0.05 mol [1]

b) 1 dm³ = 1000 cm³ [1]

1.825 × 2 [1]

= 3.65 g/dm³ [1]

13. $\Delta E = m \times c \times (T_2 - T_1)$ so $m = \Delta E \div (c \times (T_2 - T_1))$ = 5 000 000 ÷ (4200 × (40 – 15)) [1]

= 5 000 000 ÷ 105 000 [1]

= 47.6 kg [2]

Pages 142–143: Balance

Complete the example

2. $N_2 + 3H_2 \rightarrow$ **2**NH_3

Exam practice questions

1. C_2H_5OH + **3**$O_2 \rightarrow$ **2**CO_2 + **3**H_2O [1]
2. Na_2CO_3 + **2**HCl → **2**NaCl + CO_2 + H_2O [1]
3. **a)** **2**$Cl^- \rightarrow Cl_2$ + **2**e^- [1]

   b) Cu^{2+} + **2**$e^- \rightarrow$ Cu [1]
4. $4OH^- \rightarrow O_2$ + **2**H_2O + **4**e^- [2]

Pages 144–149: Measure

Complete the example

2. White blood cell = 26 mm and red blood cell = **13 mm**

   Ratio = **2** : 1
3. The value on the balance = **126.6887** g

   126.6887 ÷ 1000 = **0.1266887** kg

   = **0.13** kg

Exam practice questions

1. Width of pore – 4 mm [1]

   4 mm = 4000 μm [1]

   Magnification = ×40 [1]
2. 50 ÷ 0 1 [1]

   = 500 times [1]
3. 15 ÷ 0.03 [1]

   = 500 times [1]
4. Cylinder = 32 mm [1]

   Increase in length = 2 mm [1]

   Concentration = 0.35 mol/dm³ [1]
5. Area of cell = $\pi \times 30^2$ = 2826 mm² [1]

   Area of nucleus = $\pi \times 10^2$ = 314 mm² [1]

   So, area of cytoplasm = 2826 – 314 = 2512 mm² [1]
6. 35 μm [1]
7. **a)** 17.5 V [2]

   b) 20 ms [2]

Pages 150–157: Plan

Complete the example

2. Add the same mass and **surface area** of metals to the same **volume** and concentration of (dilute) nitric acid. Observe the temperature change or the number of **bubbles**.

   Determine conclusion:
   - Silver has no reaction.
   - Zinc has some bubbles and **an increase** in temperature.
   - Calcium has **lots of bubbles** and the **greatest increase** in temperature.
3.
   - Measure the **mass of the block**.
   - Set the block up with **the heater and thermometer inserted and the insulation in place; record the temperature of the block**.
   - Connect the heater to **the voltmeter (in parallel), the ammeter (in series) and the power supply; start timing and record the ammeter and voltmeter readings.**
   - After a set period of time, **e.g. 10 minutes, turn the heater off and record the final temperature of the block**.
   - Calculate the amount of energy transferred to the heater using **the equation ΔE = V × I × t**.
   - This can then be equated to **the amount of energy transferred to the block ΔE = m × c × (T2 – T1). In other words, c is calculated from (V × I × T)/m(T2 – T1)**.

Exam practice questions

1. Measure the distance between the lamp and the beaker. [1]

   Count the number of bubbles given off by the pondweed in a certain time. [1]

   Repeat the reading and calculate a mean / average. [1]

   Repeat this for different distances between the lamp and the beaker. [1]

   Make sure that the pondweed is left for a while before taking each reading. [1]

   Convert the distances into light intensities using $1/d^2$. [1]
2. Add excess copper(II) oxide to sulfuric acid and stir. [1]

   Filter off the excess copper(II) oxide. [1]

   Collect the filtrate. [1]

   Heat to half the volume. [1]

   Allow to crystallise. [1]

   Remove crystals and pat dry with absorbent paper / Put in a drying oven. [1]
3. Fill the eureka can/displacement can with water. [1]

   Carefully lower the irregular rock into the water [1]

   and collect the water that runs out. [1]

   Measure the volume of the displaced water using a measuring cylinder. [1]

Use a top pan balance to measure the mass in grams of the rock. **[1]**

Calculate the density by dividing the mass by the volume. **[1]**

4. Set up the length of wire on a ruler connected to a voltmeter (in parallel), an ammeter (in series), a power supply and a switch. **[1]**

Clip the wire in place. **[1]**

Decide on the lengths to be investigated and for each of these lengths adjust the distance between the connections to the rest of the circuit so that the correct length of the wire being tested is part of the circuit. **[1]**

Record the length of the wire being tested that is in the circuit, the potential difference across the ends of that length and the current flowing through it. **[1]**

For each set of readings, divide the potential difference by the current to get the resistance. **[1]**

A graph can then be drawn of length of wire against resistance. **[1]**

5. Use three or more people. Measure reaction time for left and right hand of each person. **[1]**

Use ruler drop test / computer programme to measure reaction time. **[1]**

Repeat reaction time test for each hand. **[1]**

Remove any anomalous readings. **[1]**

Calculate the mean reaction time for each hand. **[1]**

Use similar people (similar age, same gender, same time of day, same amount of food / drink / rest, same dominant hand). **[1]**

6. Mark out (grid) area in wet and dry areas / mark out a transect in each of the two areas. **[1]**

Randomly place quadrat(s) / place quadrats along transect at equal distances. **[1]**

Count / record number of daisies (in the quadrat). **[1]**

Use at least 5 quadrats in each area. Calculate the average / mean number of daisies (in each area). **[1]**

Take soil moisture readings at each site. **[1]**

Use the mean and area to calculate total number in wet area and total number in dry area. **[1]**

7. Collect up to four samples of each gas. **[1]**

As soon as the gas has been identified, no further tests are needed. **[1]**

The tests are:

Put a lighted splint in the test tube and if you hear a pop hydrogen has been identified. **[1]**

Put a glowing splint in the test tube and if it relights oxygen has been identified. **[1]**

Put in damp litmus paper and replace the stopper. If it bleaches, chlorine has been identified. **[1]**

Add a pipette of limewater and replace the stopper. Shake and if it goes cloudy then the gas is carbon dioxide. **[1]**

8. Filter the sea water to remove sand. **[1]**

Measure the volume and mass of the sample of water. **[1]**

Ensure mass measurement is in g. Ensure volume measurement is in dm^3. **[1]**

Gently heat. Evaporate all of the water away / Ensure residue is dry by using a drying oven / Pat dry with absorbent paper. **[1]**

Measure the mass of the dry residue / solid. **[1]**

Calculate the concentration of the salt by:

Concentration (g/dm^3) = mass of residu ÷ volume (dm^3) **[1]**

9. Set up a spring so that it is attached firmly at the upper end and weights can be hung on the lower end. There should be a scale fixed alongside it so that the length of the spring can be measured. **[1]**

Record the length of the spring with no weights attached. **[1]**

Now add a weight and record both the weight and the new length of the spring. Remove the weight and check that the spring returns to its original length. **[1]**

Repeat with further weights, each time checking that the spring has not been permanently deformed. **[1]**

For each load calculate the extension it caused. **[1]**

Plot a graph of load against extension. The points should form a straight line; if they start to curve then it is likely the elastic limit has been exceeded. **[1]**

Pages 158–163: Design

Complete the example

2. Measure the **unloaded length** of the spring with a ruler. Then, **hang a 100 g slotted mass carrier from the spring and measure the new length of the spring**. Calculate **the extension. As 100 g mass = 10 N weight / force, record the extension next to a force of 10N**. Repeat the measurements by adding **an extra 100g mass on the slotted mass carrier until 1000 g has been added**. Plot **a graph of the results where the x-axis is force and the y-axis is extension**. The line of best fit should be **directly proportiona**l.

Exam practice questions

1. Use a balance to measure the mass of the bolt and record this. **[1]**

Suspend the bolt from a piece of thread. **[1]**

Set up a measuring cylinder that the bolt will fit into and put water into the cylinder. The water level should be around half full. The volume of water should be measured and recorded. **[1]**

Lower the bolt on the thread into the water, ensure it is completely immersed and read the new volume. **[1]**

Subtract the old volume from the new one to get the volume of the bolt. **[1]**

Divide the mass of the bolt by its volume to get the density. **[1]**

2. Add the fungal amylase to starch solution with buffers at different pHs. Use pH buffers with the same values for bacteria and fungi. **[1]**
Test samples at regular intervals with iodine solution. **[1]**
Time how long it takes for the black colour not to appear. **[1]**
Repeat this for different pH values and with the bacterial amylase. **[1]**
Keep variables constant, such as volume / concentration of starch / amylase. **[1]**
Compare the pH that gave the shortest time for the black colour not to appear. **[1]**

3. Cut cylinders from the sweet potato and measure their masses. **[1]**
Place the cylinders in a range of concentrations of sugar solution. Remove the cylinders from the sugar solution and measure their mass. **[1]**
Calculate the percentage change in mass for each cylinder. **[1]**
Repeat with cylinders from normal potatoes. **[1]**
Plot the results on a graph and find the concentration that causes no change in mass. **[1]**
A higher concentration for zero change in mass indicates a higher concentration of sugar in cells so sweeter. **[1]**

4. The step up transformer needs to increase the voltage from 10 000 V to 50 000 V so it needs five times as many turns on the secondary coil as the primary. **[1]**
If the primary has 20 turns then the secondary coil will need 100 turns but it will work with any transformer that has a secondary coil with five times as many turns on the secondary coil. **[1]**
The step down transformer needs to reduce the voltage from 50 000 V to 100 V so there needs to be 500 times more turns on the primary than on the secondary. **[1]**
If there are 20 turns on the secondary coil there will therefore need to be 10 000 on the primary but it will work with any transformer which has 500 times more turns on the primary than the secondary. **[1]**

5. The ice should be crushed and loaded in the beaker around the heater. **[1]**
The heater should be connected to a power supply with an ammeter in series with the heater and a voltmeter in parallel with the heater. A stop watch should be available. **[1]**
The mass of the empty beaker should be measured and recorded. **[1]**
The heater should be turned on for a set period of time, say 5 minutes, and the voltage and current recorded. **[1]**
At the end of this time measure the mass of the beaker again and calculate the increase. This is the mass of the water gathered, which is the same as the mass of the ice melted. **[1]**
The amount of energy transferred to the heater is $\Delta E = V \times I \times t$ (in seconds). The amount of energy received by the ice and used to melt it is $\Delta E = m \times l$, so $l = (V \times I \times t) \div m$. **[1]**

6. Measure out two equal volumes of orange juice. **[1]**
Keep the two samples at different temperatures in a water bath. **[1]**
Measure out equal volumes of DCPIP. **[1]**
Slowly add the orange juice to the DCPIP. **[1]**
Record the volume of orange juice needed to make the DCPIP go colourless. **[1]**
The more orange juice needed then the more vitamin C has been destroyed. **[1]**

Pages 164–175: Plot

Complete the example

2. *Correct points plotted.*
Smooth curve drawn through the points.

3.

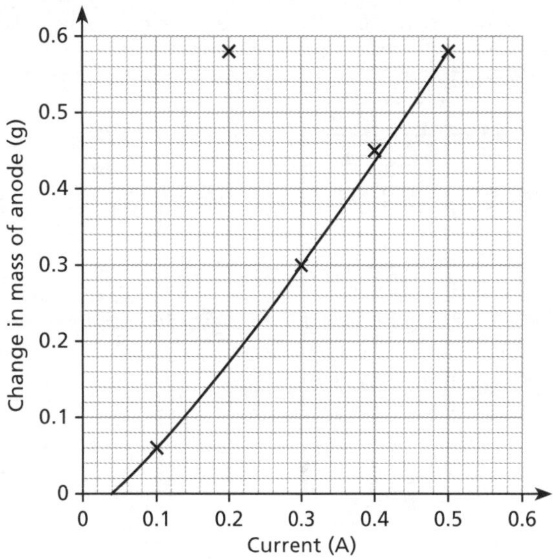

Exam practice questions

1.

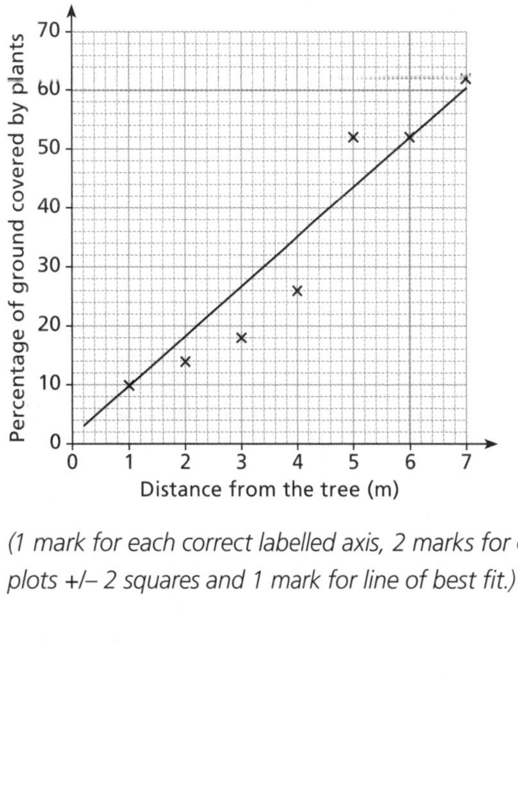

(1 mark for each correct labelled axis, 2 marks for correct plots +/– 2 squares and 1 mark for line of best fit.) **[4]**

2. a)

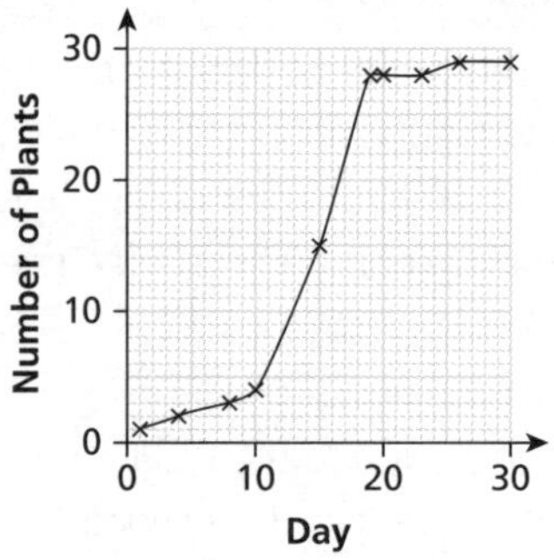

Accurately plotted points **[2]**

best curve / straight lines drawn connecting points **[1]**

3.

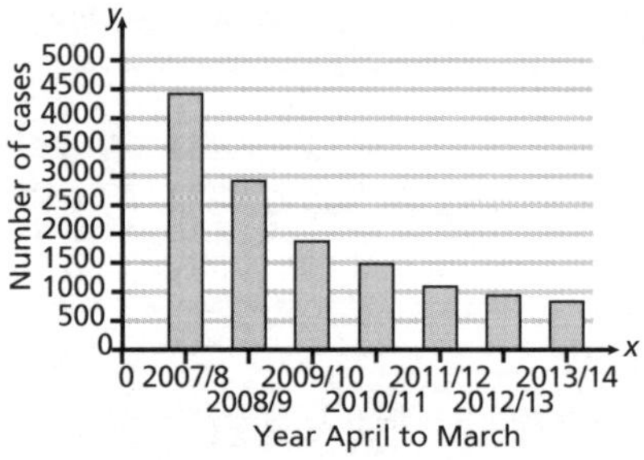

Bar must be drawn to correct height **[1]**

4.

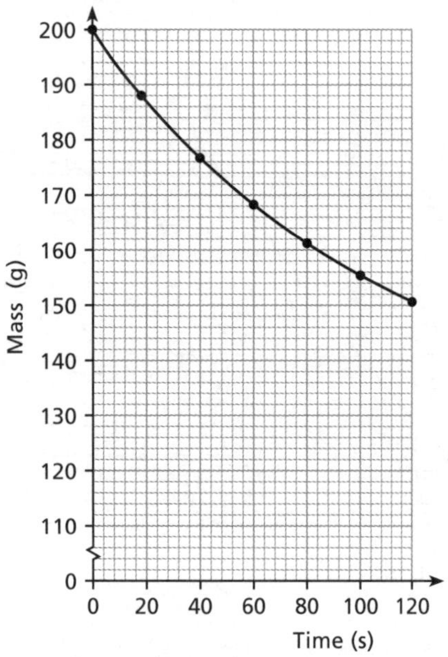

All points plotted correctly as shown (±½ small squares).
(Allow 1 mark if five or six points are correctly plotted.) **[2]**

5.

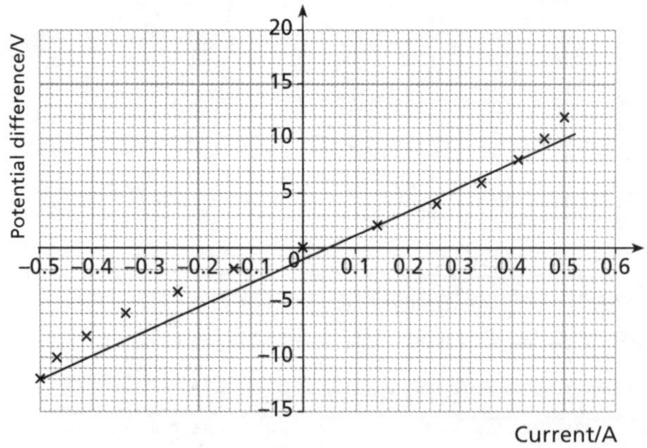

(1 mark for correct y-axis scale; 2 marks for accurate plotting of all points to plus / minus one division (1 mark if up to three are incorrect); 2 marks for line with good fit to points (1 mark if line but not well fitted).) **[5]**

6.

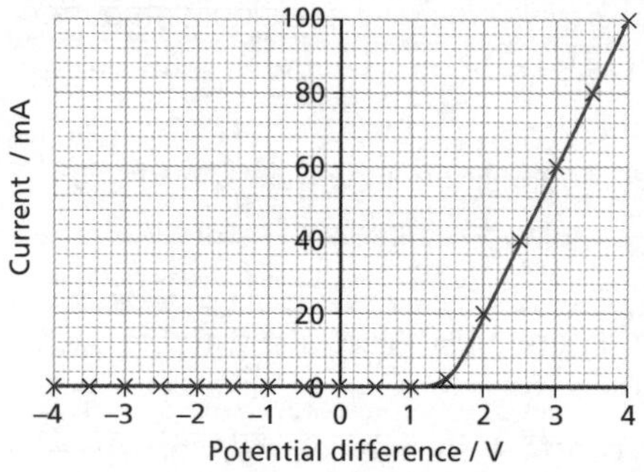

(2 marks for axes correctly labelled; 1 mark for points plotted correctly; 1 mark for line of best fit) **[4]**

7.

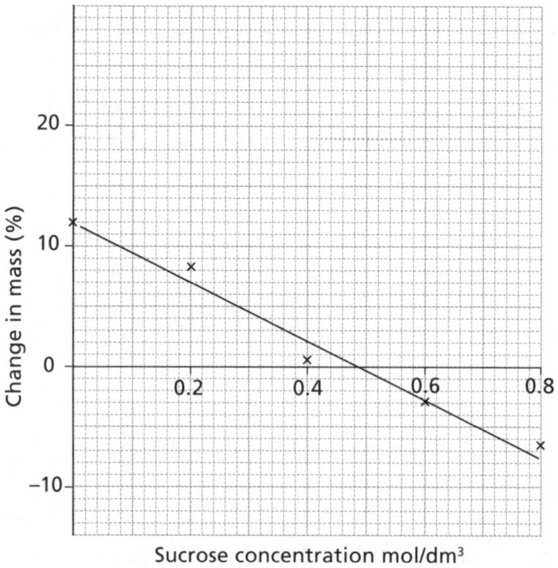

y-axis labelled with percentage change in mass. **[1]**

Suitable scale with zero on the x-axis, positive above and negative below. **[1]**

Correct plots **[2]**

Smooth curve **[1]**

8.

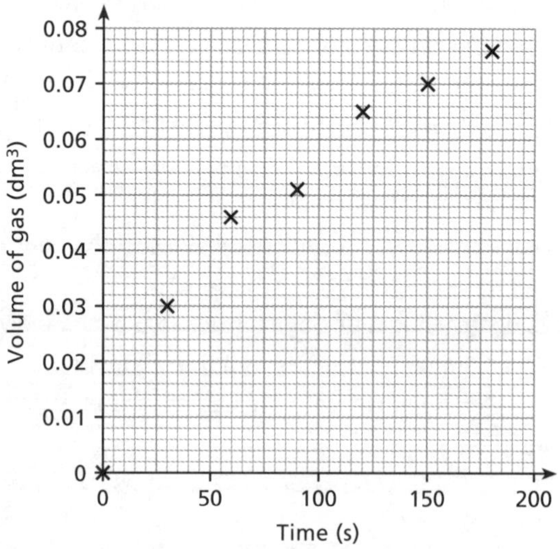

Sensible scales, using at least half the grid for the points. **[1]**

All points plotted correctly as shown (±½ small squares). **[2]**

(Allow 1 mark if five or six of the points are correct.)

9. a)

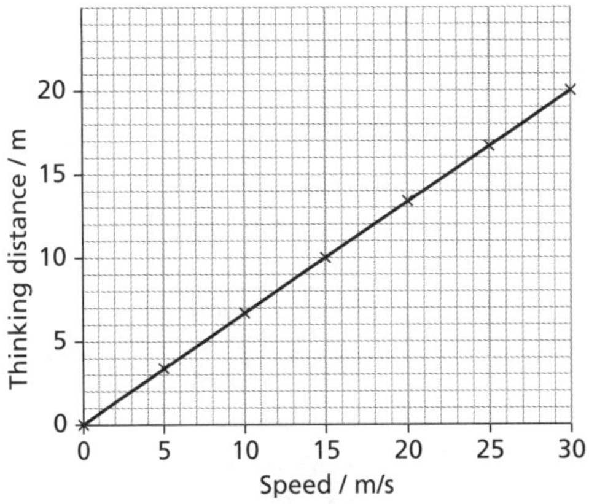

(2 marks for axes correctly labelled; 1 mark for points plotted correctly; 1 mark for line of best fit) **[4]**

b)

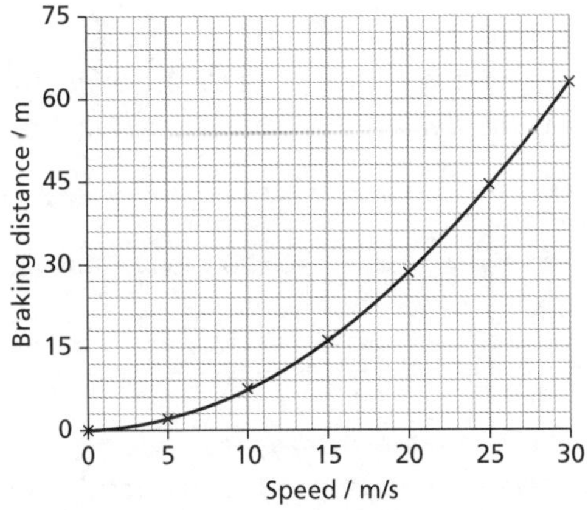

(2 marks for axes correctly labelled; 1 mark for points plotted correctly; 1 mark for line of best fit) **[4]**

Pages 176–183: Compare

Complete the example

2. Both of these reactions **supply energy for muscle contraction**.
   They are both **exothermic** reactions and use **glucose**.
   Aerobic respiration needs **oxygen**, but **anaerobic respiration does not**.
   Anaerobic respiration produces **lactic acid**, but **aerobic respiration produces carbon dioxide**.
   Less **energy** is released by **anaerobic** respiration.
3. Both ethane and pentane are **small** molecules where the atoms are held together by **covalent** bonds with **intermolecular forces of attraction** between the molecules.
   Pentane is a bigger molecule and so has a higher **melting point** and **boiling point**, meaning that pentane is a liquid at room temperature, whereas ethane is a **gas**.
   Both pentane and ethane are **hydrocarbons** as they contain only hydrogen and carbon. They can be used as fuels and undergo **combustion** to make **carbon, carbon monoxide, carbon dioxide and water**.

Exam practice questions

1. *Comparison should include four of these points:*
   All contain only carbon atoms and covalent bonds; All saturated (only contain single bonds); Diamond and graphite are giant covalent structures; Buckminsterfullerene is a simple molecule; Graphite and buckminsterfullerene have three covalent bonds on every carbon atom, whereas diamond has four covalent bonds on every carbon atom; Graphite has layers (planes) of atoms that can easily slide, whereas diamond and buckminsterfullerene do not; Graphite has electrons that are free to move, whereas diamond and buckminsterfullerene do not; Buckminsterfullerene makes a 3D cage, whereas graphite and diamond do not. **[4]**
2. *Comparison should include six of these points:*
   Fresh water only: plentiful and easy supply; fewer treatment steps; quicker to process.
   Sewage water only: more difficult to collect; more treatment steps; slower process; sedimentation (produce sewage sludge and effluent); aerobic biological digestion of effluent (reduces solid waste); sludge anaerobically digested (to remove organic matter).
   Both fresh water and sewage water: filtered / screening and grit removal to remove insoluble solids; sterilised (UV, chlorine, ozone treated). **[6]**
3. Both alpha and beta particles can travel through air. **[1]**
   However alpha particles will be stopped by paper whereas beta particles can penetrate that. **[1]**
4. Both hormones are produced in the ovaries. **[1]**
   Oestrogen is produced in a follicle and progesterone in the corpus luteum / yellow body. **[1]**
   Only oestrogen controls the female secondary sexual characteristics. **[1]**
   Oestrogen repairs the lining of the uterus and progesterone stops it breaking down. **[1]**
   Both inhibit FSH release. **[1]**
5. **a)** Both have pulses. **[1]**
   The pressure in the left ventricle varies over a wider range. **[1]**
   The maximum pressure is higher in the left ventricle. **[1]**
   b) The pressure in the aorta is higher. **[1]**
   The pressure in the aorta pulses but in capillaries it is smooth. **[1]**
   The pressure in the capillaries drops along the vessels but does not fall along the aorta. **[1]**
6. *Comparison should include four of these points:*
   Both lithium and sodium: float / less dense than water; effervesce / bubbles (*Do not accept* 'fizzing' *as this is heard and not seen*); move around on the surface; appear to disappear / get smaller (*Accept* dissolve).
   Lithium moves more slowly than sodium / sodium moves more quickly than lithium; sodium melts into a ball / lithium does not melt. **[4]**

7. The apparent path is a straight line from the object to the eye and suggests the fish isn't as far below the surface as it is. **[1]**
The actual path changes direction when it leaves the surface of the water and shows the fish to be deeper. **[1]**
8. In dish A the amylase produces no change in the lipids. **[1]**
In dish B the droplets have been broken down into smaller droplets. **[1]**
In dish C the droplets have disappeared. **[1]**
Amylase does not break down lipids as they do not fit its active site. **[1]**
Bile emulsifies lipid droplets. **[1]**
Bile emulsifies the lipids and lipase breaks them down into soluble fatty acids and glycerol. **[1]**
9. Both objects initially accelerate at a steady rate. **[1]**
Later on, both experience rapid deceleration and then a period of steady speed. **[1]**
However A has an initial acceleration of (20–0) ÷ 2 10 m/s^2 whereas B has an initial acceleration of (45 – 0) ÷ 18 = 2.5 m/s^2 **[1]**
B reaches a higher velocity than A. **[1]**
B, unlike A, reaches a steady speed before it decelerates, and in the final stage of its journey it slows to rest. **[1]**
Furthermore A appears to change velocity instantaneously whereas with B the curves show a more gradual transition from one velocity to another. **[1]**

Pages 184–189: Estimate

Complete the example

2. *Between 5 N and 5.5 N*
3. Between 63 and 64

Exam practice questions

1. *Best straight line drawn.* **[1]**
Vertical line drawn down from the line at 200 beats per minute. **[1]**
Correct reading of speed from the x-axis. (Between 46 and 48 km/h) **[1]**
2. $\frac{18 \times 10}{4}$ **[1]**
= 45 **[1]**
3. *Accept any number less than 1.* **[1]**
4. *Accept a number between –119 and 24°C.* **[1]**
5. *Accept answer between 0.50 V and 0.57 V* **[1]**
6. 25° *(±2°)* **[1]**
7. A: 53 *(±2)*; B*: 32 (±2)* **[2]**
8. *Best curve drawn using photosynthesis points.* **[1]**
Vertical lines drawn down from the two intersections of the lines. **[1]**
Correct readings of time from the x-axis (between 8am and 4pm) **[1]**
9. 0.05 ÷ 4.2 × 100 **[1]**
= 1% **[1]**

Pages 190–195: Predict

Complete the example

2. Grey / Black solid
3. **a)** The rest of the lamps will not work as there is a break in the circuit and no current will flow.
b) They will all be a little brighter as the 240 V is now divided between 19 lamps instead of 20 so each lamp will get a slightly higher potential difference across it.

Exam practice questions

1. **a)** It will increase the rate of reaction. **[1]**
b) The same maximum mass will be produced. **[1]**
c) It will increase the rate of reaction. **[1]**
2. The cup without the lid will cool down quicker **[1]**
as convection currents above the surface of the coffee are free to transfer energy to the surroundings. **[1]**
3. The oil will be on top **[1]**
as it is less dense. **[1]**
4. We can take any value and see how long it takes to halve **[1]**
so, to drop from 200 to 100 **[1]**
takes 4 days **[1]**
so three half lives takes 12 days **[1]**
(Accept 200 halves to 100, 100 to 50 and 50 to 25 (three successive halvings) and the interval between 200 and 25 is 12 days.)
5. **a)** *Any one from:* Less moles / molecules / amount of gas on the products than the reactants **[1]**
Any one from: The forward reaction will be favoured / More product / More ammonia **[1]**
b) Rate of reaction would lower **[1]**
as activation energy increases / less successful collisions in the same time **[1]**
Same yield of ammonia **[1]**
will take longer to achieve **[1]**
6. Less sulfur dioxide will be made. **[1]**
The endothermic / backwards reaction will be favoured. **[1]**

Pages 196–203: Evaluate

Complete the example

2. The shortest time is **40°C** so this supports the student's conclusion, as this is the **fastest rate of reaction**.
However, the shortest time could be anywhere between **30 and 50°C**.
This is because the student only tested **every 10°C**.
The student also **mixed the solutions** before they were allowed to reach the **correct temperature**.
Only one reading was taken at **each temperature** / there were no **repeat readings**.
3. The model is an effective one because it shows that charged particles originate in the circuit and don't all start

from **the power supply**. It also shows that these particles all set off in motion **at the same time**. The model shows that the current flow is the same **everywhere in the circuit**. If one of the pupils starts to grip the cord harder, their hand will get warmer due to friction and this shows how **resistance works**. However, the model only works for a series **circuit** and it is also inaccurate because **it doesn't show how charge is transferred**. Overall, the value of the model is **partial**.

Exam practice questions

1. Number of deaths has increased as margarine eaten increases while butter eaten decreases. **[1]**
   Then as margarine eaten decreases, the number of deaths decreases. **[1]**
   However, the increase in deaths starts before butter or margarine consumption changes. **[1]**
   A correlation does not mean a cause / there could be other factors causing the change in death rate. **[1]**
   Only data about heart disease is given in the graphs, so cannot say butter is healthier. **[1]**
   The effect of high butter consumption may take time to be seen as it may cause deaths from heart disease in the future. **[1]**
2. *Evaluation should include six of these points:*
   Both glass and plastic are finite resources; Both glass and plastic can be fully recycled an infinite amount of times; Lower temperature is used to produce plastic; Glass is re-used; Glass contains more recycled materials; Glass bottles are heavier than plastic bottles, using more fossil fuels to transport them; Glass is more brittle than plastic and bottles are more likely to get damaged leading to loss of product;
   Judgement for glass being the more sustainable:
   - Glass is a more sustainable material to make drinks bottles as it is more likely to be reused and recycled than plastic bottles;

   Judgement for plastic being more sustainable:
   - Plastic is the more sustainable material as it uses less fossil fuel during its lifespan. If the bottles could be reused and the percentage of recycled material increased in the bottle, it would be even more sustainable. **[6]**
3. *Any four from:* Both drugs reduce the risk of blood clots; Both drugs increase the risk of bleeding; Risk of bleeding is greater with warfarin than with aspirin; Increased risk of bleeding is less than the decreased risk of blood clots; So both aspirin and warfarin result in fewer total problems compared to having no drugs. **[4]**
4. Paper food plates are made from trees which are renewable but ceramic and polymer plates use finite / non-renewable resources in their production. **[1]**
   Using paper plates conserves raw materials as they use the least packaging and more paper plates fit in a box so need less transportation overall. **[1]**
   Sadly, paper plates are single use and in contrast both ceramic and polymer can be reused many times. **[1]**
   But after they are used, paper can be recycled or it biodegrades in landfill, whereas polymers can only be recycled, and ceramics cannot be recycled and do not biodegrade. **[1]**
5. This is effective as it avoids manual checks or having to stop the process. **[1]**
   Half life is suitable because it will last for a number of years **[1]**
   without being a problem if the system is no longer used. **[1]**
   The flour won't be contaminated by the process. **[1]**
   But the source will get weaker over time **[1]**
   and the system will need recalibrating. Safety measures will be needed to keep the source secure and avoid irradiation. **[1]**
6. Some features are good as it shows that a current is induced when wires cut magnetic field lines. **[1]**
   It shows there has to be continuous movement to produce continuous flow of current **[1]**
   and speed of movement will affect voltage induced. **[1]**
   Some limitations as the magnet is moving in the demonstration but is stationary in the generator. **[1]**
   Demonstration uses oscillating motion but generator uses rotating motion. **[1]**
   It has some strengths and can be used but has some limitations and needs careful explanation. **[1]**

Pages 204–211: Justify

Complete the example

2. The patient's BMI can be worked out as: $100 \div 1.8^2 = \mathbf{30.9}$. That means that they are **obese** so need to lose weight. If the patient loses 20 kg their BMI becomes **24.7**, which is in the **normal** range.
3. **a)** Repeat readings are important because there are reasons why the value obtained could vary. There might be a slight pause in **releasing the vehicle**, an error in **measuring the time** or the vehicle might **change direction slightly**.
   b) The first three readings are **very close to each other** with small gaps between, but the **final reading** is significantly different with a **much bigger gap**. Taking the mean of **the other three** will give an answer nearer to the true value.

Exam practice questions

1. **a)** Magnesium has a very slow rate of reaction with water. **[1]**
   No bubbles are observed. **[1]**
   Control is used to compare what would happen if there was no acid. **[1]**
   So, control would be pure water. **[1]**

b) A, D, C, B **[1]**

The greater the number of bubbles, the higher the reactivity. **[1]**

A has the most bubbles, then D, then C, and B has no bubbles. **[1]**

2. The ohmmeter is quicker and easier to set up so it is less likely there will be faults in the circuit. **[1]**

The ohmmeter gives a resistance reading directly, therefore no opportunities for errors. **[1]**

Easy to take repeat readings to check the value. **[1]**

3. Maximum heart rate is 200 and resting heart rate = 50 **[1]**

Therefore their VO_2 Max is 60. **[1]**

This puts them in the range of most distance runners. **[1]**

However, it is right at the lowest value so they should try and improve their fitness. **[1]**

4. Idea that the pollution from a river is found by multiplying the volume of water by the concentration of PCBs. **[1]**

Calculations: Calumet = 550, Fox = 4500, Grand = 380, St Joseph = 200 **[1]**

Adding three other rivers together = 1130 **[1]**

4500 is close to 1130 × 4 **[1]**

5. There are more heavy fractions in crude oil than is needed by world markets / industry. **[1]**

Heavy fractions would be wasted without cracking. **[1]**

There is a higher demand for fuels with small molecules than can be provided from fractional distillation of crude oil. **[1]**

Cracking can provide small molecule fuels. Products of cracking include alkenes which are important substances used to make polymers and other chemicals. **[1]**

6. System A advantages: Not dependent on a regular supply of water. **[1]**

Only has one car to maintain and it takes less space. **[1]**

System B advantages: Electricity not used to power the motor. **[1]**

Greater carrying capacity. **[1]**

(Answer should also include a clear statement as to which system is preferable.)

Pages 212-229: Mixed Questions

1. a) White blood cells **[1]**

recognise the pathogen **[1]**

and produce antibodies **[1]**

quickly. **[1]**

b) (420 ÷ 531) x 100 = 79.09% **[1]**

Percentage = 79% **[1]**

c) By air **[1]**

d) *Any one from:* Sexual contact; Contact with body fluids / blood; Sharing needles **[1]**

e) They are caused by viruses that invade cells. **[1]**

Drugs that kill the virus would also damage cells. **[1]**

Viruses are not destroyed by antibiotics. **[1]**

2. a) Homozygous **[1]**

b) 23 **[1]**

c) Testes **[1]**

d) Female, because the egg always donates X **[1]** therefore offspring will have XX, which is female. **[1]**

e) Mitosis **[1]**

f) Egg/ovum and pollen **[1]**

3. a) Low thyroxine levels cause a low metabolic rate. **[1]**

Therefore, Cerys will not release energy quickly from the food she eats – any excess will be stored as fat. **[1]**

b) Y **[1]**

c) Thyroid gland **[1]**

d) Adrenaline **[1]**

e) When glucose levels rise, the pancreas produces insulin. **[1]**

This causes the liver to convert excess glucose to glycogen for storage. It also causes glucose to move into cells. **[1]**

A return to normal glucose levels is detected by the pancreas and insulin production stops. **[1]**

This is an example of negative feedback. **[1]**

If glucose levels drop, for example during exercise, the pancreas produces glucagon **[1]**

which causes the liver to convert stored glycogen into glucose and release it into the bloodstream. **[1]**

f)

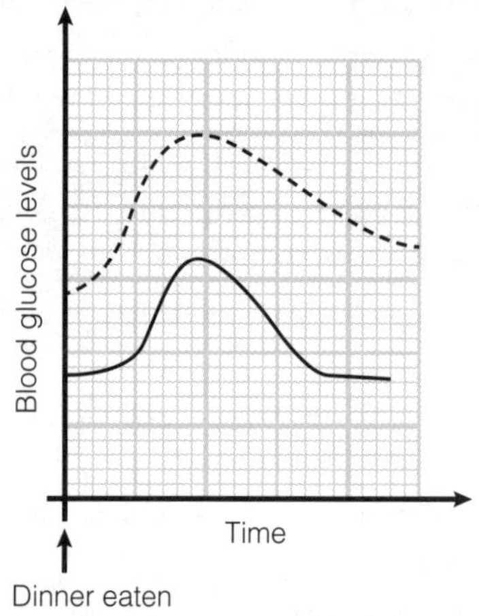

(1 mark for inserting a line above the person without diabetes; 1 mark for a slower decrease in glucose than the person without diabetes) **[2]**

g) Insulin injections **[1]**

4. a) Movement of molecules / particles **[1]**

from an area of high concentration to an area of low concentration. **[1]**

b) A = carbon dioxide; B = oxygen *(both responses needed for 1 mark)* **[1]**

c) The alveoli provide a large surface area **[1]**

have very thin walls **[1]**

have moist walls **[1]**

and an excellent blood supply. **[1]**

d) Volume / concentration of glucose solution **[1]**

volume of water **[1]**

e) 10°C took six minutes for the glucose testing stick to change colour; 20°C was twice as fast at three minutes. **[1]**

f) An increase in temperature causes the molecules / particles to move faster. **[1]**

5. a) Biotic – *any two from:* Availability of food; Number of predators; Number of pathogens **[1]**
Abiotic – *any two from:* Availability of light; temperature; water; pH; dissolved Minerals; levels of dissolved oxygen or carbon dioxide **[1]**

b) Plant plankton begin to increase in March because there is more light for photosynthesis. **[1]**
In April / May shrimp numbers increase because there is more plankton to feed on. **[1]**
Increasing numbers of shrimps eat the plankton so numbers of plant plankton decrease in May. **[1]**
This is followed by decreasing numbers of shrimps in June because their food source is decreasing. This allows plant plankton numbers to increase again in September. **[1]**

c) The deeper the rock pool, the more variety of organisms found. **[1]**

d) Shallow rock pools will have greater variation in temperature, which many organisms will not be able to tolerate / Organisms may be easier to spot by predators in shallow pools, so only those with good camouflage will inhabit them. **[1]**

6. a) Number of protons = 15 **[1]**
Number of neutrons = 16 **[1]**
Number of electrons = 15 **[1]**

b) It has five electrons in its outer shell. **[1]**

7. a) Life cycle assessment / analysis **[1]**

b) It helps them to compare products / services. **[1]**

c) *Any suitable answer, such as:* price; size; cost to run **[1]**

d) The top speed of the car. **[1]**

8. Environmental impact of paper – *any two from:* Paper is made from trees; More trees can be planted; Trees are renewable; Paper is biodegradable. **[2]**
Environmental impact of plastic – *any two from:* Plastics are made from oil; Oil is a non-renewable source; Plastic is non-biodegradable; Plastic bags can be used more times; Plastic bags do not dissolve in water and have to be thrown away. **[2]**

9. a) 14 + (4 × 1) × 2 + 32 + (4 × 16) **[1]**
= 132 **[1]**

b) 2 x 132 = 264 g **[1]**

10. a) Air contains particles made up of atoms. **[1]**
These could be hit by the alpha particles. **[1]**

b) *Beam continuing straight through the foil / drawing showing marks or particles in a central region.* **[1]**
No reflected particles at all. **[1]**

c) The 15-inch shell represents the alpha particle. **[1]**
The tissue paper represents the gold strip. **[1]**
The shell (alpha particle) was expected to pass straight through the tissue (foil). **[1]**
Instead, when the shell hit the paper it bounced straight back. **[1]**

d) The positive charge must be accumulated in the centre of the atom, rather than spread throughout it. **[1]**
The majority of the mass is concentrated in the middle of the atom (the nucleus). **[1]**

11. a) Advantage: It shows how the electrons are shared. **[1]**
Disadvantage: Suggests the electrons are different when they are really all the same. **[1]**

b) Advantage – *any one from:* It shows the metal ions are in a lattice; It explains why magnesium conducts electricity. **[1]**
Disadvantage – it does not show that the ions are vibrating. **[1]**

c) Advantage – *any one from:* It shows which atoms are joined; It shows the shape of the structure. **[1]**
Disadvantage – *any one from:* The atoms are too far apart; There aren't really sticks between the atoms. **[1]**

12. a) Carbon particles – Global dimming **[1]**
Nitrogen oxides – Acid rain (*also allow* global warming) **[1]**

b) It contains carbon and hydrogen **[1]**
only. **[1]**

c) 12.5 or 12 ½ **[1]**
8 **[1]**

d) *Any one from:* Carbon; Soot; Carbon dioxide; Water **[1]**

e) *Any one from:* It is a colourless gas; It is an odourless gas. **[1]**

f) *Any one from:* It is toxic / poisonous; It reduces the blood's ability to carry oxygen; It combines with haemoglobin in the blood. **[1]**

13. a) Light-dependent resistor / LDR **[1]**

b) 7 kilo-ohms **[1]**

c) $V = IR$
$V = 0.0003 \times 7000$ **[1]**
= 2.1 V **[1]**

14. a) Gradient indicated
$y \div x = 20 \div 300$ **[1]**
= 0.067 **[1]**

b) $\Delta E = mc\Delta\theta = Pt$
$mc(\Delta\theta) \div t = P$ **[1]**
$c = P \div (m \times \text{gradient})$
$= 54 \div (1.5 \times 0.0428)$ **[1]**
= 840.5 J / kg / °C **[1]**

15. a)

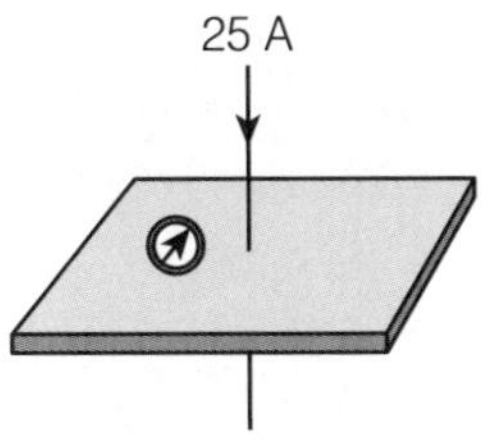

The arrow should be pointing upwards and at an angle as shown. **[1]**

b) The right-hand rule *(Accept detailed description of right-hand rule)* **[1]**
indicates that the direction of the magnetic field due to the current is in the clockwise direction. **[1]**

c)

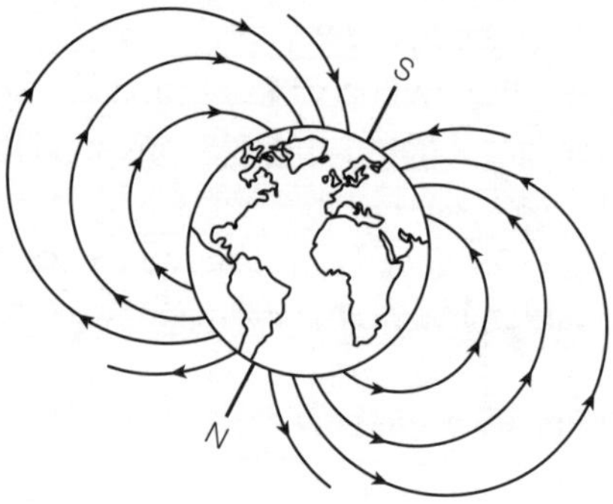

Matching field lines from N to S. **[1]**
Lines are further apart the further they are from the Earth. **[1]**

16. a) The spheres have weight in the downward direction. **[1]**
This is opposed by the force of the pendulum wire, which is equal in size so cancels the weight out. **[1]**
As the forces are balanced there is no movement. **[1]**

b)

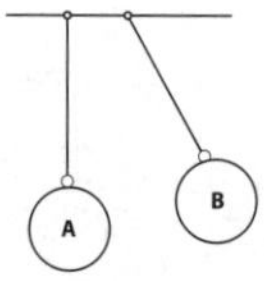

[1]

c) *Explanation should include six of these points:*
The spheres have the same mass and therefore weight
At the point it is released, sphere A has gravitational potential energy
As it falls, the energy is transferred into kinetic energy
When it hits sphere B a force is applied to the sphere
Newton's Second Law states that the acceleration of an object is proportional to the resultant force acting on the object and inversely proportional to the mass of an object
Sphere A will overcome the inertia of sphere B and cause it to accelerate
Assuming there is no air resistance, sphere B should continue moving in the same direction as sphere A was
As sphere B moves it loses kinetic energy
As sphere B gains gravitational potential energy it will reach the same height from the ground that Sphere A started at. **[6]**

d) The balls would gradually lose energy / transfer energy to the surroundings and come to a standstill. **[1]**

17. a) initial speed, $u = 31.1$ m/s, final speed, $v = 0$ m/s
Time taken to stop, $t = 5.17$ seconds; $a = ?$
$v = u + at$ **[1]**
$0 = 31.1 + 5.17 \times a$
$a = -31.1 \div 5.17$ **[1]**
$= -6.015$ m/s^2 **[1]**
$v^2 = u^2 + 2as$ **[1]**
$0 = (31.1)2 + 2 \times s \times (-6.015)$
$-967.21 = -12.03s$
$s = -967.21 \div -12.03$
$= 80.4$ m travelled before stopping. **[1]**

b) The stopping distance would have been further **[1]**
as the reaction time would have increased due to the effect of the alcohol. **[1]**

c) The lorry, having a larger momentum, would take longer to stop. **[1]**

Notes

Notes

Notes

Notes

Notes

Notes

Notes

Acknowledgements

The author and publisher are grateful to the copyright holders for permission to use quoted materials and images. Every effort has been made to trace copyright holders and obtain their permission for the use of copyright material. The author and publisher will gladly receive information enabling them to rectify any error or omission in subsequent editions. All facts are correct at time of going to press.

P.183 top photo © Sciencephoto Library Ltd.
All other images ©Shutterstock and HarperCollins*Publishers*

Published by Collins
An imprint of HarperCollins*Publishers* Limited
1 London Bridge Street, London SE1 9GF

HarperCollins*Publishers*
Macken House, 39/40 Mayor Street Upper
Dublin 1, D01 C9W8, Ireland

ISBN 978-0-00-864741-4

First published 2023

10 9 8 7 6 5 4 3 2 1

British Library Cataloguing in Publication Data.

A CIP record of this book is available from the British Library.

Publisher: Katie Sergeant
Authors: Ian Honeysett, Sam Holyman and Ed Walsh
Commissioning and Development: Richard Toms
Project Management: Katie Galloway
Inside Concept Design: Ian Wrigley and Sarah Duxbury
Layout: Rose & Thorn Creative Services Ltd and Ian Wrigley
Cover Design: Sarah Duxbury
Production: Bethany Brohm
Printed in the United Kingdom by Martins the Printers

FSC www.fsc.org MIX Paper | Supporting responsible forestry FSC™ C007454

This book contains FSC™ certified paper and other controlled sources to ensure responsible forest management.

For more information visit: www.harpercollins.co.uk/green